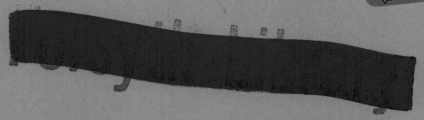

WITHDRAWN

LANGUAGE LESSONS FOR THE

SPECIAL EDUCATION CLASSROOM

Jack T. Cole
New Mexico State University
Las Cruces, New Mexico

Martha L. Cole
Las Cruces Public Schools
Las Cruces, New Mexico

AN ASPEN PUBLICATION®
Aspen Systems Corporation
Rockville, Maryland
London
1983

Library of Congress Cataloging in Publication Data

Cole, Jack T.
  Language lessons for the special education classroom.

  "An annotated bibliography of parent-involvement
materials": p. E:1.
  1. Exceptional children—Education—Language arts.
2. Language arts—Remedial teaching. 3. Language
disorders in children. I. Cole, Martha L. II. Title.
LC3973.C64 1983   371.9'044   82-24469
ISBN: 0-89443-932-4

Publisher: John Marozsan
Editorial Director: R. Curtis Whitesel
Executive Managing Editor: Margot Raphael
Editorial Services: Scott Ballotin
Printing and Manufacturing: Debbie Collins

Library of Congress Catalog Card Number: 82-24469
ISBN: 0-89443-932-4

Printed in the United States of America

To Morris
a good and tolerant friend

Table of Contents

Preface

This book is a natural outgrowth of our first book published by Aspen, *Effective Intervention with the Language Impaired Child.* Before we had even completed that manuscript, it became apparent what our next writing project had to be. So with the usual mixed feelings of reluctance to begin a major task and excitement about getting it underway, we set out to write a book specifically for the busy practitioner who is faced with teaching language to exceptional children. The challenge was to produce a product that was practical and easy to use, but also well-grounded in the philosophy of directive/data-based teaching. We hope that *Language Lessons for the Special Education Classroom* meets that challenge.

Jack T. Cole
Martha L. Cole
April 1983

Acknowledgments

It is not possible to list the names of all the special education teachers, early childhood education teachers, and speech/language pathologists who contributed to the numerous language lessons presented in this sourcebook. Nonetheless, their contributions were crucial to the completion of the project, and we thank them most sincerely.

A special thanks goes to Sue Knuth, Kathryn Ogata, and Gloria Siegel, who assisted with the field research. Their long hours of labor reflected their commitment to the education of exceptional children.

Finally, we would like to pay tribute to the late Curtis Whitesel of Aspen. He gave us the courage to write our first book and to start on this project. We only wish he could be here to participate in its completion.

Chapter 1

How To Use the Lessons

AN OVERVIEW

L *anguage Lessons for the Special Education Classroom* is intended to be a resource of effective language lessons for special education teachers and speech/language pathologists who are responsible for teaching language to children in special education programs. Chapters 2, 3, and 4 focus on considerations that are preliminary steps in organizing and developing the language curriculum. Chapters 5, 6, and 7 offer practical day-to-day language lessons to be used in the language program.

Chapter 2, Perspectives on the Language Curriculum for the Exceptional Child, deals with organizing language materials, effective physical arrangement of the classroom, managing language behaviors, techniques commonly used in language training, and children's characteristics in learning language.

Chapter 3, Coordinating the Home/School Language Training Program, is concerned with involving parents in the language intervention process. It deals with the various levels of parent involvement and presents guidelines for conducting language training in the home.

Chapter 4, Considerations for Language Training in a Multicultural Society, concerns itself with bilingual/bicultural factors in the language curriculum.

Chapters 5, 6, and 7 provide the teacher with 250 practical language remediation lessons to be used with individuals and class groups. The 250 activities that are presented have been collected from the authors' successful experiences in planning language curricula, from special education and early childhood education teachers, and from speech/language pathologists practicing in the field.

Specifically, Chapter 5, Lessons for Teaching Receptive Language Skills, provides language lessons in the following receptive areas:

- receptive phonology
- listening skills
- following directions
- concept development
- associations and comparisons
- classifying and categorizing
- comprehension
- semantic understanding of vocabulary

Chapter 6, Lessons for Teaching Expressive Language Skills, includes language lessons in the following expressive areas:

- expressive phonology
- syntax
- recalling details and describing objects and events
- expressive vocabulary
- morphology
- making changes in the basic sentence
- voice control
- social communication

To provide additional lessons designed to complement and enhance the process of learning language, Chapter 7, Lessons for Enriching the Language Environment, presents language activities involving:

- poetry
- music
- dramatics

For easy implementation, each lesson has been divided into eight sections: title, purpose, area of language stressed, duration of the lesson, lesson format, materials/equipment/physical layout, description of the lesson, and method of evaluation.

1. *Title.* The title indicates the subject of the lesson.

2. *Purpose.* Each lesson was developed with a specific learning outcome in mind. Lessons were selected to provide sequential development in receptive and expressive language skills. Lessons in poetry, music, and dramatics were included to enrich the language environment.

3. *Area of language stressed.* Here the general language areas are specified for receptive language, expressive language, and language enrichment. For example, an expressive language lesson may be categorized as one that develops morphology, or more specifically, plural forms of nouns. Thus, in the section Area of Language Stressed, the lesson would read Morphology—Plurals.

4. *Duration of the lesson.* An average time needed to complete each lesson is provided. This helps the teacher plan the instructional day in advance. The actual time needed for a particular lesson may vary from the estimated time, depending on how often the activity is repeated, how many children are participating, and whether or not the children have difficulty with the learning task.

5. *Lesson format.* The lesson format specifies whether the lesson is intended for a group of children or whether it is best suited for individual practice. If it specifies group *or* individual, it may be adapted for use with either.

6. *Materials/equipment/physical layout.* This details for the teacher the materials or equipment needed for the particular lesson. In some lessons, tape recorders, record players, magazines, and household items may be required. These instances are specified so that the teacher can prepare the materials well in advance. For the most part, the lessons utilize familiar objects that are readily available, rather than commercial materials or language programs. This enables the teacher to use a greater number of the lessons provided, since specialized materials are not required. In addition, if special seating arrangements or physical changes in the room are needed, that will be indicated. Otherwise, the teacher may use whatever group or individual seating arrangement that is preferred.

7. *Description of the lesson.* Here directions are given for conducting the lesson. In many cases, the manner of introducing the lesson is indicated.

8. *Method of evaluation.* The method of evaluation gives the teacher a means of determining whether the child achieved the stated purpose of the lesson. In some instances, the teacher will be referred to the checklist of expressive language in Appendix A. This checklist may be used to determine the level of expressive language a child used during a specific observation. In other activities, the evaluation of the child's mastery can best be obtained with the use of the generalization check in Appendix B. This instrument is designed to determine if a skill taught in a language lesson has generalized to the child's spontaneous language and whether the response has been maintained over a period of time. In still other lessons, a simple percentage of accuracy may be obtained to determine mastery of the language skill. In all instances, areas of weakness in language performance should be noted for future remedial work. For teacher convenience, each lesson may be quickly removed from the easy-to-use, three-ring binder.

THE LESSON SELECTION CHART

Table 1-1, the lesson selection chart, is provided to facilitate selection of appropriate language lessons for a child or group of children. The lessons in Chapters 5, 6, and 7 have been organized in clusters. To identify language lessons in a specific area, the teacher simply has to locate the language area in the left-hand column and its corresponding lesson numbers in the right-hand column. For example, if the teacher wishes to help a child develop language concepts of quantity, the area is first located under Receptive Language, Concept Development. There, the lessons to develop concepts of quantity are identified as Lessons 34, 35, and 36. The teacher then turns to those lessons and begins to prepare for instruction. (Relevant portions of the Table 1-1 selection chart are included as user's guides in the introduction to Chapters 5, 6, and 7.)

Table 1-1 The Lesson Selection Chart

Chapter 2

Perspectives on the Language Curriculum for the Exceptional Child

THE ROLE OF LANGUAGE IN LEARNING

Language fulfills two vital roles for the child. In a social sense, language assumes the role of helping an individual communicate and interact with others. In a cognitive sense, language serves as a functional means of inquiring and learning more about the environment. When the relationship between language and learning is examined, language performs the following functions:

- communicating
- inquiring
- describing
- interacting socially
- structuring thought
- investigating other areas of knowledge

Communicating

Even infants, in very precise ways, communicate their needs to their parents. Crying becomes the first sign of language when infants use it as a tool to inform their parents that they are hungry, wet, or uncomfortable. Toddlers likewise use gestures, grunts, and other purposeful noises to let others know their wants. Picture two toddlers playing together on the floor, amidst an array of rattles, noisemakers, and other toys. One is shaking a small chain with plastic discs. The other, seeing and hearing the noise, vocalizes and simultaneously makes a lunge and grabs for it. The child has used an initial type of language to communicate a desire for the object. In later stages of language learning, children may use such phrases as "want car," "more cookie," or "Johnny go car" to indicate their needs and desires.

At a higher developmental level, the child uses language to communicate with others in an expanded circle of relationships, such as within the neighborhood or community. Consider a young child going to the store to buy ice cream. The child must use language to make wishes known and must interact in appropriate conversation to satisfy the desire for ice cream.

At a more advanced level, the child must be able to express personal feelings through the use of language. To express emotions such as fear, happiness, or sadness or a personal idea, the child must interpret the feeling and choose the appropriate language to communicate the thought.

Language, then, in its various developmental stages, helps individuals communicate to others their needs and wants.

Inquiring

"Mommy go?" or "What that, Mommy?" represent typical questions used by small children for inquiring about events or objects. This form of language fulfills the function of inquiry. Children use language for questioning about other people (who), about the time of events (when), and about the location of events (where); for inquiring how to perform an action (how); and, of course, for posing the ever pervasive "why" questions. It is a way of finding out about immediate surroundings, the community, and the world.

Language is used to question and investigate the surrounding environment, to acquire information, and to find solutions to problems.

Describing

For young children to describe events that have occurred, a certain level of language development is required. An example of the inability to describe events is that of a child who, after hearing a story, is unable to describe the sequence of activity. This child does not have the level of language necessary to remember and explain the chain of events.

Similarly, to explain how to perform an action requires some variation in vocabulary and the ability to put several thoughts together and to verbalize them in a logical order. One child, announcing to her teacher that she had just received a new game, was asked to explain how to play the game. She replied, ''Well, you put the thing in the thing and make it go around.'' The lack of a varied vocabulary for the names of objects hindered this child in describing her game to the teacher.

Language, then, provides the child with the means of description and explanation so necessary for communication.

Interacting Socially

''No man is an island'' is an idiom often used to emphasize the interrelationships and interdependence of humans. Likewise, a child is not a solitary being in the realm of learning. Children learn to interact with others in order to fulfill social functions or to satisfy the need to make social contact. Language most likely is the tool used to make that interaction possible.

Language is used to converse with others and to communicate ideas, thoughts, and perceptions with others. Thus, language becomes a social tool that helps children learn how to get along with others in their world.

Structuring Thought

As we grow and develop, we are subjected to a variety of experiences. Our thought processes take in these experiences and, based on what is already known, react to them. These thought processes, the character of which is greatly structured and defined by language, become a receptacle for each experience. Each new experience changes the thought process to some degree, which in turn views the next experience in a slightly different fashion, thus producing learning. Learning results from the interaction between these two forces.

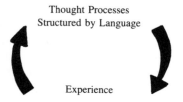

Thought Processes
Structured by Language

Experience

Cognitive development and language, then, seem to be mutually dependent upon one another. They become interdependent forces in the child's learning.

Investigating Other Areas of Knowledge

One cannot deny that there has been a vast accumulation of knowledge in the physical and social sciences since the beginning of the 20th century. And it becomes an awesome task to acquire that knowledge. Throughout a person's education, formal and informal, the written word becomes an important way of expanding the acquisition of knowledge. Books, newspapers, and other printed media help to keep people informed and further the transmission of information.

Likewise, the spoken word—especially in the form of radio, television, and telephone—aids an individual in learning more about other communities and cultures.

Language, in its various forms, becomes a key factor in transmitting information and unlocking the door to other areas of knowledge. Language is a vital element in determining a child's development and learning. It becomes the special educator's responsibility to provide experiences that will enhance the production and steady acquisition of language. This enables the child to learn more about the environment, be better equipped to communicate with others, and to acquire knowledge in the various disciplines.

PLANNING LANGUAGE EXPERIENCES FOR LEARNING

Because language is so important in the learning process of exceptional children, the special educator must make a particular effort to provide for language experiences that foster cognitive growth. This requires the careful planning of the language curriculum. Planning the curriculum includes, but is not restricted to, finding appropriate language resources, organizing these resources, and organizing the classroom.

Finding the Resources

The special education teacher should be committed to the selection and utilization of a variety of resources to provide a varied language program for children. This use of resources requires the gathering of hardware and software for use within the classroom or clinical setting.

The teacher needs to become a master of procurement and must often resort to begging or borrowing materials for use in the classroom. One should keep in mind that the type of materials used will depend upon the purpose or objective of the language instruction. For example, if the teacher wants to teach a child to describe the function of common objects found around the home, it would be necessary to gather together objects such as scissors, a comb, spatula, needle and thread, or other similar household items. In such cases, the materials would probably not be readily at hand, so planning in advance is important. However, in teaching the prepositional placement of objects, the teacher may already have available in the classroom a core of basic objects that could be used to teach the concepts of position in relation to objects. A small box, one-inch cubes, a cup, or similar objects commonly found in the classroom may demonstrate relationships such as a block *in* a cup, the cup *on* the box, or the block *under* the box. If these objects have been gathered and stored together, they may be ready to use in a moment, saving the teacher valuable planning and teaching time.

The teacher must be very careful not to become overly reliant on commercially produced language programs. This may result in language training in which the teacher attempts to fit the child to the program, rather than language training that develops a program around the needs of each individual child. A good language training program combines commercial and teacher-made materials.

The teacher must also be able to use audio and audiovisual materials judiciously. The Language Master, tape recorders, filmstrips, projectors, and other similar equipment may be utilized to give the child practice on already learned language constructions, thus giving the teacher direct teaching time with other children. However, simply using these media cannot take the place of individualized instruction, nor can machines be expected to teach the concept or construction alone in the initial teaching phase. These media are best utilized in reinforced practice, where the child is given additional opportunity to use a language construction previously learned.

The teacher should keep in mind that whatever resources are gathered, it is of utmost importance to use the following criteria while selecting materials.

- *Materials should be concrete and realistic:* To the greatest extent possible, the resources used within the learning environment should be demonstrable, visible, and concrete representations. However, many language concepts cannot be demonstrated through the use of an object or concrete experience. Therefore, picture cards may be used to depict situations or events. When pictures of language concepts are used, they should be as realistic as possible. When available, pictures of people should be real photographs or realistic drawings, rather than simple stick figures. Pictures from magazines, newspapers, and books can be used to build and organize a file designed to illustrate a language construction the teacher wishes to emphasize. One teacher known to the authors filed her pictures not only according to the language construction to be stressed but along topical categories as well. She described one occasion when, in the course of a conversation with a child, she mentioned the ocean. To a language delayed child living in a landlocked state, the word *ocean* had little meaning. When the teacher pulled out her pictures of the ocean, the child better understood the concept being discussed.

- *Materials should be interesting:* The age and interest of the child should be taken into consideration when selecting materials. Adolescents may be interested in topics such as cars, sports, and popular music while the younger child may not. Materials selected should reflect this variation of interest. If the materials are interesting and colorful, the child will likely be more motivated to participate in the language instruction.

- *Materials should be inexpensive:* Funding for classroom materials is not always at the level we, as teachers, would like. For this reason, the materials selected should at best be free, or at least inexpensive.

- *Materials should be free of sex/ethnic biases:* While the authors do not advocate the use of unisex examples, they feel that materials should be free of stereotypic displays of activity according to gender. Similarly, the depiction of ethnic minorities in stereotyped occupations or activities should be avoided.

In the language lessons in Chapters 5, 6, and 7, the materials needed to teach each lesson have been listed. In most cases, the materials selected follow the four criteria indicated above. In addition, Appendix C offers a selected list of free and inexpensive materials that may be used in organizing the language curriculum.

Organizing the Resources

The next step in planning the language curriculum for a given group of children is to organize the resources. Though initially the organization of materials will take time, in the long run it will conserve time and energy. Preplanning before the children arrive always saves valuable teaching time.

There are several techniques that may serve as starting points for organizing the resources for use in a language program. These techniques can be beneficial in organizing the materials to be used by the teacher, instructional aide, or volunteer working in the classroom.

Color Coding

Color coding is an easy way of categorizing the language materials according to general area. The teacher may wish to utilize colored stickers to code materials in two major categories: receptive language and expressive language. Within the major category of receptive language the following subheadings can be coded according to color:

- receptive phonology—green
- listening skills—yellow
- following directions—orange
- concept development—white
- associations and comparisons—black
- classifying and categorizing—gold
- comprehension—blue
- semantic understanding of vocabulary—red

Materials used to develop skills in these areas may be marked with a colored sticker and placed in a convenient location for later use. When a child or group of children needs work in one of these areas, the materials are easily located.

Similarly, expressive language materials may be coded in the following subcategories:

- expressive phonology—purple
- syntax—silver
- recalling details and describing objects and events—pink
- expressive vocabulary—brown
- morphology—tan
- making changes in the basic sentence—aqua
- voice control—lime
- social communication—rust

The teacher determines first what skill the child needs to work on and then goes immediately to the appropriate color for materials to develop that skill. Color coding is an excellent means of organizing objects, picture cards, and programs for rapid selection of materials.

Number System

A system of labeling and numbering materials may also be used to earmark items for specific use in the language program. An organization similar to the color-coding system may be used, with the exception that numbers are used instead of colors. A key can be displayed for reference by all adults teaching in the classroom. On this key, each general area under receptive and expressive language is categorized and numbered. For example, if the materials to be used to develop classification skills are all numbered the same and placed on easy-to-read labels, the teacher can quickly scan the materials for the corresponding number to obtain items designed to develop classification skills. A numbering system for labeling materials provides a means of organizing and managing materials and yields an orderly arrangement of language resources.

Folder System

Folders, manila envelopes, clipboards, or notebooks may also be utilized for organizing materials, particularly data sheets for monitoring progress, picture cards designed to depict certain language constructions, and the language portion of the Individual Education Plan (IEP). Using the folder system, the teacher provides a folder for each child receiving language instruction. For each folder, the teacher prepares data sheets so that the child's progress can be recorded. It is suggested that on the outside of the folder a summary chart be provided so that the child's mastery of the objectives on the language portion of the IEP can be carefully documented. The summary information is typed directly onto the folder, so that completion of language skills can be noted immediately and transferred to the IEP at a later date.

Exhibit 2-1 illustrates the folder of a child participating in language instruction. As illustrated, the language program for the child Max contains several skills to be developed during the year. These skills have been specified in greater detail in Max's IEP. Criteria for mastery, specific conditions for checking mastery, and other information have been omitted from inclusion on the folder, since they are contained in the IEP. The folder represents a brief summary of language skills to be stressed. In receptive language, Max will be working on categorizing and comprehension during the school year. In expressive language, Max will work on morphological markers, such as plurals, comparative adjectives, and noun/verb agreement. In addition, Max will be working on expanding sentences, communicating socially, and developing vocabulary. The materials selected for developing these skills are noted on the language folder, so that any person working with the child will see what activities and resources have been used to that point. This prevents unnecessary repetition or duplication of instruction. Starting dates and completion dates are noted on the language folder for later inclusion in the IEP. This saves time, since it eliminates looking back through numerous pages of data sheets for precise dates of mastery when updating the IEP.

Although a lengthy discussion of data collection methods is not one of the primary objectives of this book, the authors strongly advocate the use of data sheets for monitoring children's responses and daily progress toward the stated language objectives. Exhibit 2-2 illustrates a method of keeping data that has been found to be adequate for most purposes. The data sheet includes spaces for the date, the language construction being emphasized, the type of reinforcer used during the language lesson, and the final percentage of accuracy on that date. Correct and incorrect responses can be circled or checked, so that each trial of the language construction is recorded. Recording this information interjects an element of precision into the language curriculum and provides another means of accountability in the instructional process.

Exhibit 2-1 The Language Folder

MAX

Language Area	Specific Skill	Materials Used	Starting Date	Date of Completion

Receptive	1. Categorizing
	
	2. Comprehension
	  a. recalling literal details
	  b. relating cause and effect
		Category Cards, Foods & Animals	9/3	9/20

Expressive	1. Morphology
	  a. plurals
	  b. comparative adjectives
	  c. noun/verb agreement
	
	2. Expanding sentences
	
	3. Social communication
	
	4. Developing vocabulary
	  a. descriptive words
	  b. action words			

Organizing the Classroom

When one thinks of organizing a classroom or setting for developing language, the immediate reaction is to think of the physical layout of the room and how to maximize space according to the goals of the program. Too often, however, the teacher gives little thought to the development of an atmosphere for learning language and how that relates to the organization of space.

To promote talking, the room must have space where group or class activities can take place. Promoting talking in the classroom need not interfere with the quiet time, which is necessary for independent work. Rather, the children should know when it is time for quiet work, and they should be taught the rules for respecting individuals who are participating in structured language lessons with the teacher. When the group gathers together, the children should know that this time has been set aside for interaction.

The spaces provided in the classroom must accommodate two considerations: First, in a self-contained classroom, the location of two tables on opposite sides of the room provides the opportunity for conducting two individual or small group lessons at one time. This is especially important if there is an instructional aide, paraprofessional, or volunteer conducting daily language practice with children in the classroom. Second, the children's desks may be placed around the perimeter of the room, rather than clustered together in rows. This arrangement allows the teacher to conduct individualized language lessons with a minimum of disruption to other children. One should take care not to place children's desks in the line of traffic, such as close to an entry door or next to the water fountain.

Audiovisual equipment should be placed away from the children's desks to prevent interruption or disturbance while they are working independently. All too often, however, the placement of audiovisual equipment, such as a tape recorder or filmstrip viewer, is dictated by the placement of the electrical outlets in the room. For this reason, it is suggested that the teacher begin arranging the room after it is decided where the audiovisual center must be placed.

A table should be provided for science or social studies exhibits. This allows for the display of interesting items that

Exhibit 2-2 The Data Sheet

Student: _____

Date: _____	Date: _____
Construction: _____	Construction: _____
CI CI CI CI CI CI CI CI CI CI CI CI CI CI CI CI CI CI CI CI CI CI CI CI CI CI CI CI CI CI CI CI CI CI CI CI CI CI CI CI CI CI	CI CI CI CI CI CI CI CI CI CI CI CI CI CI CI CI CI CI CI CI CI CI CI CI CI CI CI CI CI CI CI CI CI CI CI CI CI CI CI CI CI CI
Reinforcer: _____	Reinforcer: _____
% Correct: _____	% Correct: _____
Date: _____	Date: _____
Construction: _____	Construction: _____
CI CI CI CI CI CI CI CI CI CI CI CI CI CI CI CI CI CI CI CI CI CI CI CI CI CI CI CI CI CI CI CI CI CI CI CI CI CI CI CI CI CI	CI CI CI CI CI CI CI CI CI CI CI CI CI CI CI CI CI CI CI CI CI CI CI CI CI CI CI CI CI CI CI CI CI CI CI CI CI CI CI CI CI CI
Reinforcer: _____	Reinforcer: _____
% Correct: _____	% Correct: _____
Date: _____	Date: _____
Construction: _____	Construction: _____
CI CI CI CI CI CI CI CI CI CI CI CI CI CI CI CI CI CI CI CI CI CI CI CI CI CI CI CI CI CI CI CI CI CI CI CI CI CI CI CI CI CI	CI CI CI CI CI CI CI CI CI CI CI CI CI CI CI CI CI CI CI CI CI CI CI CI CI CI CI CI CI CI CI CI CI CI CI CI CI CI CI CI CI CI
Reinforcer: _____	Reinforcer: _____
% Correct: _____	% Correct: _____

promote discussion and illustrate concepts in a concrete manner. A bird's nest, bees' honeycomb, snakeskins, an ant farm, or a small animal are only a few of the many objects that could be used to stimulate discussion and inquiry.

Room dividers or screens are a necessary item in any classroom, particularly if they are constructed of cardboard or lightweight wood for easy mobility. One suggestion for making inexpensive screens is to purchase folding cardboard work areas commonly used by home seamstresses. These may be found in fabric stores. Additional working spaces, interest centers, or skill areas may be temporarily created out of the dividers and then taken down when the need for that space no longer exists. Some children prefer to complete their independent work behind a screen and will elect to partition themselves off until their task is accomplished.

Study carrels can provide another option for space. If, for instance, the students' needs indicate additional concentration in a given academic area, a skill station may be set up for that purpose. For example, if several individuals need practice in a language skill such as plurals, a minilesson may be set up at a study carrel, where each child needing the lesson would go to complete a task or activity independently some time during the day. When the work on plurals is no longer necessary, another center could be created, and another skill stressed. The use of study carrels for skill stations provides an alternative to seatwork activites dominated by dittoed worksheets.

It is suggested that teachers who have the opportunity to purchase and order their own study carrels for the classroom select carrels that come equipped with electrical cords and outlets. This type of carrel not only provides lighting for the work area but allows for the placement of audiovisual equipment requiring electricity to operate.

Since field trips can be a vital part of the language curriculum, space should be provided for the display of photographs taken while out in the community. These photographs promote the recall of concrete experiences and serve as the basis for oral and written language lessons. Specifically, such pictures provide the focus for working on particular language constructions. For example, after a trip to the zoo, the teacher can use the photographs to develop verb tenses. In asking the children, "Where did we go yesterday?" the children are encouraged to use past tense verbs such as in, "We *went* to the zoo." The teacher can use subsequent questions to elicit a variety of past tense verbs:

Teacher:	What animals did we see?
Children:	We *saw* monkeys, or We *watched* the elephant.
T:	What did the elephant eat?
C:	The elephant *ate* hay.

In addition to using the photograph center for structured language lessons, it may be used as a tool for motivating interaction between children. Providing a quiet corner in the classroom should also be considered. A quiet area, preferably a carpeted space, is a welcome place for children to look through books and magazines or to listen to music.

Providing all of these features in a classroom may not be possible, given the constraints and physical restrictions of different facilities. However, Exhibit 2-3 presents a floor plan that incorporates many of the suggested features.

MANAGING BEHAVIORS IN TEACHING LANGUAGE

The S → R → S Paradigm

Whether the teacher works with children in groups, individually, or, as in most cases, a combination of both, certain teaching strategies that have been successfully utilized to manage children's behavior in language training should be noted. One is the use of the S → R → S paradigm. The S → R → S model helps to structure the language lesson so that maximum use can be made of the time available.

The teacher must strive for the most efficient use of the instructional day. The goal of each language lesson should be to elicit the greatest number of correct responses that the child is able to produce in the time allotted. However, some behaviors may limit the optimum use of instructional time. Children occasionally lose attention to the task. This lack of attention may manifest itself in the loss of eye contact, loss of concentration, or incorrect responses. If the teacher is not skilled in the proper use of behavior management techniques to keep the child on task, valuable instruction time will be wasted.

The S → R → S paradigm is based on the principle that behavior is managed by the stimulus events following a response. In other words, the way in which a child's response is reinforced will determine whether that response occurs again.

The S → R → S paradigm can be represented as a three-step process. First, the preceding stimulus (S) is presented to the child by the teacher. This stimulus may be verbal, visual, or a combination of both. Second, the child responds (R) to the preceding stimulus either verbally, by a motor response such as pointing, or by another appropriate mode. Third, depending on whether the child's response is correct or incorrect, the teacher presents the consequent stimulus (S). The consequent stimulus may consist of either positive reinforcement or some form of correction procedure. The following example illustrates the S → R → S paradigm in a language lesson.

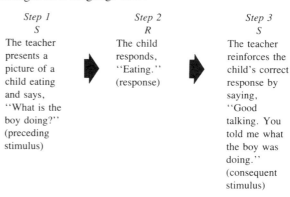

Step 1 S	*Step 2* R	*Step 3* S
The teacher presents a picture of a child eating and says, "What is the boy doing?" (preceding stimulus)	The child responds, "Eating." (response)	The teacher reinforces the child's correct response by saying, "Good talking. You told me what the boy was doing." (consequent stimulus)

Exhibit 2-3 A Sample Room Arrangement

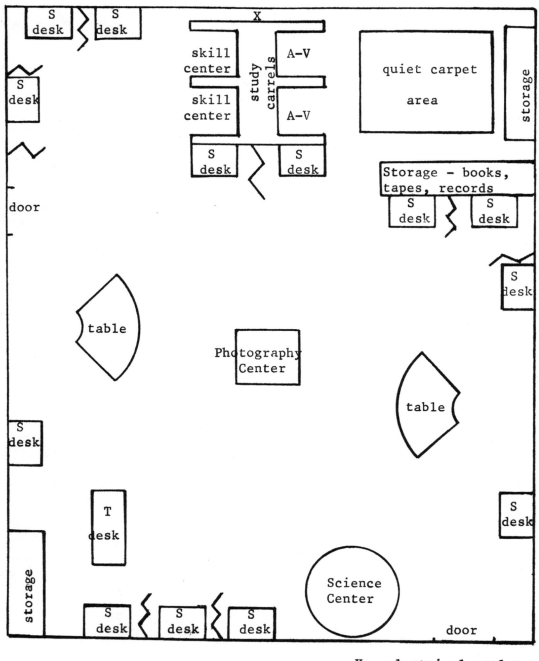

X = electrical outlet
= room divider
T = teacher
S = student
A-V = audiovisual

In this example, the teacher has reinforced the appropriate response with verbal praise, thereby increasing the likelihood that the child will respond with a similar, appropriate response the next time the stimulus is presented.

If the child responds incorrectly, the teacher should use a correction procedure by modeling, by using physical assistance if the expected response is a motor response, or by repeating the stimulus. Thus:

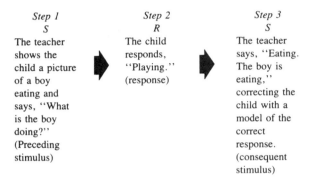

Step 1
S
The teacher shows the child a picture of a boy eating and says, "What is the boy doing?" (Preceding stimulus)

Step 2
R
The child responds, "Playing." (response)

Step 3
S
The teacher says, "Eating. The boy is eating," correcting the child with a model of the correct response. (consequent stimulus)

Use of Reinforcers

In the first illustration above, the consequent stimulus was verbal reinforcement, or praise. However, there are a multitude of reinforcers available for use as consequent stimuli. One needs only to observe the child to determine which reinforcers would be interesting to the child and produce the desired response. These reinforcers may include edible (primary) reinforcers, activity reinforcers that the child may manipulate or play with, token reinforcers that may be traded for an activity or object, and social reinforcers that represent verbal or physical approval. Use of the sample list of reinforcers in Appendix D will enable the teacher to vary the repertoire of reinforcers used in the language training process.

The use of the S ⟶ R ⟶ S paradigm and the effective use of reinforcers structures the language lesson and aids the teacher in evaluating the child's progress toward the specified objective. By also including a system of collecting data on the child's correct and incorrect responses, the teacher is able to determine when the child has mastered the desired language construction, as well as effectively manage the child's language behaviors by making it a rewarding experience to produce appropriate verbal responses.

TECHNIQUES IN LANGUAGE TRAINING

In conducting the daily language lesson, the teacher should be aware of the effective techniques commonly used in language training. These techniques include modeling, expansion, correction, and branching.

Modeling

Modeling refers to the teacher's verbatim presentation of the actual language construction desired, thus enabling the child to hear the correct usage of the construction as an example. For instance, if the child is working on the nominative pronoun *she,* the teacher first models the appropriate use of the target construction. The teacher could say, "Look at these pictures. *She* is jumping. *She* is swimming. *She* is running."

This technique is similar to what has been termed *bombardment* in the ear training phase of the Developmental Syntax Program by Coughran and Liles (1976). In this program, the child is presented with numerous repetitions of the appropriate use of the construction.

Modeling may also be used as a simple means of eliciting a response. If we consider a major goal of language training to be the gradual withdrawal of adult assistance as the child learns to produce the responses independently, then modeling would be the step that employs maximum assistance. Modeling language for the child requires an imitative response and is therefore the easiest step for the child.

One may envision the language training process as one in which the roles of the child and teacher are inversely related.

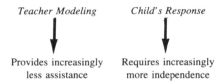

Teacher Modeling

Provides increasingly less assistance

Child's Response

Requires increasingly more independence

As the language teacher provides less modeling, the child assumes more responsibility for producing the construction independently.

Mowery and Replogle (1977) provide a five-step process that represents this relationship and leads to the generalization of the desired language construction. The following demonstration of this process uses the example previously cited, that of teaching the nominative pronoun, *she:*

Step 1. The teacher provides an imitative model of the target construction.

Teacher: She is jumping.
Desired student response: She is jumping.

Step 2. The teacher provides the target construction followed by intervening language. Here, the child is required to remember the construction for a longer period of time.

Teacher: She is jumping. What is *she* doing?
Desired student response: She is jumping.

Step 3. The teacher provides the construction in an alternative form, in this case, as a question.

> *Teacher:* What is *she* doing?
> *Desired student response: She* is eating.

Step 4. The teacher elicits the target construction by asking an open-ended question. Note that the model *she* is not included.

> *Teacher:* Tell me about the girl.
> *Desired student response: She* is running.

Step 5. The teacher provides a natural setting where the child's use of the target language construction can be observed. In this step, there is no prompting of the child.

Thus, as the teacher reduces the verbal assistance given to the child, the child gradually generalizes the correct use of the construction.

Modeling, then, may be used to initiate or elicit a response in the initial phases of language training, taking care to gradually move the child away from the imitation of target constructions.

Expansion

Expansion refers to enlarging the child's response in conversation:

> *Child:* Cat drinking.
> *Teacher:* Yes, the cat is drinking milk.

The syntax in the child's original phrase is preserved, yet the teacher has expanded it to include the article *the,* the auxiliary verb *is,* and a direct object *milk.*

Research evidence suggests that expansion to the next highest level of language construction is an effective technique in language training (Stremel & Ruder, 1973). Combined with other techniques, expansion can help a child be successful in learning language.

Correction

The commonly used practice of correcting a child's errors in spontaneous conversation has not proven to be as effective as one might assume.

> *Child:* The dog runned.
> *Teacher:* No, we say the dog *ran.*

In most cases, the child will continue to make the same errors, despite the good intentions of the correcting adult.

However, if we look at correction as a procedure in the formal language training process, its effectiveness becomes more apparent. In a formal language lesson, when the child

makes errors, the teacher should make use of correction procedures by providing the child with the appropriate model of the response. By effective use of the S $\longrightarrow$ R $\longrightarrow$ S model and by withholding reinforcement for incorrect responses, the child should make fewer and fewer errors.

Branching

Branching is a technique used to provide intermediate steps to help the child over problem areas in a language program. Branching may be contained within the content of a language program, its sequence of steps, or in the method of presentation by the teacher. For example, if a child is having difficulty discriminating between objects placed *in* and *on* a table when presented together, branching steps should be included. These branching steps reteach the prepositions *in* and *on* separately, using concrete objects. When the child has met the criterion for each preposition separately, then the two are combined again. Branching provides the child with a way to learn successfully a discrimination task in smaller steps.

The teacher must be able to utilize the data collected in the training process, evaluate it, and determine how and when to branch. Gray and Ryan (1973) have developed charting configurations that aid in determining the relative effectiveness of the language program. By observing the performance as graphed in percentages of correct responses, the teacher can examine whether the steps are too big and if branching is necessary.

Table 2-1 presents five types of chart configuration collected by Gray and Ryan in language training. Though the data are specific to their language program, the information gathered from such data can be more universally applied.

The teacher must be continually aware of the day-to-day progress of the child, so that the language program may be task analyzed, if necessary, to provide for branching from one step to the next. When providing language training these four techniques should be utilized as needed:

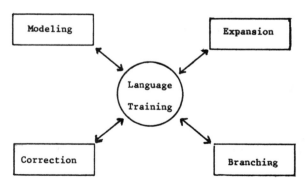

These techniques represent ways in which the teacher can individualize language training and improve instructional effectiveness.

Table 2-1 Five Types of Chart Configurations

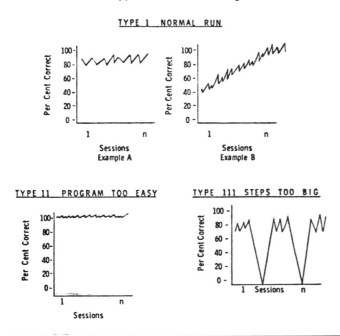

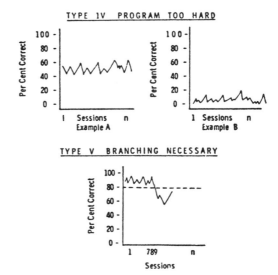

Source: Reprinted from Burl B. Gray and Bruce P. Ryan, *A Language Program for the Nonlanguage Child,* Champaign, Ill., 1973, with permission of Research Press.

LEARNER CHARACTERISTICS IN THE ACQUISITION OF LANGUAGE

Children who are learning language exhibit certain characteristics at different developmental stages. Knowing these characteristics not only helps in evaluating the stage of the child's language development but also assists the teacher in planning language training. These characteristics include overextension, overgeneralization, buttressing, self-correction, and buildup.

Overextension

Overextension refers to the child's incorrect reference of a word meaning to objects with similar features (Clark, 1973). A child may use the label *car* for all multiwheeled vehicles, including trains, trucks, and motorcycles. In overextension, the child's concept of the word is limited, applying a small set of features as defining characteristics to a broad number of objects. This is a commonly found characteristic among children who are beginning to learn language. As the child's language develops, more specific features are perceived, and objects are more clearly distinguished from others. The child learns that these objects carry distinctive labels of their own.

Overgeneralization

Overgeneralization refers to the child applying grammatical rules to more specific cases than is required. For

example, "he runned" demonstrates a child overgeneralizing the regular past tense verb ending *ed* to an irregular verb.

Buttressing

Buttressing, according to Muma and Muma (1979), involves backing up one form of language construction with another. This frequently occurs when the child is learning to use pronouns. For example, the child may say, "Boy, he ran home." In this instance, the child had been using *him* as the subject pronoun rather than the more appropriate form *he*. When the child moved to the correct pronoun, *he* in the subject place, the word *boy* was inserted to back up the new form. As children learn new forms of words and begin to refine their language, buttressing often occurs. It serves as the child's base of confidence when trying new linguistic forms.

Self-Correction

Self-correction in learning language is just as its name implies—a correction that children make in their own use of language. Self-correction frequently occurs when the child is working on the next highest language construction. For example, suppose the child's language up to a certain point has been characterized by the use of only present tense verbs. As the child begins to develop the higher form of past tense verbs, self-correction is often the intermediate step in this process of language refinement. For example: "The boy run. The boy ran."

Buildup

After a particular language construction is firmly established in the child's repertoire, there is a natural tendency for the child to build up this construction by including additional qualifying words (Muma & Muma, 1979). An example of a child using buildup is illustrated by the following statements: "I make soup. I make big soup. I eat it. I eat it all." This exemplifies a child who is extending language from a constant system or security base to the use of more refined language constructions.

The way in which a child uses techniques such as overextension, overgeneralization, buttressing, self-correction, and buildup provides the teacher with information on the child's development in acquiring language. Careful observation of the child's existing language serves as a guide for the teacher who must plan the language curriculum.

SUMMARY

There is a strong interrelationship between language and cognitive development. The special education teacher's responsibility is to develop an effective language curriculum that maximizes the child's development. When developing the language curriculum, attention must be given to the selection of instructional materials, organization of resources, methods of monitoring student performance, and the design of the classroom setting. The teacher must also be able to make the most efficient use of the instructional day by utilizing effective behavioral management strategies and language training techniques, including modeling, expansion, correction, and branching.

Finally, the teacher must be aware of major learner characteristics in the acquisition of language. Behavioral characteristics such as overextension, overgeneralization, buttressing, self-correction, and buildup provide the teacher with important information regarding the child's current language developmental level.

REFERENCES

Clark, E. What's in a word. In T.E. Moore (Ed.), *Cognitive development and the acquisition of language*. New York: Academic Press, 1973.

Coughran, L., & Liles, B. *Developmental syntax*. Austin, Tex.: Learning Concepts, 1976.

Gray, B., & Ryan, B. *A language program for the nonlanguage child*. Champaign, Ill.: Research Press, 1973.

Mowery, C., & Replogle, A. *Developmental language lessons*. Boston: Teaching Resources, 1977.

Muma, J., & Muma, D. *Muma assessment program*. Lubbock, Tex.: Natural Child Publication, 1979.

Stremel, K., & Ruder, K. *Utilization of grammatical expansions in language training* (Bureau of Child Research Working Paper). Lawrence, Kans.: University of Kansas, 1973.

Chapter 3

Coordinating the Home/School Language Training Program

THE PARENT/TEACHER INSTRUCTIONAL TEAM

Some Potential Problems

In recent years great emphasis has been placed on the inclusion of parents in the education of the exceptional child. Research evidence suggests that not only are parents helpful in the educational process but they may be crucial to its success.

Stile and Cole (1978) state that parental involvement has been encouraged in special education programs for several reasons:

1. Parents have a special relationship with their child.
2. Participation by parents increases manpower resources.
3. Parent participation reduces the cost of instruction.
4. Parent involvement is a means of solving the unique problems of time and distance in providing education to handicapped students in sparsely populated, rural areas.

Program Design

While parent involvement in the educational process is crucial, attempts at getting parents involved have not always been successful. Some of the best-intended parent involvement programs have failed or met with limited success because of a failure to design the training program in such a way that it supports effective involvement. For example, too many programs offer only token involvement for parents.

Under these conditions, parents soon feel of little value and drop out.

Another potential problem area centers around the failure to provide adequate monitoring and follow-up. This is a special problem for home-based language training programs. Parents who are given a single training session without a mechanism for regular feedback and monitoring often experience frustration and disappointment in their efforts.

More than ever before in the history of this country we find many families in which both parents hold full-time jobs. In addition, there is an increasing number of single-parent families. This change in family dynamics usually results in parents having limited amounts of time to spend with their children. Obviously, then, language training that requires great amounts of the parents' time may be unreasonable in terms of program expectations and is probably doomed to failure. Furthermore, short, intensive language training sessions seem to be more effective than long, drawn-out activities that leave both parent and child fatigued.

In home-based training programs, the special education teacher must be careful that the training objectives are in agreement with the perceived needs of the parents. For example, if the program focuses exclusively on developing expressive language skills when the parents' greatest need is to reduce the child's tantruming behavior, the results may be disappointing. Sometimes it is necessary to help the parents begin a program working on skills that they view as having priority before starting the desired language training program.

Parent-Staff Interaction

One of the easiest ways to lose parent participation is to have key staff members who are not parent oriented. The teacher must make sure that the parents' contact with ancillary personnel and paraprofessionals is positive and supportive.

Another problem can occur when there is disagreement between the parent and teacher over teaching styles or philosophies. Discipline is a typical area of disagreement. Fortunately, most of these disagreements can be avoided if the teacher anticipates potential problem areas and discusses them with the parents.

Occasionally, there may arise a sense of competition between staff and parent for the child's attention, or over who is doing the most effective teaching. These, of course, are immature feelings and must be recognized as being counterproductive. It then becomes the job of the teacher to reestablish the attitude that the parent and program staff are crucial parts of the same team, working toward the same language development goals for the child.

Problems in Family Dynamics

Some parents become discouraged with language training programs because their original expectations were much too high and the child's progress is much too slow. The teacher must be careful to explain fully that language development and language training are often slow, step-by-step processes, especially with children who have language problems. Reasonable goals and objectives must be established by the teacher so that parents have guidelines for their own expectations.

Problems can arise if only one parent is committed to the language training program. This is especially true in home-based training programs that require time commitments and family cooperation. In this case, the teacher should make every effort to gain the support, if not the total involvement, of both parents.

Some families can be viewed as "multiple problem families" (Neifert & Gayton, 1973). These families have a difficult time maintaining involvement in the training program because of problems involving things like finances, health, and marital relations. Such families usually must focus on the most immediate crisis, and expectations for extended involvement in a language training program may be quite unrealistic.

Parent Mobility

Finally, we must look at parent mobility. Interestingly, problems may arise both when there is too much mobility and when there is too little mobility. Dr. Anne Garner-Gallegos (1979) conducted a survey in which parents were asked what might prevent them from participating in a parent training program. She found the following cited reasons: (1) The training was at inconvenient times. (2) The training was not conveniently located. (3) The training sessions conflicted with other activities. (4) Some parents preferred not to go out alone at night.

Some Solutions

The teacher, then, has a number of variables to take into account when soliciting the help of parents in the language training program. In an effort to facilitate this process, Stile and Rimac (1979) suggest dividing parent involvement strategies into preprogram, program, and postprogram efforts. The following summarizes their suggestions and adapts them to a language training program:

1. **Preprogram Stategies**
   - Provide some type of program orientation. For example, parents may be encouraged to visit programs already in progress and to talk with current participants.
   - Establish a contractual agreement with the parents. Make sure that the parents are provided with information that clearly outlines the extent of their involvement. This acceptance into the program should be based on their willingness to accept these conditions. It is important to note that not all parents should necessarily be required to have the same level of participation.
   - Assess the individual needs of each child and make sure that the parents are aware of those needs.
   - Make sure that parents have an opportunity for input with regard to their child's needs as they see them.

2. **Program Strategies**
   - Be sure that each child's program is truly individualized.
   - Provide daily home carryover activities.
   - Require regular feedback from the home regarding the child's language development.
   - Develop a method of keeping in frequent contact with the home. This is most often done through regularly scheduled conferences.
   - If possible, provide transportation to the program site for parents who are in need of it.
   - Lend parents language training materials for use in home-based programs.

3. **Postprogram Strategies**
   - Use former parent participants as trainers in subsequent parent involvement programs.
   - Assist parents with follow-up services, such as contacting other agencies or programs where the child may receive services.
   - Have parents participate in evaluating the program.

COMMUNICATING WITH PARENTS OF EXCEPTIONAL CHILDREN

Effective communication with parents is certainly one of the keys to a successful language training program. However, it is interesting to note that, though teachers are supposedly experts at communicating with children and youth, we do not always transfer these important skills when interacting with parents. A favorite story of the authors is about the woman who, after all her children had been raised and left home, surprisingly found herself pregnant again. While she was prepared to face the loss of the freedom she had so anticipated, she couldn't bear the thought of 13 more years of parent/teacher conferences.

A common parent reaction to a poor parent/teacher conference is a feeling of frustration, and sometimes anger. Too often, the teacher spends the entire conference listing all the child's negative behaviors without making any constructive suggestions or mentioning the child's strengths. This usually results in the parent dreading and even avoiding future conferences, and the teacher becomes disappointed at what appears to be a lack of interest on the part of the parents. Ultimately, the child is the real loser when situations like this develop.

One of the authors spent four years as an elementary school counselor/psychologist and observed teachers who were both effective at interacting and those who were less successful. From those experiences, the following ten steps for successful communication with parents have evolved:

1. Do not wait until small problems become large ones. Make contact with the parents while the problem is still manageable.
2. Send home "good work slips" as well as "bad work slips." Do not make your only contact with parents during periods when the child is having problems.
3. Try to have the parent conference in a comfortable environment. If the conference is to be held at school, make sure that the parents have adult size chairs to sit in, and arrange for the conference to be held in private. Sometimes it is better to hold a conference in the parents' home where they feel most comfortable. This is especially important for parents who feel threatened in the school setting.
4. Remember to point out the child's strengths, not only the problem areas. All children have some strengths worthy of mention.
5. Whether you are discussing a child's strengths or weaknesses, be sure to be behavior specific. Simply telling parents that their child has immature language is of little value. Instead, examples of the child's language should be cited to give a clearer picture of the language problem. Recorded language samples are one of the best ways to do this.
6. Avoid excessive use of technical jargon. Education, along with other helping professions such as psychology, medicine, and law, has often been guilty of hiding behind a smoke screen of technical jargon that is incomprehensible to the lay person. Too often this jargon has served as a way to avoid saying, "I am not quite sure how to solve your child's problems." Speaking succinctly, with an understandable vocabulary will result in better teacher-parent communication.
7. Avoid the hazards involved in "talking down" to parents. Some teachers talk to parents as if they were lecturing their students. Parents, like students, will come with varying levels of intelligence and sophistication in the field of education. The skilled teacher can quickly adjust to the appropriate level of communication.
8. Listen to what parents have to say. They know their child better than anyone else. Ask them for their ideas on how best to work with their child. Besides providing a source of valuable information, this shows parents that you respect them as key members of the educational team.
9. Keep a written summary of each conference in your files. It is difficult, if not impossible, to remember the exact contents of all parent conferences without recording the pertinent facts.
10. Finally, if possible, provide the parents with some type of feedback after the conference, especially if new ideas, strategies, or objectives have evolved. This is a personal touch that most parents greatly appreciate. A brief note or telephone call does the job nicely.

PARENTS AS TEACHERS IN THE LANGUAGE TRAINING PROCESS

Parent-Teacher Interaction

Most special education teachers concerned with effective language training are well aware that six hours a day of formal instruction, five days a week, is simply not enough for most exceptional children. Furthermore, there may be regression in language development over the summer if the child does not participate in some type of summer school program. In order to maximize language development and to prevent regression in learning, the only logical solution seems to be some degree of parent involvement in the instructional process.

There is, however, resistance to parental involvement by some educators. The authors are well aware of the old argument that parents do not have the professional training that is necessary to teach their children. On close examination, this argument does not make much sense, since the average parent spends more time teaching the child in the home environment than all the combined instructional time the child will ever receive in the school setting. It is true that the parent's involvement may not constitute formal instruction, but teaching and learning occur nevertheless. It is also true that some parents are better teachers than others, but all parents can be taught a few skills to make them an effective part of the instructional team in the home.

First, the parents must establish a specific time of the day to work with their child on identified language skills. This is often difficult for busy families, but it is crucial to a successful home-based program. This time must be as dependable as the dinner hour.

Formal instruction sessions should be kept brief. A typical lesson might last 15-20 minutes. A surprising amount of instruction can take place in a short period of time if the parents are aware of the need to stay on the task and adhere to a regular daily schedule. As previously mentioned, long, drawn-out sessions tend to be frustrating for both parent and child.

In the beginning, the parent should not focus on the teaching of more than one or two language skills at a time. As the parents become more comfortable with the teaching sessions, one or even two more skills may be added. The general rule of thumb, however, is to focus on not more than two or three skill areas at a time.

The need for short, regularly scheduled formal training sessions should again be emphasized. In addition to this, informal training in language may take place any time the parent and child interact. Language, unlike many other skills, is a natural human activity that occurs continuously. Parents should always seize the opportunity to elicit language from their children.

Parents must be made aware of the need to reinforce appropriate language during the regular language training sessions. The teacher can help the parent establish reinforcers that can be used in the home. (See Appendix D for various types of reinforcers appropriate for use in the home and school.) Parents must understand that the most effective instruction takes place when the focus is on positive child behaviors.

The teacher should show the parents how to keep daily records of the child's progress. Simple charts and graphs can be developed and used in the home. Use of daily records is important for maintaining coordination between the home and school.

Finally, it helps to be able to lend or give parents language training materials and ideas to be used in the home. There are available well-programmed commercial language materials that would be excellent for this purpose. In addition, the teacher can show parents how to make their own language training materials, such as flashcards and picture cards. The parents may also be shown how to use books, magazines, and other objects found in the home as focal points for discussion.

Managing Language Experiences in the Home

Parents have a significant impact on the communication skills of their child. They interact with the child in a way no other adults do and thus play important roles as natural teachers of language. The home becomes a center of learning, where the child can experience and learn language in uncontrived situations. If the parent is aware of language, and of the many opportunities that exist in the home for teaching language, these learning experiences can become even more meaningful for the child.

There may be several components to a parent-assisted language program in the home. The nature of the parent participation, and therefore of the parameters of the training, will depend on the needs of the child involved.

Training Parents in Behavior Management Skills

Behavior problems can be common among children with learning handicaps; thus the need to help parents manage behavior in the home becomes a high priority in the training program. Parents must often deal with noncompliant behavior in their children, such as tantruming, lack of attention, and failure to follow directions. Training programs that aid parents in handling these problem behaviors do much to enhance the conditions of learning and the readiness of the child to participate in more specific language training.

In addition, the application of behavior management skills and contingency management, such as the $S \longrightarrow R \longrightarrow S$ paradigm in the learning of language within the home, facilitates earlier and more comprehensive generalization of language skills. Appropriate use of the $S \longrightarrow R \longrightarrow S$ technique can be modeled for the parent by the teacher. When the parent tries it, the teacher can provide feedback. Such feedback gives the parent the skill and confidence to utilize the technique in the home.

Even though parents already teach language, they can be taught to be more efficient at it. If they are skilled in the techniques of differentially reinforcing appropriate language constructions and applying contingencies to specific language behaviors, the child's acquisition and refinement of language will proceed more rapidly.

In their coordinated efforts, the home-school team of parents and teacher can provide consistency in the content and methods used in the language training program. This consistency ensures that the child will make continuous progress toward the desired language goal.

Parental Understanding of Normal Language Development

Ideally, parents should be aware of the development of language in the normal child, as a guide for the language development of their own child. Parents should be familiar with sequences of language constructions and when they are commonly acquired by the normally developing child. It becomes the responsibility of the teacher to communicate such information to the parents.

Knowledge of developmental milestones in language will aid the parents in listening to and observing their own child. It will give them guidelines for initiating instruction and for selecting activities that are appropriate and meaningful to their child's current level of language functioning.

Parent Follow-Up

Another component of parent participation in the language intervention process consists of training the parent to check for the generalization of language skills learned in the classroom. Central to the learning of language is the carryover or generalization of an elicited language construction to the child's spontaneous language repertoire. One cannot claim success in a school-based language training program unless the child actually uses the newly learned language skills across all settings. Training parents in what to listen for, in charting language in the home, and in communicating the child's progress enables the teacher to determine if generalization has taken place. The carryover of language training in the home setting provides consistency in working with the child and maximizes the potential for successful acquisition of language.

Teaching Parents How To Provide Language Stimulation in the Home

Parents must be made aware of the many opportunities for learning language that exist in the home. There are hundreds of daily, routine activities in the home that can be transformed into language learning for the child. Encouraging the parent to provide these experiences will foster cognitive development and accelerate the language learning process. For example, if the child is asked to put clean silverware into a divided drawer, the child will be sorting according to physical properties or function. By placing all forks, knives, and spoons in their respective compartments, the child is practicing categorization of objects. Sorting clothes, setting the table, and putting away toys provide similar classification practice and are easily performed in the home.

There are other considerations for parents who want to positively affect their child's language development. The following guidelines will facilitate language training in the home:

- Talk *with,* not at, the child. Though this seems simplistic, it nevertheless forms the basis for the home language training program. The more practice in talking and interacting the child has, the more proficient the child will become in using language for its various purposes.

- Point out to the child the names and labels for common objects and activities in the home or community. For example, the parent might say, "Look, there is a road grader. It is pushing the dirt to the side of the road. They are going to pave the road." Naming and labeling will increase the child's receptive and expressive vocabulary and enlarge the child's core of usable words.

- Expand the child's sentences. Expansions provide a more mature, correct form of language construction and help the child develop longer sentences. If the child uses a two-word phrase such as "cat eat," enlarge the phrase by providing a model of the adult form. "Yes, the cat is eating" would be an appropriate expansion of the child's statement.

- Make language functional for the child. Encourage the child to use language for the satisfaction of needs. Instead of pointing, the child should be required to verbalize what is wanted. "I want cookie" or "want juice" would be appropriate alternatives to gestures.

- Read to the child and discuss what has been read. Set aside a daily time when the parent and child can read, listen, and evaluate together the events of a story. This promotes recognition of a sequence of activities and furthers comprehension of what is heard.

- Employ music, rhythm, and singing to develop the child's sense of rhythm, sequence of words, and awareness of sound—all important aspects in learning language. Family singing, listening to the stereo, or playing with musical toys can provide valuable language experiences. As these experiences are provided, talk about them with the child. For example, using a toy xylophone, strike a chord and say, "Oh, I hit a *high* sound. Let's see if we can hit a *low* sound." Or, "Make the drum beat *fast*. Make it *slow*." Talking about these experiences as the child is participating not only makes the child aware of the musical qualities of rhythm, pitch, tone and tempo but also increases the understanding of the language concepts associated with these characteristics.

- Hold dinner conversations in which the child is included. This makes the child aware of the social purpose of language and communication.
- Allow the child to help with tasks around the house. As the parent and child perform an activity, there should be discussion about the action, such as "We're folding clothes, aren't we? The socks go here. The shirts go here. Put the pants there." Again, this calls the child's attention to the names of objects and gives practice in classifying.
- Control the environment of the language lesson by turning off radios and television, quieting other children in the home, and removing family pets. Removing distracting visual and auditory stimuli will allow the child to direct full attention to the language task.
- Utilize newspapers, magazines, and catalogs commonly found around the house as points of interest for the child. Pictures in these publications can provide a focal point for discussion of objects and events.
- Encourage the child's interaction with peers. Allow the child to play with other children by inviting children to the house and by letting the child seek friends in the neighborhood outside the house. This encourages social communication.

- Ask the child questions that require more than a one-word response. Open-ended questions, such as, "Tell me what is happening," require the child to give a longer verbal response than statements like, "Tell me what the man is doing."

When these guidelines are applied, the atmosphere for stimulating language in the home will be greatly enhanced. The home environment will then become a place where the child learns to use language to communicate, inquire, describe, and investigate. (Appendix E provides the reader with an annotated bibliography of parent involvement materials for both parents and professionals.)

SUMMARY

Several levels of parent involvement may be explored in providing language training for the child. The one selected by the teacher will depend upon the goals and objectives of the language training program. Parents may be utilized to provide carryover of skills learned at school into the home, or they may be used as natural teachers of language in the home environment. The participation of parents in the language training program provides a much needed human resource to complete the makeup of the instructional team.

REFERENCES

Garner-Gallegos, A. *An examination of two delivery models with regard to program effectiveness and extent of parent involvement.* Unpublished dissertation, New Mexico State University, 1979.

Neifert, T., & Gayton, W.F. Parents and the home program approach in the remediation of learning disabilities. *Journal of Learning Disabilities,* 1973, *6,* 85-89.

Stile, S.W., & Cole, J.T. *Parent attrition in programs for exceptional children: Extent of the problem, associated factors and strategies for minimizing the phenomenon.* Paper presented at the annual conference of the Council for Exceptional Children, Kansas City, Mo., May 3, 1978. (ERIC Document Reproduction Service No. ED 153 420)

Stile, S.W., & Rimac, R.T. *Parent Attrition in First Chance Projects: A Survey.* Unpublished manuscript, 1979.

Chapter 4

Considerations for Language Training in a Multicultural Society

THE MELTING POT vs. MULTICULTURALISM

Much of the greatness of the United States can be attributed to its cultural diversity. However, this diversity has not always been a valued goal of our society. In fact, the emergence of 19th century nationalism and the period of isolationism following World War I contributed greatly to what became known as the "melting pot" theory. The melting pot theory promoted a one country, one culture concept. The intent was for all new immigrants to be assimilated into one large American culture with English as the common language (Mackey, 1978). The role of the schools was to assist in this assimilation process by discouraging language and cultural diversity while supporting the evolution of a single American culture (McLaughlin, 1978).

In recent years, the melting pot theory has come under heavy criticism by many Americans, both minorities and nonminorities. These people say that the melting pot ideology has failed and that we must accept the fact that multiculturalism is in the best interest of Americans. Multiculturalism can be defined as the simultaneous existence of two or more cultures. This coexistence allows for parity and equal respect among all cultures regardless of size or power (Stent, Hazard, & Rivlin, 1973).

MULTICULTURAL EDUCATION

At one time, children who entered the public schools with language or cultural differences were often automatically placed in special education classrooms. That minority children were so readily diagnosed as having learning handicaps brought about accusations of discrimination and violation of individual rights.

Two major factors were responsible for the cessation of these practices and for the progression toward multicultural education. First, research in education and the behavioral sciences revealed the biasing effects of measuring the cognitive abilities of minority children with traditional standardized tests. Second, federal laws now require certain procedures before minority children can be identified as having learning handicaps.

With regard to the measurement of the cognitive abilities of minority children, Mercer (1975) found that a disproportionate number of minority children were enrolled in special education classrooms. Specifically, "300% more Mexican-American and 50% more Blacks than their proportion in the general population . . . but only 60% as many Anglo-Americans . . . as would be expected" (p. 133).

In addition, de Burciaga (1974) found that teachers with little understanding of cultural diversity often made instructional recommendations and decisions based on the findings of intelligence tests. de Burciaga also found that schools that placed great emphasis upon the results of intelligence tests often allowed students to go long periods of time without intellectual reevaluations. This type of research has called attention to the many injustices minority children have traditionally faced in the schools.

The second major source or reform has involved litigation in the courts and legislation. The courts have made it clear that traditional standardized tests are of questionable value when attempting to determine a minority child's intellectual ability (*Diana v. Board of Education of California*, 1973; and *Larry P. v. Riles*, 1972).

In addition to judicial decisions, the federal government has implemented important legislation affecting multicultural education. Singletary, Collings, and Dennis (1977) have pointed out that the Education for All Handicapped Children Act of 1975 (P.L. 94-142) is based upon prior litigation in the courts. P.L. 94-142 clearly points out that multicultural education is to be considered in guaranteeing an equal educational opportunity for handicapped minorities. Furthermore, the law mandates a "free and appropriate" education for handicapped children and requires the development of an individual education plan (IEP) for each child. This plan must take into consideration multicultural education, where appropriate, for minority children.

With respect to the language of minority children, a note of caution must be emphasized. When determining the language skills of minority children, care must be taken not to mislabel a child's difficulty in learning English as a communication disorder. Cole and Cole (1981) warn about confusing bilingualism with a language delay:

The student diagnosed as language delayed may actually be a minority child who would be better served in a bilingual education program or in an English as a Second Language (ESL) program.

This does not imply that children of ethnic minorities do not exhibit language problems. However, it becomes the responsibility of the language practitioner to determine the difference and assist other professional personnel in determining the most appropriate placement for the child. (p. 38)

Table 4-1 Multicultural Education Competencies for the Language Training Program

Competency	Content	Procedures
1.0 Ideological, sociological, and historical awareness	1.0 Attitudes and beliefs about learning handicaps and language problems	1.0 Beliefs, values, and attitudes of some cultures regarding children who are intellectually or physically handicapped stem from religious beliefs and/or teachings. Some of the beliefs about the handicapped may be considered superstitions. Whatever their source, special educators must be aware of these attitudes if they are to interact effectively with these children and their parents.
	1.1 Parental attitudes about education and the schools	1.1 Parental involvement is crucial to all special education programs. A major obstacle with some minority parents involves their role as parents in the special education program. For many undereducated parents, the school setting is a foreign, even threatening, environment. Some minority parents believe that school is for children only and that parents should not "interfere" with their child's education. In many cases, the need for involvement has never been properly explained to minority parents. Language and cultural barriers frequently prohibit effective communication between parent and teacher. A sincere and continued effort on the part of the educator is needed to overcome these obstacles.
	1.2 Family structure	1.2 The educator must be aware of the place of the family structure within the particular culture. Special attention must be given to family customs and traditions as well as to the role of religion in the family.

CONSIDERATIONS FOR LANGUAGE TRAINING

No discussion of language training would be complete without consideration of the multicultural society that we live in and the important implications this has in the area of language development. An awareness of cultural differences will personalize language training and increase the minority child's interest in the language learning process. The teacher should be sensitive to and cognizant of cultural differences, so that when the language intervention program is planned, cultural experiences may be utilized to enrich the language environment. King, Barrera, Gorena, Fernandez, and Saenz (1976) suggest consideration of the following cultural factors when developing an instructional program that includes minority children:

- historical background
- important celebrations
- arts and crafts
- foods of the ethnic group
- poems, songs, and games
- dances
- legends, fables, and stories

Table 4-1, an adaptation of the work of Rodriguez, Cole, Stile, and Gallegos (1979), provides the teacher with guidelines to implement these cultural factors within the broader spectrum of the language curriculum and to include multicultural education in the language training program. The table presents three multicultural competencies: (1) ideological, sociological, and historical awareness; (2) parental and

Table 4-1 continued

Competency	Content	Procedures
2.0 Parental and community inclusion	2.0 Accept family and home in the classroom	2.0 Children should be encouraged to share with their classmates the unique features of their culture as demonstrated through the family. Photographs and stories about family members and family life should be promoted.
	2.1 Provide for direct parental participation	2.1 Minority parents should be encouraged to participate in classroom activities. Parents are great resources for the teacher. At first, there might be some hesitation on the parents' part, so encouragement and perseverance will be necessary.
	2.2 Communication in the dominant language	2.2 This is a difficult area to deal with since it is not reasonable to assume that the teacher will be able to communicate in the dominant language of the child and the child's parents. The teacher, therefore, should make a concerted effort to find someone in the school or community who can assist and has the necessary bilingual skills. A home visitor, aide, or another parent is preferable; but the teacher should not hesitate to ask secretaries, custodians, or even bus drivers for help in communicating, if necessary. Communication in the dominant language is particularly important when conferencing with parents regarding things such as program placement, IEPs, and the child's progress.
3.0 Multicultural curriculum for language training	3.0 Artistic creations a. folklore b. dress c. foods d. music e. dance	3.0 The special educator should incorporate artistic and musical work found in the targeted cultures. Children can easily participate in popular cultural songs and dances. The in-class preparation of common foods and the wearing of native costumes are also popular activities with children. The folklore of a culture is always fascinating and provides an excellent vehicle for language training activities.
	3.1 Multicultural language arts	3.1 This is obviously an important area for the minority handicapped child. Most of the language activities presented in Chapters 5, 6, and 7 can easily be modified and adapted to meet the needs of the minority handicapped child.

Source: Adapted from R. Rodriguez, J. Cole, S. Stile, and R. Gallegos. Bilingualism and biculturalism for the special education classroom. *Teacher Education and Special Education*, 1979, 2, 69–74, with permission of *Teacher Education and Special Education*.

community inclusion; and (3) the multicultural curriculum for the language training program. Next, the content of each competency area is outlined. Finally, suggested procedures for the implementation of each competency are briefly presented.

Providing for specific cultural experiences in the language curriculum is easily accomplished. The language lessons for the special education classroom in Chapters 5, 6, and 7 can be adapted to include dances, games, legends, stories, celebrations, and ethnic foods in the language training process.

With minor variations, many of these lessons emphasize ethnic or cultural customs.

SUMMARY

In recent years, the melting pot theory has come under a great deal of criticism. What has emerged is the concept of multiculturalism. With the belief in a multicultural society has come an emphasis on multicultural education. The language curriculum provides a natural area for the inclusion of ethnic and cultural factors.

REFERENCES

Cole, M., & Cole, J. *Effective intervention with the language impaired child.* Rockville, Md.: Aspen Systems Corporation, 1981.

de Burciaga, C. Towards quality education for Mexican-Americans. *Mexican-American educational study.* Washington, D.C.: Commission on Civil Rights, February 1974. (ERIC Document Reproduction Service No. ED 086 407)

Diana v. State Board of Education of California, Civil Action No. C-70, 37 RFP (N.D. Cal. 1973).

King, R.; Barrera, M.; Gorena, M.; Fernandez, I.; & Saenz, M. *Information and materials to teach the cultural heritage of the Mexican-American child.* Austin, Tex.: Dissemination and Assessment Center for Bilingual Education, 1976.

Larry P. v. Riles, 374 F. Supp. 1306 (1972).

Mackey, F. "Foreword" in T. Anderson & M. Boyer (Eds.), *Bilingual schooling in the United States* (2nd ed.). Austin, Tex.: National Education Laboratory Publishers, 1978.

McLaughlin, B. *Second-language acquisition in childhood.* Hillsdale, N.J.: Lawrence Erlbaum Associates, 1978.

Mercer, J. Psychological assessment and the rights of children. In N. Hobbs (Ed.), *Issues in the classification of children.* San Francisco, Calif.: Jossey Bass, 1975.

Rodriguez, R.; Cole, J.; Stile, S.; & Gallegos, R. Bilingualism and biculturalism for the special education classroom. *Teacher Education and Special Education,* 1979, 2, 69-74.

Singletary, E.; Collings, G.; & Dennis, H. *Law briefs on litigation and the rights of exceptional children, youth, and adults.* Washington, D.C.: University Press of America, 1977.

Stent, M.; Hazard, W.; & Rivlin, H. *Cultural pluralism in education: A mandate for change.* New York: Appleton-Century-Crofts, 1973.

Chapter 5

Lessons for Teaching Receptive Language Skills

USER'S GUIDE

RECEPTIVE LANGUAGE

PURPOSE:
To identify words beginning with a specific consonant

AREA OF LANGUAGE STRESSED:
Receptive phonology—Recognizing phonemes in their initial position

DURATION OF LESSON:
Fifteen minutes

LESSON FORMAT:
Group or individual

LESSON 1: CLAP WHEN YOU HEAR IT

MATERIALS/EQUIPMENT/PHYSICAL LAYOUT:
None

DESCRIPTION OF THE LESSON:
Explain that the children will play a listening game. Specify the initial consonant sound that the children will listen for, such as *m*. Give a number of words orally in succession, some that begin with *m*, others that do not. For example, present the words *me, ball, man, mix, see, mop, pat,* and *mug.* The children's task is to clap each time they hear a word beginning with the specified sound. Repeat this procedure for other sounds.

METHOD OF EVALUATION:
Determine the percentage of correct responses by dividing the number of correct responses by the total number of responses possible.

$$\frac{\text{Correct responses}}{\text{Total responses}} = \text{Percentage correct}$$

RECEPTIVE LANGUAGE

PURPOSE:
To identify words beginning with a specific consonant

AREA OF LANGUAGE STRESSED:
Receptive phonology—Recognizing phonemes in their initial position

DURATION OF LESSON:
Fifteen minutes

LESSON FORMAT:
Group or individual

LESSON 2: SISTER SUE

MATERIALS/EQUIPMENT/PHYSICAL LAYOUT:
Teacher-made story cards emphasizing specific phonemes

DESCRIPTION OF THE LESSON:
Read a story to the children. The story should emphasize a specific sound for the children to identify. For example, have the children listen for the sound *s*. Read or tell the story in which the sound is frequently used in the initial position of a word. Example: "Sue has a little sister. Sue loves to help her sister say silly things. She says soup, sawdust, sandwich, suds, and salamander." As the children listen to the story, they listen for the *s* sound and identify words beginning with *s* by raising their hands. This procedure may be repeated for other initial consonants.

METHOD OF EVALUATION:
Determine the percentage of correct responses by dividing the number of correct responses by the total number of responses possible.

$$\frac{\text{Correct responses}}{\text{Total responses}} = \text{Percentage correct}$$

RECEPTIVE LANGUAGE

PURPOSE:
   To recognize phonemes in their initial position

AREA OF LANGUAGE STRESSED:
   Receptive phonology—Recognizing phonemes in their initial position

DURATION OF LESSON:
   Fifteen minutes

LESSON FORMAT:
   Group or individual

LESSON 3: A TRIP TO THE ZOO

MATERIALS/EQUIPMENT/PHYSICAL LAYOUT:
   None

DESCRIPTION OF THE LESSON:
   Say to the children, "Let's pretend that we are going on a trip to the zoo. I see an animal. Its name begins with S. Guess what it is." If the children respond with "snake," "seal," or another appropriate animal whose name begins with S, record the response as correct. Repeat the procedure for other consonants.

METHOD OF EVALUATION:
   Determine the accuracy of the child's responses. It is suggested that an anecdotal record of the child's ability to recognize various phonemes in the initial position be maintained.

RECEPTIVE LANGUAGE

PURPOSE:
   To identify syllables using rhythm

AREA OF LANGUAGE STRESSED:
   Receptive phonology—Listening for syllables

DURATION OF LESSON:
   Twenty minutes

LESSON FORMAT:
   Group or individual

LESSON 4: WORD RHYTHMS

MATERIALS/EQUIPMENT/PHYSICAL LAYOUT:
   Rhythm sticks

DESCRIPTION OF THE LESSON:
   Explain to the children that words are made up of several sounds, or syllables. Model how the sounds of those words have a rhythm and may be tapped out using the rhythm sticks. Give the children a word and have them tap out the syllables with their sticks. The following are good words to use:

- ham-burg-er
- mo-tor-cy-cle
- el-e-phant
- choc-o-late
- ba-nan-a
- ap-pen-di-ci-tis

METHOD OF EVALUATION:
   Determine if the child can repeat the rhythm of the multi-syllable word by observing the child during the activity. It is suggested that an anecdotal record be kept on each child.

RECEPTIVE LANGUAGE

PURPOSE:
To match auditory stimuli

AREA OF LANGUAGE STRESSED:
Listening skills—Identifying environmental sounds

DURATION OF LESSON:
Fifteen minutes

LESSON FORMAT:
Individual

LESSON 5: SHAKE-A-CAN

MATERIALS/EQUIPMENT/PHYSICAL LAYOUT:
Use pairs of small coffee cans, each pair containing identical objects. For example, one paired set may contain a button in each can, while another set contains small rubber balls. Other objects that may be used are rice, sand, pins, water, and small blocks.

DESCRIPTION OF THE LESSON:
Hold one set of cans while the child holds the other set. Shake one of the cans and ask, "Can you find the can with the same sound?" The child must listen to the sound made by the object shaken in the teacher's can and must shake each of the cans in the other set until the one that makes the same sound is found.

METHOD OF EVALUATION:
Determine the percentage of correct responses by dividing the number of correct responses the child made by the total number of responses possible.

$$\frac{\text{Correct responses}}{\text{Total responses}} = \text{Percentage correct}$$

RECEPTIVE LANGUAGE

PURPOSE:
To locate environmental sounds

AREA OF LANGUAGE STRESSED:
Listening skills—Identifying environmental sounds

DURATION OF LESSON:
Fifteen minutes

LESSON FORMAT:
Group

LESSON 6: HUM-A-TUNE

MATERIALS/EQUIPMENT/PHYSICAL LAYOUT:
Blindfold

DESCRIPTION OF THE LESSON:
Choose one child to be a "hummer" and another child to be blindfolded. After one child has been blindfolded, the other child (the hummer) moves quietly across the room to a far corner or wall. The hummer begins to hum a favorite tune. The blindfolded child must point to the direction from which the sound is coming.

A variation of this lesson would be to identify one child as "it." The other children put their heads down on their desks. As one child in the group hums, the child who is "it" must find the source of the sound.

METHOD OF EVALUATION:
Observe to determine if the child can accurately identify the location of the sound.

RECEPTIVE LANGUAGE

PURPOSE:
To identify environmental sounds

AREA OF LANGUAGE STRESSED:
Listening skills—Identifying environmental sounds

DURATION OF LESSON:
Twenty minutes

LESSON FORMAT:
Group or individual

LESSON 7: LISTENING WALK

MATERIALS/EQUIPMENT/PHYSICAL LAYOUT:
None

DESCRIPTION OF THE LESSON:
Take the children outside. Tell them, "Listen. What do you hear? Name all of the sounds you can hear." The children may in response name such things as birds, cars, machinery, wind, or other similar environmental sounds. The activity may have to be started by calling the children's attention to one or two obvious sounds.

METHOD OF EVALUATION:
Determine the extent to which the child is sensitive to sounds in the environment by noting the number of responses given.

RECEPTIVE LANGUAGE

PURPOSE:
To identify auditory stimuli in the school environment

AREA OF LANGUAGE STRESSED:
Listening skills—Identifying environmental sounds

DURATION OF LESSON:
Forty-five minutes

LESSON FORMAT:
Group

LESSON 8: SOUNDS AROUND US

MATERIALS/EQUIPMENT/PHYSICAL LAYOUT:
A piece of butcher paper, approximately 3′ × 6′, and crayons

DESCRIPTION OF THE LESSON:
Introduce the activity by telling the children that they will be listening for sounds they commonly hear around their school. The class then goes on a listening walk, and, as the sounds are identified, one child or the teacher lists them. When the class returns, a mural may be made in map form, indicating the sounds indentified and the location of the sounds in the school. Common sounds that may be identified include:

- cafeteria sounds—lunch trays, silverware noises
- a typewriter
- a heater fan blowing
- children swinging
- a piano or other musical instruments
- duplicating machines

METHOD OF EVALUATION:
Observe and record the number of sounds each child identifies.

RECEPTIVE LANGUAGE

PURPOSE:
To identify environmental sounds

AREA OF LANGUAGE STRESSED:
Listening skills—Identifying environmental sounds

DURATION OF LESSON:
Twenty minutes

LESSON FORMAT:
Group or individual

LESSON 9: WHAT SOUND DO YOU HEAR?

MATERIALS/EQUIPMENT/PHYSICAL LAYOUT:
Audiotape recordings of animal and environmental sounds and picture cards of the corresponding sound-producing objects

DESCRIPTION OF THE LESSON:
First, ask the children to listen to a sound on tape and pair the sound with the corresponding picture. Next, as the children listen to a sound, ask them to tell what animal or object makes it, without the benefit of picture stimuli as clues. Then, make a sound and ask the children to identify the source. Initially, play or make one sound at a time. As the children become more proficient, they may be asked to remember a series of sounds.

METHOD OF EVALUATION:
Determine the percentage of correct responses by dividing the number of correct responses the child made by the total number of responses possible.

$$\frac{\text{Correct responses}}{\text{Total responses}} = \text{Percentage correct}$$

RECEPTIVE LANGUAGE

PURPOSE:
To identify environmental sounds

AREA OF LANGUAGE STRESSED:
Listening skills—Identifying environmental sounds

DURATION OF LESSON:
Fifteen minutes

LESSON FORMAT:
Individual

MATERIALS/EQUIPMENT/PHYSICAL LAYOUT:
The following objects may be used:

- ball
- chair
- paper
- chalk
- coins
- water
- cup
- scissors
- keys
- blindfold (optional)

LESSON 10: ACTION SOUNDS

DESCRIPTION OF THE LESSON:
Ask the child to close both eyes or use a blindfold. Then perform a common action with one of the above-mentioned objects, such as bouncing a ball. The child's task is to identify the action sound accurately. The following common action sounds may be used:

- jingling keys
- wadding up paper
- pouring water into a cup
- scooting a chair
- writing on the chalkboard
- placing coins on a table
- cutting paper
- leafing through a book

METHOD OF EVALUATION:
Evaluate the child's ability to identify environmental sounds by recording correct and incorrect responses. To obtain a percentage of correct responses, divide the number of correct responses made by the total number of responses possible.

$$\frac{\text{Correct responses}}{\text{Total responses}} = \text{Percentage correct}$$

RECEPTIVE LANGUAGE

PURPOSE:
   To identify animal sounds accurately

AREA OF LANGUAGE STRESSED:
   Listening skills—Identifying environmental sounds

DURATION OF LESSON:
   Fifteen to twenty minutes

LESSON FORMAT:
   Group

LESSON 11: ANIMAL SOUNDS

MATERIALS/EQUIPMENT/PHYSICAL LAYOUT:
   Safety pins or tape, gummed animal stickers, or 3″ × 5″ cards depicting animals

DESCRIPTION OF THE LESSON:
   Put a sticker or card on each child's shirt. After the children are seated at the table, ask "What animal goes quack, quack?" The child with the picture of the duck must stand up. Continue by asking, "What animal goes moo? What animal goes hee-haw?"

METHOD OF EVALUATION:
   Determine whether the child can associate an animal with its sound and then record correct and incorrect responses.

RECEPTIVE LANGUAGE

PURPOSE:
   To identify noisy and quiet sounds

AREA OF LANGUAGE STRESSED:
   Listening skills—identifying environmental sounds

DURATION OF LESSON:
   Forty-five minutes

```
┌─────────────────────┐
│  Quiet Things       │
│                     │
│    clouds           │
│                     │
│    snowfall         │
│                     │
│  plants growing     │
└─────────────────────┘
```

LESSON FORMAT:
   Group

LESSON 12: QUIET/NOISY

MATERIALS/EQUIPMENT/PHYSICAL LAYOUT:
   Paper, crayons, and felt markers

DESCRIPTION OF THE LESSON:
   After a discussion of how some objects and events make tremendous noise while others are soundless, ask the children to brainstorm by naming all the quiet and noisy things they can think of. As they identify these objects and events, write them on two separate charts. After the list is completed, the children should illustrate these objects on paper. These may become the focal point for a bulletin board display.

```
┌─────────────────────┐
│  Noisy Things       │
│                     │
│    thunder          │
│                     │
│  firecrackers       │
│                     │
│ waves on a beach    │
└─────────────────────┘
```

METHOD OF EVALUATION:
   Evaluate the child's ability to identify noisy and quiet items by the number of items the child lists.

RECEPTIVE LANGUAGE

PURPOSE:
To identify specific words embedded in conversation

AREA OF LANGUAGE STRESSED:
Listening skills—Listening for detail

DURATION OF LESSON:
Fifteen minutes

LESSON FORMAT:
Group or individual

LESSON 13: LISTEN TO MY STORY

MATERIALS/EQUIPMENT/PHYSICAL LAYOUT:
A children's storybook depicting a variety of animals, foods, or toys

DESCRIPTION OF THE LESSON:
Explain to the children that they will have to listen carefully for specific classes of words in a story. Depending upon the book selected, ask the children to listen for animal words, foods, or toys. As the story is read, the children must stand every time they hear a word representing an animal, food, or toy.

METHOD OF EVALUATION:
Determine the child's ability to listen for specific detail by counting the number of times the child correctly stood up when a class word was mentioned.

RECEPTIVE LANGUAGE

PURPOSE:
To identify specific words embedded in conversation

AREA OF LANGUAGE STRESSED:
Listening skills—Listening for detail

DURATION OF LESSON:
Fifteen minutes

LESSON FORMAT:
Group or individual

LESSON 14: LISTENING FOR OPPOSITES

MATERIALS/EQUIPMENT/PHYSICAL LAYOUT:
A set of sentences illustrating opposite relationships

DESCRIPTION OF THE LESSON:
After a discussion of opposites, ask the child to listen for opposites embedded in sentences presented orally. The child must listen to each sentence, then identify the two words that represent opposite relationships. For example:

- The *boys* liked the cars, but the *girls* liked the dolls.
- First he went to the *big* house, then to the *little* one.
- During the *day* I work, but at *night* I watch television.
- Do you like *sweet* or *sour* oranges?
- If you have *cold* water, you can heat it until it gets *hot*.
- I looked *high* and *low* for my book, but I couldn't find it.

METHOD OF EVALUATION:
Determine whether the child can identify opposite words within a sentence and derive a percentage of correct responses by dividing the number of correct responses made by the total number of responses possible.

$$\frac{\text{Correct responses}}{\text{Total responses}} = \text{Percentage correct}$$

RECEPTIVE LANGUAGE

PURPOSE:
To recall simple directions

AREA OF LANGUAGE STRESSED:
Listening skills—Listening for detail

DURATION OF LESSON:
Fifteen to twenty minutes, depending upon how many times the lesson is repeated

LESSON FORMAT:
Group

LESSON 15: SECRET MESSAGE

MATERIALS/EQUIPMENT/PHYSICAL LAYOUT:
A small group of chairs, placed in a circle

DESCRIPTION OF THE LESSON:
Whisper into the ear of the child seated to the right of you. The message is an action that must be performed by the last child who receives it. Each child must pass the information to the right until it reaches the last child. The children rotate so that several children have an opportunity to perform the action. The activity may be started with simple directions, such as "stand up," or "tap your head," and the detail and number of the actions the children must perform may then be gradually increased.

METHOD OF EVALUATION:
Determine the general extent to which the children passed on the information correctly. Evaluation of individual recall of detail is difficult in this lesson.

RECEPTIVE LANGUAGE

PURPOSE:
To recall detail from visual and auditory stimuli

AREA OF LANGUAGE STRESSED:
Listening skills—Listening for detail

DURATION OF LESSON:
Twenty to twenty-five minutes

LESSON FORMAT:
Group or individual

LESSON 16: PLAY IT AGAIN

MATERIALS/EQUIPMENT/PHYSICAL LAYOUT:
Filmstrip projector and filmstrip with audio cassette

DESCRIPTION OF THE LESSON:
Show a filmstrip with an audio cassette. Then show the filmstrip again without the auditory comment on cassette. Each child narrates one frame of the filmstrip.

METHOD OF EVALUATION:
Determine if the child can recall detail. This may be measured by a percentage of correct responses. For example, if the child recalled five details, how many of them were accurate? To derive the percentage of correct responses, divide the number of correct responses made by the total number of responses possible.

$$\frac{\text{Correct responses}}{\text{Total responses}} = \text{Percentage correct}$$

RECEPTIVE LANGUAGE

PURPOSE:
To imitate a sentence model

AREA OF LANGUAGE STRESSED:
Listening skills—Increasing auditory memory

DURATION OF LESSON:
Ten to fifteen minutes

LESSON FORMAT:
Individual

LESSON 17: SENTENCE IMITATION

MATERIALS/EQUIPMENT/PHYSICAL LAYOUT:
None

DESCRIPTION OF THE LESSON:
Give the child a model sentence. The child must repeat the sentence verbatim. Begin with sentences of two or three syllables, and increase the length of each sentence gradually:

- I eat. (two syllables)
- He eats meat. (three syllables)
- Tom ran quickly. (four syllables)
- I went to the store. (five syllables)
- The boys ate bananas. (six syllables)

METHOD OF EVALUATION:
Determine and record the length of a sentence or the specific number of syllables the child is able to remember.

RECEPTIVE LANGUAGE

PURPOSE:
To recall a sequence of words given verbally

AREA OF LANGUAGE STRESSED:
Listening skills—Increasing auditory memory

DURATION OF LESSON:
Fifteen to twenty minutes

LESSON FORMAT:
Small group

LESSON 18: TRIP TO THE MOON

MATERIALS/EQUIPMENT/PHYSICAL LAYOUT:
None

DESCRIPTION OF THE LESSON:
Explain the game by saying, "We are going on a trip to the moon. We have to take many things with us on the spaceship. You have to remember all of the things we are taking." Then begin by saying, "I'm going to the moon, and I'm going to take my toothbrush." The first child must repeat the phrase and add an item: "I'm going to the moon and I'm going to take my toothbrush and my pajamas." Each child repeats the sequence and adds another item to the list.

METHOD OF EVALUATION:
Record how many items each child is able to recall.

RECEPTIVE LANGUAGE

PURPOSE:
   To follow oral directions

AREA OF LANGUAGE STRESSED:
   Following directions—Following simple commands

DURATION OF LESSON:
   Fifteen minutes

LESSON FORMAT:
   Individual

LESSON 19: DRESS THE DOLL

MATERIALS/EQUIPMENT/PHYSICAL LAYOUT:
   Doll and doll clothes, such as a shirt, pants, shoes, hat, socks, and a bathing suit

DESCRIPTION OF THE LESSON:
   Give the child a doll and doll clothes. Direct the child to "put the sock on the doll's foot, put the arm in the sleeve, put the hat on the doll's head." This process is continued until the doll is entirely clothed.

METHOD OF EVALUATION:
   Determine the percentage of correct responses for the task of following directions by dividing the number of correct responses the child made by the total number of responses possible.

$$\frac{\text{Correct responses}}{\text{Total responses}} = \text{Percentage correct}$$

RECEPTIVE LANGUAGE

PURPOSE:
   To follow directions in planning and cooking a meal

AREA OF LANGUAGE STRESSED:
   Following directions—Following simple commands

DURATION OF LESSON:
   To be completed over a period of days

LESSON FORMAT:
   Group

MATERIALS/EQUIPMENT/PHYSICAL LAYOUT:
   The following materials are used:

   - toaster oven
   - hot plates
   - cooking utensils
   - dishes
   - food
   - cookbooks

LESSON 20: LET'S BE CHEFS

DESCRIPTION OF THE LESSON:
   The children first plan a menu for a meal. If, for example, a social studies unit on Thanksgiving has been studied, the class can plan a Thanksgiving meal. However, it may be preferable to start out on a smaller scale, such as baking a single item. First, the children must decide the ingredients they need to purchase and how much they cost. Use this as an opportunity to take a field trip in order to purchase the necessary items. Later, the children must delegate duties in the preparation of the meal. Finally, they must follow directions from the recipe.
   This activity may be extended to include foods from other ethnic or cultural groups. For example, in observance of the Hispanic culture, a dish such as enchiladas can be planned and prepared.

METHOD OF EVALUATION:
   Precise determination of each child's ability to follow directions is difficult in this group activity, so evaluation is best done through observation. It is suggested that an anecdotal record be kept on each child's performance, based on your observations.

RECEPTIVE LANGUAGE

PURPOSE:
To follow oral directions in a game

AREA OF LANGUAGE STRESSED:
Following directions—Following simple commands

DURATION OF LESSON:
Twenty minutes

LESSON FORMAT:
Group

LESSON 21: DIRECTION RACE

MATERIALS/EQUIPMENT/PHYSICAL LAYOUT:
This activity should be held outside or in a gym or multipurpose room. Several objects are needed, such as a chair, balance beam, a chalkboard eraser, and bucket.

DESCRIPTION OF THE LESSON:
Divide the children into teams of equal numbers. Then give a verbal direction to be performed on the obstacle course, for example, "Run to the chair, jump over the balance beam." The first person to perform the activity correctly gains a point for that person's team. The team with the most points wins. Directions are made increasingly difficult for children who can recall longer sequences.

METHOD OF EVALUATION:
Determine and record which children are having difficulty in recalling and executing the directions and will require further practice.

RECEPTIVE LANGUAGE

PURPOSE:
To follow verbal directions in a game

AREA OF LANGUAGE STRESSED:
Following directions—Following simple commands

DURATION OF LESSON:
Fifteen to twenty minutes

LESSON FORMAT:
Individual

LESSON 22: NUMBERS EVERYWHERE

MATERIALS/EQUIPMENT/PHYSICAL LAYOUT:
Small cards, each containing a number between one and ten

DESCRIPTION OF THE LESSON:
Give the child verbal direction: "Put a one on the table and a two on the bookshelf." The child must follow the directions in sequence. Begin with one-phase directions, and increase the difficulty of the task by asking the child to remember longer sequences of directions.

METHOD OF EVALUATION:
Determine the percentage of correct responses by dividing the number of correct responses the child made by the total number of responses possible.

$$\frac{\text{Correct responses}}{\text{Total responses}} = \text{Percentage correct}$$

RECEPTIVE LANGUAGE

PURPOSE:
To follow oral directions in a game

AREA OF LANGUAGE STRESSED:
Following directions—Following simple commands

DURATION OF LESSON:
Twenty minutes

LESSON FORMAT:
Pairs of children

LESSON 23: BLOCK BUILDER

MATERIALS/EQUIPMENT/PHYSICAL LAYOUT:
Two sets of blocks or one-inch cubes, identical in number and colors

DESCRIPTION OF THE LESSON:
Two children sit on the floor with their backs to each other. One child builds a shape using different colors and patterns. The child then gives the second child directions on how to build an identical shape. The children are not allowed to look at each other's work. To vary this activity, a time limit may be imposed, or the child may give additional clues to what the final product should look like.

METHOD OF EVALUATION:
Observe the child to determine how well the directions are followed in building the shape.

RECEPTIVE LANGUAGE

PURPOSE:
To follow directions in an art lesson

AREA OF LANGUAGE STRESSED:
Following directions—Following verbal directions through art

DURATION OF LESSON:
Thirty minutes

LESSON 24: SHAPES ALIVE

MATERIALS/EQUIPMENT/PHYSICAL LAYOUT:
Glue or paste, colored construction-paper shapes, such as circles, squares, half-circles, rectangles, and triangles

DESCRIPTION OF THE LESSON:
Tape-record or give verbally a series of directions that, if followed correctly, will result in a completed art product: "Take a large circle. At the top, glue a medium-sized circle. On top of that, glue a triangle with the point up. Now use three small circles and place them for eyes and a nose. Now take a small triangle for the mouth." Other figures may resemble the following:

LESSON FORMAT:
Group or individual

METHOD OF EVALUATION:
Examine the final product to determine if the child followed the sequence of directions correctly.

RECEPTIVE LANGUAGE

PURPOSE:
To follow verbal directions in an art lesson

AREA OF LANGUAGE STRESSED:
Following directions—Following verbal directions through art

DURATION OF LESSON:
Twenty minutes

LESSON FORMAT:
Individual

LESSON 25: CONNECT THE DOTS

MATERIALS/EQUIPMENT/PHYSICAL LAYOUT:
Graph paper, a geometric picture on graph paper with written directions, and a pencil

DESCRIPTION OF THE LESSON:
Give the child a sheet of graph paper with one dot on it. Hiding the picture from the child, tell the child to start on the first dot. Then give step-by-step directions instructing the child where to make each dot. After all the dots are placed, the child connects the dots to make a picture.

METHOD OF EVALUATION:
Examine the child's shape to determine if the child has followed the directions correctly.

RECEPTIVE LANGUAGE

PURPOSE:
To follow verbal directions in an art lesson

AREA OF LANGUAGE STRESSED:
Following directions—Following verbal directions through art

DURATION OF LESSON:
Twenty minutes

LESSON FORMAT:
Individual

LESSON 26: OBJET D'ART

MATERIALS/EQUIPMENT/PHYSICAL LAYOUT:
The following materials may be used:

- sticks of gum
- scissors
- one-inch cubes
- Lifesavers
- index cards
- large paper clips
- paper
- pencils
- bottle and jar lids

DESCRIPTION OF THE LESSON:
Give the child an assortment of objects. As you give an oral direction, such as, ''Make a circle the size of the finger holes in your pair of scissors,'' or ''Make a line the length of a stick of gum,'' the child draws the shape, using the object as a guide. Other directions may include:

- Make an oval shape using the inside of a paper clip.
- Make a line the size of two block sides.
- Make a circle the size of the lid.

METHOD OF EVALUATION:
Determine the child's ability to follow verbal directions by noting if the child can draw each shape with no repetition of the directions and if the shape is accurately represented.

RECEPTIVE LANGUAGE

PURPOSE:
To follow verbal directions in an art lesson

AREA OF LANGUAGE STRESSED:
Following directions—Following verbal directions through art

DURATION OF LESSON:
Thirty minutes

LESSON FORMAT:
Individual

LESSON 27: THREE RED APPLES

MATERIALS/EQUIPMENT/PHYSICAL LAYOUT:
The following materials are needed:

- paper divided into ten numbered boxes
- tape recorder
- audio cassette tape
- pencil
- crayons

DESCRIPTION OF THE LESSON:
This is a good free-time activity for children. In preparation for the lesson, tape-record the directions for the drawing activity on an audio cassette tape. Ask the child to listen to the recorded directions. The word *stop* at the end of each direction will tell the child to turn off the tape recorder and draw the object requested. When the child is finished drawing the first item in Box 1, the child continues with Box 2 by starting the tape recording again. Thus:

- "Box 1: Make two cats. Color them black. Stop."
- "Box 2: Draw a house. Color it yellow. Stop."
- "Box 3: Make four red flowers. Stop."

METHOD OF EVALUATION:
Check the child's paper for accuracy. To determine the percentage of correct responses divide the number of correct responses made by the total number of responses possible.

$$\frac{\text{Correct responses}}{\text{Total responses}} = \text{Percentage correct}$$

RECEPTIVE LANGUAGE

PURPOSE:
To follow verbal directions in an art lesson

AREA OF LANGUAGE STRESSED:
Following directions—Following verbal directions through art

LESSON 28: DRAW A SHAPE

MATERIALS/EQUIPMENT/PHYSICAL LAYOUT:
Two children are seated at a table, separated by a screen. A set of cards containing geometric designs is held by one child. The other child has a paper and pencil.

DESCRIPTION OF THE LESSON:
The first child chooses a card with a geometric figure such as one of the following:

DURATION OF LESSON:
Fifteen to twenty minutes

The first child must give directions on how the second child is to proceed in drawing the figure. The figures get increasingly complex. After the child is finished, the figure is compared with the model. The children then change roles.

METHOD OF EVALUATION:
Observe while the child is drawing to determine how well the directions are followed.

LESSON FORMAT:
Pairs of children

RECEPTIVE LANGUAGE

PURPOSE:
To develop the ability to follow oral directions

LESSON 29: A PLACE ON THE MAP

MATERIALS/EQUIPMENT/PHYSICAL LAYOUT:
Each child has a pencil and a dittoed sheet resembling the following street intersection:

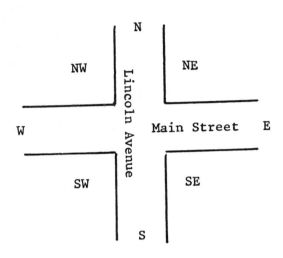

AREA OF LANGUAGE STRESSED:
Following directions—Following verbal directions using maps

DURATION OF LESSON:
Twenty minutes

LESSON FORMAT:
Group or individual

DESCRIPTION OF THE LESSON:
Explain to the children that they must help finish the street map by listening very carefully to the directions:

- There is a store on the southeast corner of Main Street. Draw a square and write the word *store* in it.
- Susie lives in the third house from the northwest corner of Lincoln Avenue. Draw Susie's house.
- Make a bakery right across the street from Susie's house.
- There is a school on the southwest corner of Main Street. Make a circle showing the school.
- Show the route that Susie takes when walking to school.

METHOD OF EVALUATION:
Observe the child's map to determine if the child accurately followed the verbal directions.

RECEPTIVE LANGUAGE

PURPOSE:
To develop the ability to follow oral directions

AREA OF LANGUAGE STRESSED:
Following directions—Following verbal directions using maps

DURATION OF LESSON:
Twenty minutes

LESSON FORMAT:
Group or individual

LESSON 30: THE TREASURE HUNT

MATERIALS/EQUIPMENT/PHYSICAL LAYOUT:
A simple map dittoed on paper, one per child

DESCRIPTION OF THE LESSON:
Show the map shown below to the children. Say to the children, "Let us pretend we are going on a treasure hunt. A big chest of gold was hidden in this town by a pirate who came to shore. Let's see if we can find it. Start at the lighthouse. Go up Elm Street two blocks. Turn left on Daisy Avenue. Go one block. Turn right at the skating rink. Go one block and turn left on Tulip Avenue. Go left one block and turn left on Oak Street. Go two blocks and turn right on Rose Avenue. Turn left at the bakery. At the corner of the bakery take ten steps and dig. There is the treasure!''

METHOD OF EVALUATION:
Determine if the child followed verbal directions by observing whether the child finished in the correct spot.

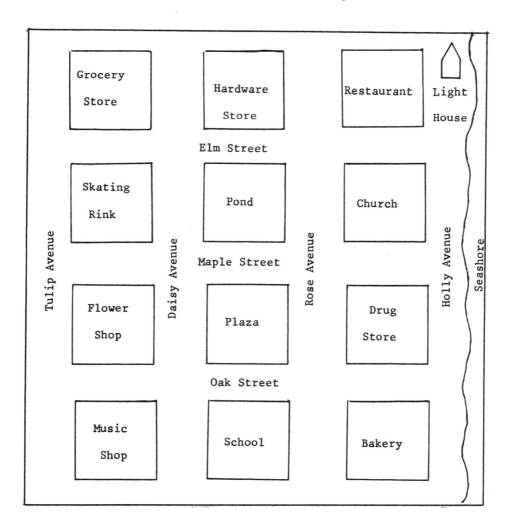

RECEPTIVE LANGUAGE

PURPOSE:
To develop the ability to follow verbal directions

AREA OF LANGUAGE STRESSED:
Following directions—Following verbal directions using maps

DURATION OF LESSON:
Twenty to thirty minutes

LESSON FORMAT:
Group or individual

LESSON 31: FOLLOW THE MAP

MATERIALS/EQUIPMENT/PHYSICAL LAYOUT:
Paper and pencils

DESCRIPTION OF THE LESSON:
First, give the children practice in drawing a map of their room or school. The map may include desks, tables, study carrels, bookcases, and similar room furnishings. In a subsequent activity, ask the children to draw a map of the school and its surrounding neighborhood, including streets, stores, churches, and houses. After discussing directional concepts (north, south, east, west), ask the children to follow verbal directions such as: "Go west two blocks, then north three blocks. Where are you?"

METHOD OF EVALUATION:
Determine if the child can follow verbal directions in the final lesson by observing whether the child finishes in the correct spot on the map.

RECEPTIVE LANGUAGE

PURPOSE:
To develop an understanding of the concepts of body parts

AREA OF LANGUAGE STRESSED:
Concept development—Body parts

DURATION OF LESSON:
Fifteen to twenty minutes

LESSON FORMAT:
Individual

LESSON 32: BODY LANGUAGE

MATERIALS/EQUIPMENT/PHYSICAL LAYOUT:
Instruct the children to make life-sized drawings of themselves by having each of them lie down on a separate piece of butcher paper. Trace their outlines and have them fill in details such as eyes, ears, nose, mouth, hands, feet, and clothing.

DESCRIPTION OF THE LESSON:
Using the child's drawing, ask the child to identify body parts by using the following directions: Touch your nose, find your feet, where are your ears? etc. For young children whose primary language is not English, the body part may need to be given in the child's primary language, paired with the appropriate English word.

METHOD OF EVALUATION:
Observe the child's performance. To determine the percentage of correct responses, divide the number of correct responses made by the total number of responses possible.

$$\frac{\text{Correct responses}}{\text{Total responses}} = \text{Percentage correct}$$

RECEPTIVE LANGUAGE

PURPOSE:
To develop understanding of basic language concepts

AREA OF LANGUAGE STRESSED:
Concept development—Body parts

DURATION OF LESSON:
Fifteen to twenty minutes

LESSON FORMAT:
Individual

LESSON 33: BODY IMAGES

MATERIALS/EQUIPMENT/PHYSICAL LAYOUT:
Large laminated picture cards depicting distinct body parts and a grease pencil or crayon

DESCRIPTION OF THE LESSON:
Say to the children, "Point to your nose. Where is the man's nose? Mark it." The children first point to their own body parts and then to the corresponding body part on the laminated picture. This process continues until all major body parts have been identified.

METHOD OF EVALUATION:
Observe the child's performance. To determine the percentage of correct responses, divide the number of correct responses made by the total number of responses possible.

$$\frac{\text{Correct responses}}{\text{Total responses}} = \text{Percentage correct}$$

RECEPTIVE LANGUAGE

PURPOSE:
To develop concepts of quantity

AREA OF LANGUAGE STRESSED:
Concept development—Quantity

DURATION OF LESSON:
Fifteen minutes

LESSON FORMAT:
Individual

LESSON 34: MORE OR LESS?

MATERIALS/EQUIPMENT/PHYSICAL LAYOUT:
Small bowls of dry macaroni, beans, and noodles

DESCRIPTION OF THE LESSON:
Instruct the child to place the objects randomly in two groups. Ask, "Which has more? Which has less?" Then instruct the child to divide the objects into three unequal groups. Ask, "Which group has the *least*? Which has *more* than the first group? Which group has the *most*?" Other directions emphasizing concepts of quantity may include: "Pick up a *pair* of beans, give me a *few* noodles, give me a *lot* of macaroni, give me *some* beans."

METHOD OF EVALUATION:
Observe the child's performance. To determine the percentage of correct responses, divide the number of correct responses made by the total number of responses possible.

$$\frac{\text{Correct responses}}{\text{Total responses}} = \text{Percentage correct}$$

RECEPTIVE LANGUAGE

PURPOSE:
To develop concepts of quantity

AREA OF LANGUAGE STRESSED:
Concept development—Quantity

LESSON 35: SURVEY PROJECT

MATERIALS/EQUIPMENT/PHYSICAL LAYOUT:
Paper, pencil, and graph paper

DESCRIPTION OF THE LESSON:
The child conducts a survey, using classmates as respondents. The child may survey favorite foods, sports, colors, or television programs. The child interviews other children to determine their preferences and records the tallies in each category on a paper. When the survey is completed, the child illustrates the results using a simple bar graph.

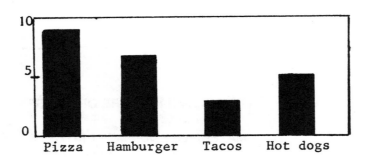

Simple tally

Bar Graph

The child is encouraged to explain the results and share some of the problems encountered in conducting the survey.

DURATION OF LESSON:
To be completed over a period of days

METHOD OF EVALUATION:
Determine each child's understanding of the concept of quantity by asking questions such as: What food did children like the most? The least? How many more children liked pizza than hot dogs? To determine the percentage of correct responses, divide the number of correct responses made by the total number of responses possible.

LESSON FORMAT:
Group or individual

$$\frac{\text{Correct responses}}{\text{Total responses}} = \text{Percentage correct}$$

RECEPTIVE LANGUAGE

PURPOSE:
To develop the concept of quantity

AREA OF LANGUAGE STRESSED:
Concept development—Quantity

LESSON 36: BIRTHDAYS IN BUNCHES

MATERIALS/EQUIPMENT/PHYSICAL LAYOUT:
Tagboard and marking pen

DESCRIPTION OF THE LESSON:
Make a chart with the children's names down the left side and the 12 months across the top. Ask the children to name the month of their birthdays. As each child responds, the teacher puts an X under the appropriate birthday month.

	Jan.	Feb.	Mar.	April	May	June	July	Aug.	Sept.	Oct.	Nov.	Dec.
Ann		X										
Bob							X					
Ray				X								
Ted										X		
Sue							X					
Ed					X							

After recording each child's birthday month, ask the following questions: Which month has the most birthdays? How many birthdays are there in that month? Which month has the least birthdays? How many birthdays are there in that month? How many more does July have than May? How many do July and April have combined?

METHOD OF EVALUATION:
Evaluate each child's understanding of quantity concepts by determining the number of correct responses. To obtain the percentage of correct responses, divide the number of correct responses made by the total number of responses possible.

$$\frac{\text{Correct responses}}{\text{Total responses}} = \text{Percentage correct}$$

DURATION OF LESSON:
Twenty minutes

LESSON FORMAT:
Group

RECEPTIVE LANGUAGE

PURPOSE:
To identify five basic shapes

AREA OF LANGUAGE STRESSED:
Concept development—Shapes

DURATION OF LESSON:
Fifteen to twenty minutes

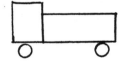

LESSON FORMAT:
Individual

LESSON 37: SHAPE UP

MATERIALS/EQUIPMENT/PHYSICAL LAYOUT:
The following materials are used:

- small objects of differing shapes such as blocks or beads (shapes must include a circle, square, rectangle, oval, and triangle)
- flannelboard with five felt shapes
- objects for shape painting
- paint
- construction paper shapes
- glue
- paper

DESCRIPTION OF THE LESSON:
Use the flannelboard and felt shapes to introduce the five shapes. Depending upon the abilities of the child, you may wish to stress only one shape per session. Next, take the child on a walk to find the shape(s) discussed. At a later session, give the child several objects and instruct the child to sort them by shape. Finally, using the objects, the child makes shape prints by dipping an object in a saucer of paint and pressing it on paper to make a design. A follow-up lesson may consist of an art activity in which the children make pictures from construction paper shapes. Each child is given a variety of shapes and is required to make a picture, gluing the shapes to a 9″ × 12″ piece of construction paper.

METHOD OF EVALUATION:
After teaching all five shapes, observe the child's performance. To determine the percentage of correct responses, divide the number of correct responses made by the total number of responses possible.

$$\frac{\text{Correct responses}}{\text{Total responses}} = \text{Percentage correct}$$

RECEPTIVE LANGUAGE

PURPOSE:
To develop an understanding of the concept of size

AREA OF LANGUAGE STRESSED:
Concept development—Size

DURATION OF LESSON:
Fifteen to twenty minutes

LESSON FORMAT:
Individual

LESSON 38: BIGGER OR SMALLER

MATERIALS/EQUIPMENT/PHYSICAL LAYOUT:
Picture cards of animals

DESCRIPTION OF THE LESSON:
Ask the child to compare pictures of two objects that are grossly different in size, such as an ant and an elephant. Ask, "Which is bigger, the ant or the elephant?" Continue the activity, selecting objects that are closer to the same size. Ask the child to make finer levels of discrimination in size. The following pairs may be used for comparison:

- ant—elephant
- man—boy
- bee—tree
- rabbit—horse
- puppy—dog
- horse—elephant
- rhinoceros—monkey
- monkey—gorilla

METHOD OF EVALUATION:
Observe the child's performance. To determine the percentage of correct responses, divide the number of correct responses made by the total number of responses possible.

$$\frac{\text{Correct responses}}{\text{Total responses}} = \text{Percentage correct}$$

RECEPTIVE LANGUAGE

PURPOSE:
To develop an understanding of time concepts and related vocabulary

AREA OF LANGUAGE STRESSED:
Concept development—Time

DURATION OF LESSON:
Twenty minutes

LESSON FORMAT:
Group or individual

LESSON 39: TOMORROWS AND YESTERDAYS

MATERIALS/EQUIPMENT/PHYSICAL LAYOUT:
A set of 3″ × 5″ index cards

DESCRIPTION OF THE LESSON:
Ask the children to brainstorm words that represent temporal concepts. For example:

noon	yesterday	early
in the morning	dawn	late
before	evening	sundown
tomorrow	afternoon	until

As the children list the concepts of time, write each of them on a card. Then ask the children to think of activities that commonly occur at certain times of the day; for example, in the *afternoon* we have math, at *noon,* we eat lunch.

METHOD OF EVALUATION:
Determine at a later date whether the new vocabulary words have generalized to spontaneous language by taking a language sample and using the generalization check in Appendix B.

RECEPTIVE LANGUAGE

PURPOSE:
To understand concepts of time represented on a calendar

AREA OF LANGUAGE STRESSED:
Concept development—Time

DURATION OF LESSON:
Twenty to thirty minutes

LESSON FORMAT:
Individual

LESSON 40: CALENDAR CONCEPTS

MATERIALS/EQUIPMENT/PHYSICAL LAYOUT:
A current calendar; seven index cards, each containing the name of a day of the week; and a circular spinner board with the numbers 1 through 31 printed around the perimeter

DESCRIPTION OF THE LESSON:
Ask the child to name the days of the week orally. Then ask the child to match the day cards with the corresponding days of the week on the calendar. The child spins the spinner until it points to one of the numbers from 1 through 31. The child must read the number and find the day that corresponds with the date in a particular month. For example, if the spinner points to 15, the child must look at the calendar and determine what day of the week the 15th will fall on.

METHOD OF EVALUATION:
To determine the child's understanding of how to locate dates on a calendar, observe the child's performance. To compute the percentage of correct responses, divide the number of correct responses made by the total number of responses possible.

$$\frac{\text{Correct responses}}{\text{Total responses}} = \text{Percentage correct}$$

RECEPTIVE LANGUAGE

PURPOSE:
To match colors

AREA OF LANGUAGE STRESSED:
Concept development—Color

DURATION OF LESSON:
Twenty minutes

LESSON FORMAT:
Individual

LESSON 41: COLOR CUES

MATERIALS/EQUIPMENT/PHYSICAL LAYOUT:
Small, colored squares of paper—orange, green, red, blue, yellow, purple, and brown

DESCRIPTION OF THE LESSON:
With the young child beginning to learn colors, play the following game: Place the colored squares on the table in front of the child. Instruct the child, ''I am going to name a food. You must point to the square that is the same color as the food.'' For example:

- banana—yellow
- apple—red
- grape jello—purple
- peas—green
- chocolate cookie—brown
- cherries—red

METHOD OF EVALUATION:
Observe the child's accuracy in associating the named object with its color. The percentage of correct responses is determined by dividing the number of correct responses made by the total number of responses possible.

$$\frac{\text{Correct responses}}{\text{Total responses}} = \text{Percentage correct}$$

RECEPTIVE LANGUAGE

PURPOSE:
To identify objects of a specified color

AREA OF LANGUAGE STRESSED:
Concept development—Color

DURATION OF LESSON:
Twenty minutes

LESSON 42: COLOR PALETTES

MATERIALS/EQUIPMENT/PHYSICAL LAYOUT:
Tagboard or construction paper shaped like paint palettes, each of a different color, and pictures with objects representing the various colors of the palettes

DESCRIPTION OF THE LESSON:
After a discussion of colors, the children place on the paint palettes a list or set of pictures of the items that represent each color.

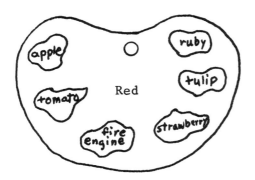 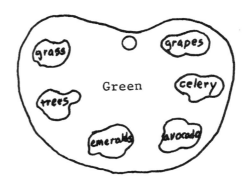

METHOD OF EVALUATION:
Count the number of correct items on the child's palette. To determine the percentage of correct responses, divide the number of correct responses made by the total number of responses possible.

$$\frac{\text{Correct responses}}{\text{Total responses}} = \text{Percentage correct}$$

LESSON FORMAT:
Group

RECEPTIVE LANGUAGE

PURPOSE:
To develop concepts of direction and position

AREA OF LANGUAGE STRESSED:
Concept development—Direction/position

DURATION OF LESSON:
Twenty minutes

LESSON FORMAT:
Group

LESSON 43: MOTHER MAY I?

MATERIALS/EQUIPMENT/PHYSICAL LAYOUT:
The children stand in a circle.

DESCRIPTION OF THE LESSON:
Give a direction to a child. The child must first ask, "Mother may I?" and then perform the action. Begin with simple directions at first, such as, "Put your hand *on top of* your head," and progress to more difficult directions, such as "Put your *right* hand on your *left* knee." Other directional and positional concepts that may be emphasized in this manner include:

below	over	on/off
behind	right/left	between
next to	in/out	up/down
under	beside	away from

METHOD OF EVALUATION:
Determine if the child understands the directional/positional concept by observing the child's performance. Determine the percentage of correct responses by dividing the number of correct responses made by the total number of responses possible.

$$\frac{\text{Correct responses}}{\text{Total responses}} = \text{Percentage correct}$$

RECEPTIVE LANGUAGE

PURPOSE:
To develop associations between objects

AREA OF LANGUAGE STRESSED:
Associations and comparisons—Developing associations

DURATION OF LESSON:
Twenty minutes

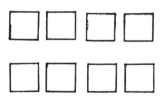

LESSON FORMAT:
Individual

LESSON 44: SPIN—A—PICTURE

MATERIALS/EQUIPMENT/PHYSICAL LAYOUT:
On a cardboard wheel (the type used for pizza), pictures are mounted around the perimeter of the circle. On separate cards kept in a pocket on the back of the wheel are pictures that can be associated in some way with the pictures on the front.

DESCRIPTION OF THE LESSON:
The child turns the spinner, identifies the picture, and then finds a picture to go with it. Associations might include:

- pencil—eraser
- cup—saucer
- bed—pillow
- shoe—sock
- lock—key
- knife—fork

The teacher may make this game more difficult by selecting objects with more abstract relationships.

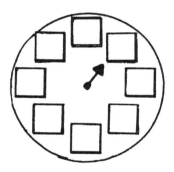

METHOD OF EVALUATION:
Determine the percentage of correct responses by dividing the number of correct responses the child made by the total number of responses possible.

$$\frac{\text{Correct responses}}{\text{Total responses}} = \text{Percentage Correct}$$

RECEPTIVE LANGUAGE

PURPOSE:
To match pictures associated by their whole-part relationship

AREA OF LANGUAGE STRESSED:
Associations and comparisons—Developing associations

DURATION OF LESSON:
Twenty minutes

LESSON FORMAT:
Individual

LESSON 45: ASSOCIATION BEANBAG

MATERIALS/EQUIPMENT/PHYSICAL LAYOUT:
Table size plastic or paper mat, approximately 24″ × 36″, divided into boxes in which there are pictures; a beanbag; and picture cards that are in some way associated with the pictures on the mat by whole-part relationships

DESCRIPTION OF THE LESSON:
The mat is placed on the table. The child stands three to five feet away and tosses the beanbag onto a picture. The task of the child is to find a picture card that goes with the picture on the mat. For example:

- lamp—light globe
- wagon—wheel
- car—tire
- shoe—shoelace
- door—doorknob
- wagon—handle

METHOD OF EVALUATION:
Determine the percentage of correct responses by dividing the number of correct responses the child made by the total number of responses possible.

$$\frac{\text{Correct responses}}{\text{Total responses}} = \text{Percentage correct}$$

RECEPTIVE LANGUAGE

PURPOSE:
To match objects according to smell

AREA OF LANGUAGE STRESSED:
Associations and comparisons—Developing associations

DURATION OF LESSON:
Fifteen minutes

LESSON FORMAT:
Individual

LESSON 46: SMELL AND TELL

MATERIALS/EQUIPMENT/PHYSICAL LAYOUT:
The following items are needed:

- baby food jars
- pieces of gauze wrapped around fragrant items
- corresponding pictures or drawings of items to be smelled

The items to be smelled may include a cinnamon stick, perfume, orange peelings, peanut butter, a chocolate square, and so on.

DESCRIPTION OF THE LESSON:
Say to the child, "In each one of these jars I have wrapped up something for you to smell. What does it smell like to you? Can you find a picture of what you think it is?" After the child has matched the items and the cards, continue by saying something like, "Give me the jar of something you put on bread to make a sandwich. Find one that is sweet tasting. Find the jar with something ladies might wear." Cultural or ethnic foods may be included to expand this lesson.

METHOD OF EVALUATION:
Determine the percentage of correct responses by dividing the number of correct responses the child made by the total number of responses possible.

$$\frac{\text{Correct responses}}{\text{Total responses}} = \text{Percentage correct}$$

RECEPTIVE LANGUAGE

PURPOSE:
To demonstrate facial expressions associated with certain foods

AREA OF LANGUAGE STRESSED:
Associations and comparisons—Developing associations

DURATION OF LESSON:
Fifteen minutes

LESSON FORMAT:
Group or individual

LESSON 47: TASTE EXPRESSIONS

MATERIALS/EQUIPMENT/PHYSICAL LAYOUT:
The following materials are used:

- lemon
- sugar
- orange
- cookie
- jelly
- rhubarb
- salt
- pepper
- ice cream

DESCRIPTION OF THE LESSON:
After tasting several items and discussing the taste sensation and consequent facial expression associated with certain highly spiced or pungent foods, ask a child to show the facial expression of a person who has just eaten sauerkraut, a lemon, pepper, salt, chocolate, sugar, ice cream, rhubarb, and an onion.

METHOD OF EVALUATION:
Determine if the child correctly associates facial expressions with certain foods by observing the child's facial features after the food is named.

RECEPTIVE LANGUAGE

PURPOSE:
To identify words associated with concepts

AREA OF LANGUAGE STRESSED:
Associations and comparisons—Developing associations

DURATION OF LESSON:
Fifteen to twenty minutes

LESSON FORMAT:
Group or individual

LESSON 48: THINK OF A WORD

MATERIALS/EQUIPMENT/PHYSICAL LAYOUT:
Individual cards, each with a key word written on it, or a list of key words to be used by the teacher

DESCRIPTION OF THE LESSON:
The child chooses a card that has a key word on it, or the teacher may read a word to the child, such as red. Then say, "Tell me as many words as you can when you think of the word red." Points may be given for each word the child names. Apple, fire hydrant, cherry, and a stop sign are examples of acceptable associations for red. Other key words that may evoke associations are:

flower	elephant	fast
ocean	sad	happy
love	little	strong
war	big	hurt
fight	hot	cold

METHOD OF EVALUATION:
Record the number of associations each child is able to identify correctly.

RECEPTIVE LANGUAGE

PURPOSE:
To compare objects using a minimum of four characteristics

AREA OF LANGUAGE STRESSED:
Associations and comparisons—Making comparisons

DURATION OF LESSON:
Twenty minutes

LESSON FORMAT:
Individual

LESSON 49: ALIKE BECAUSE

MATERIALS/EQUIPMENT/PHYSICAL LAYOUT:
Objects or pictures of items that have similarities

DESCRIPTION OF THE LESSON:
Show the child two objects or pictures of items that have a number of similarities or share the same characteristics, such as an apple and a cherry. Say to the child, "Name at least four ways these are alike." For example, an apple and a cherry may be alike in these characteristics:

- They are both red when ripe.
- They both grow on trees.
- They are both fruits.
- They both have seeds or pits.

Other pairs of objects that may be used for comparison are:

- bee—ant
- plane—train
- lettuce—cabbage
- cat—dog

METHOD OF EVALUATION:
Determine if the child can name a minimum of four similarities for each pair of objects.

RECEPTIVE LANGUAGE

PURPOSE:
To distinguish differences in objects

AREA OF LANGUAGE STRESSED:
Associations and comparisons—Making comparisons

DURATION OF LESSON:
Fifteen to twenty minutes

LESSON FORMAT:
Individual

LESSON 50: DIFFERENT BECAUSE

MATERIALS/EQUIPMENT/PHYSICAL LAYOUT:
Pairs of pictures or objects

DESCRIPTION OF THE LESSON:
Give the child two objects or two pictures of objects. Then ask the child to describe how the two objects are different. The following pairs may be used:

- car—boat
- orange—ball
- spider—bee
- whale—goldfish
- plane—bird
- gorilla—monkey

Encourage the child to explain the differences according to size, shape, function, other physical properties, or class of species.

METHOD OF EVALUATION:
Determine if the child can state at least one difference for each pair of objects.

RECEPTIVE LANGUAGE

PURPOSE:
To identify words to complete a simile

AREA OF LANGUAGE STRESSED:
Associations and comparisons—Making comparisons

DURATION OF LESSON:
Fifteen to twenty minutes

LESSON FORMAT:
Group or individual

LESSON 51: SIMILE STARTERS

MATERIALS/EQUIPMENT/PHYSICAL LAYOUT:
A list of simile starters

DESCRIPTION OF THE LESSON:
Read a simile in which the last word has been omitted. The child must complete the simile with an appropriate word or words.

as fast as. . . .	as tiny as. . . .
as cute as. . . .	as dark as. . . .
as big as. . . .	as hot as. . . .
as hungry as. . . .	as cold as. . . .
as happy as. . . .	as sweet as. . . .
as mad as. . . .	as sour as. . . .
as tired as. . . .	as far as. . . .
as thirsty as. . . .	as near as. . . .

METHOD OF EVALUATION:
Determine if the word or words used to complete the simile are appropriate.

RECEPTIVE LANGUAGE

PURPOSE:
To develop the ability to make comparisons using a simile

AREA OF LANGUAGE STRESSED:
Associations and comparisons—Making comparisons

DURATION OF LESSON:
Thirty minutes

LESSON FORMAT:
Group or individual

LESSON 52: GREETING CARDS

MATERIALS/EQUIPMENT/PHYSICAL LAYOUT:
Several used greeting cards, construction paper, and crayons

DESCRIPTION OF THE LESSON:
Show the children several greeting cards, pointing out different messages and their meanings. With construction paper and crayons, the children then design their own greeting cards. Using similes, they think of messages to write on their cards, for example:

- Hoping your day is as nice as. . . .
- You're as sweet as. . . .
- We wish you a birthday as happy as. . . .

METHOD OF EVALUATION:
Determine whether the child can create an appropriate simile in greeting card format.

RECEPTIVE LANGUAGE

PURPOSE:
To develop the ability to make comparisons using a simile

AREA OF LANGUAGE STRESSED:
Associations and comparisons—Making comparisons

DURATION OF LESSON:
Thirty minutes

LESSON FORMAT:
Group or individual

LESSON 53: POSTER PARTY

MATERIALS/EQUIPMENT/PHYSICAL LAYOUT:
Poster board or large construction paper, tempera, and crayons

DESCRIPTION OF THE LESSON:
Suggest a topic or theme for a poster-making activity. Topics such as fire prevention, or an antilittering campaign would be appropriate. The children paint or color their posters and make up slogans to fit the theme, using similes to illustrate their messages. For example, if the topic is fire prevention, the slogan may read, ''Playing with fire is as dangerous as. . . .'' An antilitter campaign may proclaim, ''Littering is as messy as. . . .''

METHOD OF EVALUATION:
Determine whether the child can create an appropriate simile in a slogan format.

RECEPTIVE LANGUAGE

PURPOSE:
To develop classification skills

AREA OF LANGUAGE STRESSED:
Classifying and categorizing—Simple classification

DURATION OF LESSON:
Thirty minutes

LESSON FORMAT:
Teams of three or four, or an individual

LESSON 54: SCAVENGER HUNT

MATERIALS/EQUIPMENT/PHYSICAL LAYOUT:
Mail order catalogs or magazines and scissors

DESCRIPTION OF THE LESSON:
The children are divided into teams of three or four and are instructed to find and cut out a series of picture items. For example, Team 1 must find three brown shoes, four towels, two cars, and five plants. Team 2 must find three toothbrushes, one boat, two airplanes, and four plates. The team that finds all of its items first is the winner. After all the teams have located their assigned pictures, they tell how their pictures in each category are alike and how they are different. This lesson may also be conducted with an individual child.

METHOD OF EVALUATION:
Observe each child during the lesson to determine the child's ability to find appropriate items for each category. It is suggested that an anecdotal record of each child's performance be maintained, based on your observations.

RECEPTIVE LANGUAGE

PURPOSE:
   To develop skill in classification of objects

AREA OF LANGUAGE STRESSED:
   Classifying and categorizing—Simple classification

DURATION OF LESSON:
   Twenty minutes

LESSON FORMAT:
   Small group

LESSON 55: PERSONS, PLACES, THINGS

MATERIALS/EQUIPMENT/PHYSICAL LAYOUT:
   A game board with pictures of objects, a spinner board with numbers, and a place marker for each child

DESCRIPTION OF THE LESSON:
   Each child turns the spinner, which indicates how many spaces the child may advance on the game board. As the child lands on a picture on the game board, the picture must be classified as a person, place, or thing. The object of the game is to finish first.

METHOD OF EVALUATION:
   Observe each child during the game to determine the number of correct responses. To obtain the percentage of correct responses, divide the number of correct responses made by the total number of responses possible.

$$\frac{\text{Correct responses}}{\text{Total responses}} = \text{Percentage correct}$$

RECEPTIVE LANGUAGE

PURPOSE:
   To develop skill in classification of events

AREA OF LANGUAGE STRESSED:
   Classifying and categorizing—Simple classification

DURATION OF LESSON:
   To be completed over a period of weeks

LESSON FORMAT:
   Group or individual

LESSON 56: WEATHER TALLY

MATERIALS/EQUIPMENT/PHYSICAL LAYOUT:
   Butcher paper and pencils

DESCRIPTION OF THE LESSON:
   Construct a weather chart divided into three sections: cloudy, rainy, and sunny.

The task of the children is to classify each day's weather into one of the three categories and to make a tally mark daily. When a two- to four-week period has passed, the class may discuss the results.

METHOD OF EVALUATION:
   Observe each child's classification of the weather. It is suggested that an anecdotal record of each child's performance be maintained, based on your observations.

RECEPTIVE LANGUAGE

PURPOSE:
To identify specific examples within a category

AREA OF LANGUAGE STRESSED:
Classifying and categorizing—Simple classification

DURATION OF LESSON:
Fifteen minutes

LESSON FORMAT:
Group

LESSON 57: CLASSIFICATION BALL GAME

MATERIALS/EQUIPMENT/PHYSICAL LAYOUT:
A rubber playground ball

DESCRIPTION OF THE LESSON:
The children stand in a circle while a child in the center names a class of objects, such as *fruit*. The child bounces the ball to another child in the circle who must name within five seconds a specific example in that class. Using the example *fruit*, if the child names apple, banana, or another appropriate fruit within five seconds, the game continues with that child as the new leader. An example may be used only once.

METHOD OF EVALUATION:
Observe each child's ability to name a specific example within a category. Determine the percentage of correct responses by dividing the number of correct responses made by the total number of responses possible.

$$\frac{\text{Correct responses}}{\text{Total responses}} = \text{Percentage correct}$$

RECEPTIVE LANGUAGE

PURPOSE:
To develop skill in the classification of objects

AREA OF LANGUAGE STRESSED:
Classifying and categorizing—Simple classification

DURATION OF LESSON:
Forty-five minutes

LESSON FORMAT:
Group or individual

LESSON 58: WHO, WHAT, WHERE BOOKS

MATERIALS/EQUIPMENT/PHYSICAL LAYOUT:
Mail order catalogs, magazines, scissors, paste or glue, and 9″ × 12″ tagboard

DESCRIPTION OF THE LESSON:
Initiate the activity by discussing the meaning of questions. Who questions most often refer to people; what questions indicate objects, and where questions refer to location or places. The children are given catalogs and magazines. They find pictures to be placed in a who book or collage. A vocabulary of people's labels may be developed as the children are pasting pictures. A mailman, farmer, policeman, chef, and truck driver are a few of the labels that may be identified for the who book. This process may be repeated for a what book of objects and a where book of locations.

METHOD OF EVALUATION:
Observe the child's classification skills. It is suggested that an anecdotal record of each child's performance be maintained, based on your observations.

RECEPTIVE LANGUAGE

PURPOSE:
To develop skill in the classification of objects

AREA OF LANGUAGE STRESSED:
Classifying and categorizing—Simple classification

DURATION OF LESSON:
Fifteen minutes

LESSON FORMAT:
Individual

LESSON 59: SORTING JUNK

MATERIALS/EQUIPMENT/PHYSICAL LAYOUT:
A collection of "junk" items such as:

cans	old silverware	clothespins
string	buttons	wire
boxes	bottle caps	toothpicks
keys	baseball cards	spools
rubber bands	material scraps	corks

DESCRIPTION OF THE LESSON:
Place the items of junk on a table and say, "Find some things that go together." The child may classify according to shape, size, color, function, or any other attribute. The child must describe a rationale for classifying the objects.

METHOD OF EVALUATION:
Observe the child's method of classifying objects. It is suggested that an anecdotal record be kept, based on observations of the child's performance.

RECEPTIVE LANGUAGE

PURPOSE:
To develop skill in the classification of objects

AREA OF LANGUAGE STRESSED:
Classifying and categorizing—Simple classification

DURATION OF LESSON:
Twenty minutes

LESSON FORMAT:
Group

LESSON 60: FAMILY FEUD

MATERIALS/EQUIPMENT/PHYSICAL LAYOUT:
The group is divided into two teams, lined up and facing each other. A small toy or object is placed on a chair between the teams. Chalk and a chalkboard are needed to record team scores.

DESCRIPTION OF THE LESSON:
The first child from one team stands facing the first child from the other team, with the chair between them. The teacher names a category, such as animals. The first child to grab the toy from the chair gets a chance to name something from that category. If the child's response is correct, other members of that child's team may also name something from that category. Each correct item named receives a point for the team. When someone misses or cannot name an item within five seconds, the other team gets a turn. When a new category is identified, a different member from each team gets a chance to be the first to compete. Categories may range from simple topics such as animals or fruits, to more complex topics such as U.S. presidents or states.

METHOD OF EVALUATION:
Determine if each child's response fits within the general category named. It is suggested that an anecdotal record of each child's performance be maintained, based on your observations.

RECEPTIVE LANGUAGE

PURPOSE:
To develop skill in the classification of objects

AREA OF LANGUAGE STRESSED:
Classifying and categorizing—Simple classification

DURATION OF LESSON:
Fifteen minutes

LESSON FORMAT:
Individual

LESSON 61: FLANNELBOARD CLASSIFICATION

MATERIALS/EQUIPMENT/PHYSICAL LAYOUT:
A flannelboard and felt objects or picture cards with felt backing representing fruit, vegetables, animals, household items, and other specific categories

DESCRIPTION OF THE LESSON:
Place several objects on the table and say, "Find all the fruits," or, "Find all the things that go in a house." The child must sort by category. Next, place four felt objects or picture cards on the flannelboard, three of them in the same category, one of them different. Say to the child, "Find the one that does not belong." After selecting the one that does not go with the others, the child must explain why it is different.

METHOD OF EVALUATION:
Determine the percentage of correct responses by dividing the number of correct responses the child made by the total number of responses possible.

$$\frac{\text{Correct responses}}{\text{Total responses}} = \text{Percentage correct}$$

RECEPTIVE LANGUAGE

PURPOSE:
To identify a general class of objects from several examples given

AREA OF LANGUAGE STRESSED:
Classifying and categorizing—Simple classification

DURATION OF LESSON:
Fifteen minutes

LESSON FORMAT:
Group or individual

MATERIALS/EQUIPMENT/PHYSICAL LAYOUT:
None

LESSON 62: CATEGORIES GALORE

DESCRIPTION OF THE LESSON:
Say to the children, "I am going to name three or four things. You have to tell me what the things are":

- eagle, robin, sparrow (birds)
- Texas, Rhode Island, Maine, Washington (states)
- Kennedy, Reagan, Washington, Roosevelt (presidents)
- butterfly, ant, bees (insects)
- apple, peach, orange, pineapple (fruit)
- cobra, rattler, garter, coral (snakes)
- shepherd, collie, boxer, poodle (dogs)
- cello, bass, piano, flute (musical instruments)

METHOD OF EVALUATION:
Observe the child's ability to categorize. To determine the percentage of correct responses, divide the number of correct responses made by the total number of responses possible.

$$\frac{\text{Correct responses}}{\text{Total responses}} = \text{Percentage correct}$$

RECEPTIVE LANGUAGE

PURPOSE:
To identify the contents of various containers

AREA OF LANGUAGE STRESSED:
Classifying and categorizing—Classifying by physical property

DURATION OF LESSON:
Fifteen to twenty minutes

LESSON FORMAT:
Individual or small group

LESSON 63: CONTAINER CAPERS

MATERIALS/EQUIPMENT/PHYSICAL LAYOUT:
Procure empty containers of all sizes and shapes, such as a:

- cereal box
- cottage cheese container
- soup can
- camera film box
- milk carton
- shoe box

The labels on these containers may be covered to make the lesson more difficult.

DESCRIPTION OF THE LESSON:
Say to the child, "I have some containers. I want you to tell me what comes in this type of container." The child must look at the container and respond with the object or substance contained. Other containers that may be used include:

- hairspray can
- tea box
- coffee can
- cellophane candy wrapping
- cracker box
- playdough can
- crayon box
- light bulb box
- detergent box
- puzzle box

METHOD OF EVALUATION:
Determine the percentage of correct responses by dividing the number of correct responses the child made by the total number of responses possible.

$$\frac{\text{Correct responses}}{\text{Total responses}} = \text{Percentage correct}$$

RECEPTIVE LANGUAGE

PURPOSE:
To classify objects by physical properties

AREA OF LANGUAGE STRESSED:
Classifying and categorizing—Classifying by physical property

DURATION OF LESSON:
Twenty minutes

LESSON FORMAT:
Group or individual

LESSON 64: WHAT'S IT MADE OF?

MATERIALS/EQUIPMENT/PHYSICAL LAYOUT:
Objects made of cloth, plastic, glass, metal, rubber, paper, and wood; cards with the same categories written on them (optional); and seven aluminum pie tins

DESCRIPTION OF THE LESSON:
Place one object from each of the seven categories in each pie tin. Introduce the activity by asking a child to choose one of the objects. Ask, "Do you know what it is made of? Is it made of cloth? Is it rubber?" Then say, "Feel it. Find an object that is made of the same material." Each child selects objects and classifies them by their physical properties. The following objects may be used:

- wood: pencil, wooden spoon, clothespin
- plastic: comb, small plastic car, tape dispenser
- cloth: cloth napkin, handkerchief, doll dress
- metal: paper clip, nail, jar lid, tin can, scissors
- paper: paper napkin, notebook paper, playing cards
- glass: baby food jar, perfume bottle, pair of prescription glasses, mirror
- rubber: elastic band, piece of rubber tire, a rubber washer

METHOD OF EVALUATION:
Observe the child's ability to classify by physical properties. Determine the percentage of correct responses by dividing the number of correct responses made by the total number of responses possible.

$$\frac{\text{Correct responses}}{\text{Total responses}} = \text{Percentage correct}$$

RECEPTIVE LANGUAGE

PURPOSE:
To classify objects by location

AREA OF LANGUAGE STRESSED:
Classifying and categorizing—Classifying by location

DURATION OF LESSON:
Fifteen to twenty minutes

LESSON FORMAT:
Group

LESSON 65: MOVING IN

MATERIALS/EQUIPMENT/PHYSICAL LAYOUT:
The following materials are needed:

- doll house
- doll furniture
- mail-order catalog
- glue
- simple floor plan of a house on 18″ × 36″ tagboard

DESCRIPTION OF THE LESSON:
Explain that it is moving day and the children will have to help the furniture movers place the furniture in proper rooms. Assign each child in the group a room of the house. Then hold up a piece of furniture and name it. The children must raise their hands when a piece of furniture belonging to their room is named.

In a variation, name a room of the house, such as the kitchen. The children must then name all of the items that that room could contain. In another variation, the children may cut out pictures of household objects from a mail order catalog and place them in the appropriate room on the floor plan.

METHOD OF EVALUATION:
Determine the percentage of correct responses by dividing the number of correct responses the child made by the total number of responses possible.

$$\frac{\text{Correct responses}}{\text{Total responses}} = \text{Percentage correct}$$

RECEPTIVE LANGUAGE

PURPOSE:
To classify objects by location

AREA OF LANGUAGE STRESSED:
Classifying and categorizing—Classifying by location

DURATION OF LESSON:
Twenty minutes

LESSON FORMAT:
Group (teams)

LESSON 66: FRIENDLY FACES

MATERIALS/EQUIPMENT/PHYSICAL LAYOUT:
Butcher paper strips, approximately 18″ × 24″

DESCRIPTION OF THE LESSON:
Divide the children into teams. Explain that, "We can find many friendly faces, even animal friends, if we look hard enough." Encourage the children to imagine animal friends that could be found in the water, in trees, under logs, in holes. Have the children work in teams to list the animals found in those locations. After the teams complete their lists, they can share their results with the class.

METHOD OF EVALUATION:
Keep an anecdotal record of each child's performance based on classroom observations.

RECEPTIVE LANGUAGE

PURPOSE:
   To classify objects by location

AREA OF LANGUAGE STRESSED:
   Classifying and categorizing—Classifying by location

DURATION OF LESSON:
   Fifteen to twenty minutes

LESSON FORMAT:
   Group

LESSON 67: EVENTS AND PLACES

MATERIALS/EQUIPMENT/PHYSICAL LAYOUT:
   Chalk and chalkboard

DESCRIPTION OF THE LESSON:
   Ask the children to name events that take place in a specific location. For example, the children may list events that take place at home, such as sleeping, eating, or watching television. Or they may list things that take place at school, such as eating, working, and playing. Write these activities on the board as the children identify them. Then ask the children to name the events that take place in both locations (playing, eating, etc.). Other comparisons of locations might include church—school, picnic—camping, city—country, and beach—park.

METHOD OF EVALUATION:
   Observe each child's ability to classify events by location. Determine the percentage of correct responses by dividing the number of correct responses made by the total number of responses possible.

$$\frac{\text{Correct responses}}{\text{Total responses}} = \text{Percentage correct}$$

RECEPTIVE LANGUAGE

PURPOSE:
   To classify objects by location

AREA OF LANGUAGE STRESSED:
   Classifying and categorizing—Classifying by location

DURATION OF LESSON:
   Forty-five minutes

LESSON FORMAT:
   Group or individual

LESSON 68: CLASSIFICATION COLLAGE

MATERIALS/EQUIPMENT/PHYSICAL LAYOUT:
   Glue, paper, magazines, scissors, mail-order catalogs, and pictures of stores typically found in a community, such as a restaurant, grocery store, clothing store, or hardware store.

DESCRIPTION OF THE LESSON:
   Encourage the children to find pictures of objects that belong in each type of store. Have the children cut the pictures out and paste them in a collage.

METHOD OF EVALUATION:
   After the child cuts out a picture, determine if the child associated it with the appropriate store. Determine the percentage of correct responses by dividing the number of correct responses made by the total number of responses possible.

$$\frac{\text{Correct responses}}{\text{Total responses}} = \text{Percentage correct}$$

RECEPTIVE LANGUAGE

PURPOSE:
To classify objects by location

AREA OF LANGUAGE STRESSED:
Classifying and categorizing—Classifying by location

DURATION OF LESSON:
Twenty to thirty minutes

LESSON FORMAT:
Group or individual

LESSON 69: LET'S GO SHOPPING

MATERIALS/EQUIPMENT/PHYSICAL LAYOUT:
Newspaper advertisements for restaurants, pet shops, clothing stores, car repair shops, toy stores, shoe stores, jewelry stores, and pharmacies

DESCRIPTION OF THE LESSON:
Ask the children to name some of the frequently visited stores in their community. Using the newspaper, read an advertisement without divulging the name of the store. Ask the children to identify the store in which they would find a particular item from the advertisement.

METHOD OF EVALUATION:
Observe the child's response in categorizing. If sufficient trials are presented, the percentage of correct responses for the child may be determined by dividing the number of correct responses made by the total number of responses possible.

$$\frac{\text{Correct responses}}{\text{Total responses}} = \text{Percentage correct}$$

RECEPTIVE LANGUAGE

PURPOSE:
To classify objects by function

AREA OF LANGUAGE STRESSED:
Classifying and categorizing—Classifying by function

DURATION OF LESSON:
Fifteen to twenty minutes

LESSON FORMAT:
Group or individual

MATERIALS/EQUIPMENT/PHYSICAL LAYOUT:
None

LESSON 70: BRAINSTORMING

DESCRIPTION OF THE LESSON:
Say to the children, "See how many things you can name that are things to wear." The children may name such items as a blouse, coat, shirt, pants, hat, bracelet, ring, or swimsuit. Then say, "Name all the things we can ride in." Appropriate responses would be a car, boat, train, wagon, plane, or helicopter. Ask the children to classify by function using the following:

- things we write with
- things we cook with
- things we work with
- things we use in sports

METHOD OF EVALUATION:
Observe the child's ability to classify by function. To determine the percentage of correct responses, divide the number of correct responses made by the total number of responses possible.

$$\frac{\text{Correct responses}}{\text{Total responses}} = \text{Percentage correct}$$

RECEPTIVE LANGUAGE

PURPOSE:
To develop the ability to understand the meaning of common street signs

AREA OF LANGUAGE STRESSED:
Comprehension—Recalling detail from a visual stimulus

DURATION OF THE LESSON:
Thirty minutes

LESSON FORMAT:
Group or individual

LESSON 71: READ A SIGN

MATERIALS/EQUIPMENT/PHYSICAL LAYOUT:
The following materials are required:

- magazines
- glue
- scissors
- tagboard
- dictionaries

DESCRIPTION OF THE LESSON:
Begin the discussion by asking the children why signs are needed. A good idea is to take the group on a tour of the school or community to identify common signs. Upon returning to the classroom, have the children find similar signs in magazines and mount them on tagboard. The task of the children is to identify each sign and tell where it might be located. Difficult words on some signs may need to be looked up in the dictionary. The following list may be used if you wish to have the children make signs themselves:

telephone	exit	walk
restrooms	no trespassing	dangerous
no admittance	wait	bus stop
fire alarm	for sale	do not enter
employees only	railroad crossing	high voltage
wet paint	school zone	watch your step
no swimming	dead end	emergency exit
fire escape	keep out	beware of dog

METHOD OF EVALUATION:
Determine by an informal check whether the child understands the meaning of common signs. Hold up the sign; if the child can identify the meaning of the sign, a correct response can be recorded. All signs on the list can be checked in this manner. Determine the percentage of correct responses by dividing the number of correct responses made by the total number of responses possible.

$$\frac{\text{Correct responses}}{\text{Total responses}} = \text{Percentage correct}$$

RECEPTIVE LANGUAGE

PURPOSE:
To summarize visual detail in a single caption

AREA OF LANGUAGE STRESSED:
Comprehension—Recalling detail from a visual stimulus

DURATION OF LESSON:
Fifteen to twenty minutes

LESSON FORMAT:
Individual

LESSON 72: NAME THE STORY

MATERIALS/EQUIPMENT/PHYSICAL LAYOUT:
A set of pictures mounted on 9″ × 12″ tagboard

DESCRIPTION OF THE LESSON:
The child chooses a picture and is encouraged to write a caption for it. The child must first write a one-word title, then a two-word title, and so on. For example, a picture of an animal in a cage may be captioned in this manner:

- one-word caption: Caught
- two-word caption: The Catch
- three-word caption: The Big Hunt

METHOD OF EVALUATION:
Observe the child's ability to synthesize the content of the picture and to develop appropriate titles for it. It is suggested that an anecdotal record of the child's performance be kept, based on your observations.

RECEPTIVE LANGUAGE

PURPOSE:
To recall detail from a visual stimulus

AREA OF LANGUAGE STRESSED:
Comprehension—Recalling detail from a visual stimulus

DURATION OF LESSON:
Twenty minutes, if repeated for more than one frame

LESSON FORMAT:
Group or individual

LESSON 73: NOW YOU SEE IT, NOW YOU DON'T

MATERIALS/EQUIPMENT/PHYSICAL LAYOUT:
Filmstrip of a factual nature and a filmstrip projector

DESCRIPTION OF THE LESSON:
Using a filmstrip, ask the children to observe one frame very carefully. Then turn the filmstrip projector off. One child must describe the visual detail from memory. Repeat to give each child the opportunity to respond.

METHOD OF EVALUATION:
Observe the children's performance. It is suggested that an anecdotal record of each child's performance be kept, based on your observations.

RECEPTIVE LANGUAGE

PURPOSE:
To determine whether statements based on a story are true or false

AREA OF LANGUAGE STRESSED:
Comprehension—Recalling detail from an auditory stimulus

DURATION OF LESSON:
Fifteen minutes

LESSON FORMAT:
Group or individual

LESSON 74: TRUE OR FALSE?

MATERIALS/EQUIPMENT/PHYSICAL LAYOUT:
A children's book or story

DESCRIPTION OF THE LESSON:
Read a story to the child. After the story is completed, make simple declarative statements about the story, some of which depict true events, some of which do not. The child must indicate whether the statement is true or false. This activity may be expanded to include ethnic or cultural considerations, using a folktale or historical event from a culture previously studied.

METHOD OF EVALUATION:
Determine the percentage of correct responses by dividing the number of correct responses the child made by the total number of responses possible.

$$\frac{\text{Correct responses}}{\text{Total responses}} = \text{Percentage correct}$$

RECEPTIVE LANGUAGE

PURPOSE:
To recall literal details from a story

AREA OF LANGUAGE STRESSED:
Comprehension—Recalling detail from an auditory stimulus

DURATION OF LESSON:
Twenty minutes

LESSON FORMAT:
Group or individual

LESSON 75: DRAW A STORY

MATERIALS/EQUIPMENT/PHYSICAL LAYOUT:
A descriptive story, paper, pencil, and crayons

DESCRIPTION OF THE LESSON:
Tell or read a descriptive story to the children. The story should contain specific references to the color of objects. For example: "The girl walked by the red house with the white fence. She had her brown dog with her." After the story is finished, have the children draw and color their pictures according to the description given.

METHOD OF EVALUATION:
It is suggested that an anecdotal record of each child's ability to recall details be kept, based on your observations.

RECEPTIVE LANGUAGE

PURPOSE:
   To sequence the events of a story

AREA OF LANGUAGE STRESSED:
   Comprehension—Sequencing events

DURATION OF LESSON:
   Twenty minutes

LESSON FORMAT:
   Group or individual

LESSON 76: SEQUENCING A STORY

MATERIALS/EQUIPMENT/PHYSICAL LAYOUT:
   Sets of teacher-made picture cards that tell a story in a sequence of events, or comic strips cut into separate frames

DESCRIPTION OF THE LESSON:
   Say to the children, "These cards tell a story. I mixed them up. Can you put them back in order and tell me the story?"
   In a variation of this lesson, have the children order the sequence of events and then assign children to play the characters of the story. The children act out the story in the proper sequence. In another variation, expand the activity to include pictures of ethnic fables or folktales.

METHOD OF EVALUATION:
   Observe to determine if the children can sequence a series of story events. It is suggested that an anecdotal record of each child's performance be kept, based on your observations.

RECEPTIVE LANGUAGE

PURPOSE:
   To identify absurdities

AREA OF LANGUAGE STRESSED:
   Comprehension—Identifying absurdities and nonessential information

DURATION OF LESSON:
   Fifteen minutes

LESSON FORMAT:
   Group or individual

LESSON 77: THE MIX UP

MATERIALS/EQUIPMENT/PHYSICAL LAYOUT:
   A bulletin board made with construction paper cutouts or a flannelboard with felt figures

DESCRIPTION OF THE LESSON:
   Construct a bulletin board with several objects in obviously inappropriate situations. For example, a cat may be wearing a boy's baseball cap, a fish may be in a tree, or a flower may be growing upside down. The child must be able to identify the absurdities and tell the teacher what is wrong.

METHOD OF EVALUATION:
   Observe the child to see how many absurdities can be identified. It is suggested that an anecdotal record of each child's performance be kept, based on your observations.

RECEPTIVE LANGUAGE

PURPOSE:
   To develop the ability to recognize absurdities and visual inconsistencies

AREA OF LANGUAGE STRESSED:
   Comprehension—Identifying absurdities and nonessential information

DURATION OF LESSON:
   Twenty minutes

LESSON FORMAT:
   Group or individual

LESSON 78: WHAT'S WRONG?

MATERIALS/EQUIPMENT/PHYSICAL LAYOUT:
   What's Wrong Cards (Teaching Resources Corporation, 50 Pond Park Road, Hingham, MA 02043): a set of pictures depicting ridiculous events—a turtle on the dinner table, a man sitting in a baby's highchair, a picture upside down on a wall, a woman with a beard, and so on.

DESCRIPTION OF THE LESSON:
   Introduce the activity by saying, ''I am going to show you a picture that has some silly things in it. Can you find out what is silly about the picture?'' The child must identify the absurdities in each picture.

METHOD OF EVALUATION:
   Observe to determine whether the child can correctly identify all of the absurdities. Determine the percentage of correct responses by dividing the number of correct responses made by the total number of responses possible.

$$\frac{\text{Correct responses}}{\text{Total responses}} = \text{Percentage correct}$$

RECEPTIVE LANGUAGE

PURPOSE:
   To develop the ability to identify absurdities

AREA OF LANGUAGE STRESSED:
   Comprehension—Identifying absurdities and nonessential information

DURATION OF LESSON:
   Fifteen minutes

LESSON FORMAT:
   Individual

MATERIALS/EQUIPMENT/PHYSICAL LAYOUT:
   None

LESSON 79: HOW ABSURD!

DESCRIPTION OF THE LESSON:
   Introduce the activity by stating, ''I am going to say some sentences. Some of the things I say will be true. Others will not be. If the sentence is true, say yes. If it isn't, say no.''

- Horses eat hay.
- Candy grows on trees.
- Elephants like jello.
- A cow can fly.
- The moon is made of cheese.
- Dogs can bark.

METHOD OF EVALUATION:
   Observe to see if the child can identify all the absurd statements. Determine the percentage of correct responses by dividing the number of correct responses made by the total number of responses possible.

$$\frac{\text{Correct responses}}{\text{Total responses}} = \text{Percentage correct}$$

RECEPTIVE LANGUAGE

PURPOSE:
To develop the ability to identify nonessential information

AREA OF LANGUAGE STRESSED:
Comprehension—Identifying absurdities and nonessential information

DURATION OF LESSON:
Twenty minutes

LESSON FORMAT:
Group or individual

LESSON 80: WHICH ONE DOESN'T BELONG?

MATERIALS/EQUIPMENT/PHYSICAL LAYOUT:
A set of short paragraphs, each with a sentence that does not follow the topic

DESCRIPTION OF THE LESSON:
Explain that a paragraph will be read and that one sentence will not fit the topic. The child's task is to identify the sentence that is nonessential to the topic.

- Example 1: On Saturday, the two boys decided to play together. First they played ball. Then they played marbles. The flowers on the doorstep were tall. Soon the boys got on their bikes and rode to another friend's house.
- Example 2: Monkeys are very smart animals. They can be trained to help people. Some monkeys have been taught to use sign language. I like cats because they are soft. Monkeys are funny animals too. They make funny noises and make people laugh.

METHOD OF EVALUATION:
Determine if the child can identify the nonessential sentences. To obtain a percentage of correct responses, divide the number of correct responses made by the total number of responses possible.

$$\frac{\text{Correct responses}}{\text{Total responses}} = \text{Percentage correct}$$

RECEPTIVE LANGUAGE

PURPOSE:
To make inferences from auditory clues

AREA OF LANGUAGE STRESSED:
Comprehension—Interpreting and evaluating

DURATION OF LESSON:
Fifteen to twenty minutes

LESSON FORMAT:
Group or individual

LESSON 81: MYSTERY ME

MATERIALS/EQUIPMENT/PHYSICAL LAYOUT:
Short riddles

DESCRIPTION OF THE LESSON:
Read a riddle: "I see water and shells. I am getting sunburned making castles in the sand. Where am I? Who am I? What time of the day is it?" The child must answer questions by recalling from the auditory clues given. Here are two other examples that may be used:

- I hear horns honking. I look out the window and see tall buildings lit up by thousands of lights. Where am I? What time of the day is it?
- I am going bump, bump as I ride. The animal I am riding on is trotting very fast. I see a cactus. Where am I? What am I doing?

METHOD OF EVALUATION:
Observe the child and determine the accuracy of answers to the riddles. To obtain a percentage of correct responses, divide the number of correct responses made by the total number of responses possible.

$$\frac{\text{Correct responses}}{\text{Total responses}} = \text{Percentage correct}$$

RECEPTIVE LANGUAGE

PURPOSE:
To describe personal choices in making purchasing decisions

AREA OF LANGUAGE STRESSED:
Comprehension—Interpreting and evaluating

DURATION OF LESSON:
Twenty to twenty-five minutes

LESSON FORMAT:
Group or individual

LESSON 82: PLAYING SANTA CLAUS

MATERIALS/EQUIPMENT/PHYSICAL LAYOUT:
Several mail-order catalogs complete with order blanks

DESCRIPTION OF THE LESSON:
Ask the children to pretend that they will each be given a specified sum of money, $100 for example, and with that money they must purchase Christmas gifts for each member of the family. Encourage the children to consider each family member's sizes and tastes in colors, styles, and interests. The children may complete the order forms if their reading and writing skills permit. The children may also tell the class of their shopping decisions and their rationale for choosing certain items.

METHOD OF EVALUATION:
Observe the children's performance. It is suggested that an anecdotal record of each child's performance be kept, based on your observations.

RECEPTIVE LANGUAGE

PURPOSE:
To identify the main idea of a story

AREA OF LANGUAGE STRESSED:
Comprehension—Interpreting and evaluating

DURATION OF LESSON:
Fifteen minutes

LESSON FORMAT:
Individual

LESSON 83: TITLE MATCHES

MATERIALS/EQUIPMENT/PHYSICAL LAYOUT:
Construction paper; an envelope; tagboard strips, approximately 2″ × 7″; and 8½″ × 11″ plain white paper, cut in half width-wise

DESCRIPTION OF THE LESSON:
Write several short stories or paragraphs, one on each half sheet of paper. On the tagboard strips, write appropriate titles to fit the stories. Place the titles in the envelope, and mount the stories on the construction paper. The child must read the paragraphs and select a title that summarizes the main idea of the story.

METHOD OF EVALUATION:
Determine whether the child can identify the main idea of a story by counting correct matches of the titles and stories. To obtain a percentage of correct responses, divide the number of correct responses made by the total number of responses possible.

$$\frac{\text{Correct responses}}{\text{Total responses}} = \text{Percentage correct}$$

RECEPTIVE LANGUAGE

PURPOSE:
To understand relationships in a story and verbally summarize the contents

AREA OF LANGUAGE STRESSED:
Comprehension—Interpreting and evaluating

DURATION OF LESSON:
Twenty minutes

LESSON FORMAT:
Group or individual

LESSON 84: CAPTIONED PICTURES

MATERIALS/EQUIPMENT/PHYSICAL LAYOUT:
Pictures clipped from magazines and mounted on tagboard or construction paper

DESCRIPTION OF THE LESSON:
Read a story and ask the child to give a descriptive sentence or caption for the picture. The captions may be factual or humorous.

METHOD OF EVALUATION:
Determine whether the child's caption is appropriate for the picture being presented. It is suggested that an anecdotal record of the child's performance be kept, based on your observations.

RECEPTIVE LANGUAGE

LESSON 85: A FAVORITE STORY

PURPOSE:
To increase comprehension of a story plot

MATERIALS/EQUIPMENT/PHYSICAL LAYOUT:
The following materials are needed:

- a classic children's story book
- puppets
- flannelboard
- felt
- clay
- shoeboxes
- paint
- paper

AREA OF LANGUAGE STRESSED:
Comprehension—Interpreting and evaluating

DESCRIPTION OF THE LESSON:
After a story is read orally to the class, the children may participate in the following activities:

- Make up a play based on the story.
- Use puppets to act out the story.
- Create a flannelboard scene from the story.
- Make a diorama of a favorite part in the story.
- Paint a picture of a favorite part in the story.
- Retell the story by making a scroll for the scroll theater.

DURATION OF LESSON:
Variable

METHOD OF EVALUATION:
Observe the children's performance. It is suggested that an anecdotal record of each child's performance be kept, based on your observations.

LESSON FORMAT:
Group

RECEPTIVE LANGUAGE

LESSON 86: WHO SAID THAT?

PURPOSE:
To develop the ability to interpret dialogue

MATERIALS/EQUIPMENT/PHYSICAL LAYOUT:
Introduce the lesson by saying, "I have cut apart a comic strip. The pictures have been separated, so that the characters and what they said are mixed up. Can you match up the characters with what they said?" The children must match the dialogue with the appropriate character.

AREA OF LANGUAGE STRESSED:
Comprehension—Interpreting and evaluating

METHOD OF EVALUATION:
Determine the accuracy of the child's character-dialogue matches. The percentage of correct responses may be obtained by dividing the number of correct responses made by the total number of responses possible.

DURATION OF LESSON:
Twenty minutes

$$\frac{\text{Correct responses}}{\text{Total responses}} = \text{Percentage correct}$$

LESSON FORMAT:
Group or individual

RECEPTIVE LANGUAGE

PURPOSE:
To interpret a problem and develop a solution

AREA OF LANGUAGE STRESSED:
Comprehension—Interpreting and evaluating

DURATION OF LESSON:
Thirty minutes

LESSON FORMAT:
Group

LESSON 87: DEAR ABBY

MATERIALS/EQUIPMENT/PHYSICAL LAYOUT:
Index cards, 3″ × 5″, and a cardboard box covered with butcher paper, with a small slit in the top

DESCRIPTION OF THE LESSON:
To introduce this lesson, select several appropriate "Dear Abby" columns from the newspaper.

Read the problem letters and Abby's responses. Explain that each child will have an opportunity to play Abby, to help another child with a problem. Each child must write out a problem and place it in the problem box. The problem may be one encountered in the home, at school, or with the child's peers.

For example, the class may first respond as a group to this representative problem:

> Dear Abby,
>
> My sister and I take turns doing the dishes. Every time it is my sister's turn, she says she has homework. What should I do?

Encourage the group to think of possible solutions to this problem. Then appoint a child to reach in the box and choose another problem to respond to independently.

METHOD OF EVALUATION:
Determine the children's ability to create an appropriate solution to a problem. It is suggested that an anecdotal record of each child's performance be maintained, based on your observations.

RECEPTIVE LANGUAGE

PURPOSE:
To develop the ability to interpret and locate items from advertisements

AREA OF LANGUAGE STRESSED:
Comprehension—Interpreting and evaluating

DURATION OF LESSON:
Thirty minutes

LESSON FORMAT:
Group

LESSON 88: CLASSIFIED ADS

MATERIALS/EQUIPMENT/PHYSICAL LAYOUT:
Each child is supplied with a section of newspaper containing the classified ads.

DESCRIPTION OF THE LESSON:
The children must have some reading ability to participate in this activity. Introduce the activity by saying, ''Advertisements in the newspaper help people find the things they want or the services they need.'' Discuss the major headings and how they can be used to locate specific items. Then ask, ''Under what heading would I look for a kitten? A job? An apartment to rent? A used refrigerator?'' Have the children look in the help wanted column. Ask them to count how many ads offer jobs for males. For females. Ask the children to write an ad for an item they want to sell.

METHOD OF EVALUATION:
Through observation, determine the children's ability to interpret classified ads. It is suggested that an anecdotal record of each child's performance be kept, based on your observations.

RECEPTIVE LANGUAGE

PURPOSE:
To develop the ability to evaluate information

AREA OF LANGUAGE STRESSED:
Comprehension—Interpreting and evaluating

DURATION OF LESSON:
Fifteen to twenty minutes

LESSON FORMAT:
Group or individual

LESSON 89: THE DAILY NEWS

MATERIALS/EQUIPMENT/PHYSICAL LAYOUT:
Two stories from two different newspapers, each an account of the same event

DESCRIPTION OF THE LESSON:
Read, or have a child read, two different stories to the class. After the two accounts are read, ask the children, ''How are these stories different? Which one do you think is most correct? Why?''

Read one statement or sentence from the news story and ask, ''Is this a fact or an opinion? What makes you think so?''

METHOD OF EVALUATION:
Observe the children's ability to compare and contrast the two stories. It is suggested that an anecdotal record of each child's performance be kept, based on your observations.

RECEPTIVE LANGUAGE

PURPOSE:
To develop the ability to predict outcomes

AREA OF LANGUAGE STRESSED:
Comprehension—Predicting outcomes

DURATION OF LESSON:
Fifteen to twenty minutes

LESSON FORMAT:
Small group or individual

LESSON 90: PREDICTING OUTCOMES

MATERIALS/EQUIPMENT/PHYSICAL LAYOUT:
A story book to be read by the teacher

DESCRIPTION OF THE LESSON:
Read a story orally to the child, stopping at a point approximately one-third through the story, or at a point just before a significant event in the story. To know the best place to stop, you must be familiar with the story. Ask the child to predict what will happen next. Then continue reading so that the child may determine if the prediction was correct. At a point just before the end of the story, again stop reading and ask the child to predict the outcome. Then complete the story, giving the child feedback as to whether the prediction was correct.

METHOD OF EVALUATION:
Observe the children's ability to predict outcomes. It is suggested that an anecdotal record of each child's performance be kept, based on your observations.

RECEPTIVE LANGUAGE

PURPOSE:
To increase descriptive vocabulary

AREA OF LANGUAGE STRESSED:
Semantic understanding of vocabulary—Expanding vocabulary

DURATION OF LESSON:
Twenty minutes

LESSON FORMAT:
Group

MATERIALS/EQUIPMENT/PHYSICAL LAYOUT:
Chalk and chalkboard

LESSON 91: PRETTY WORDS

DESCRIPTION OF THE LESSON:
Say to the children, "Some words make us feel pleasant and some do not. Let's name all the 'pretty' words we can think of—words that make us feel good or give us a nice feeling." Examples are words like heavenly, elegant, gently, soft, fresh, natural, delicate, and sparkling. This process may be repeated with ugly words (snarled, selfish, scarred, rotten, spoiled, decay) or delicious words (spicy, savory, steaming, moist, fruity). Other types of words that may be used are:

- sad words
- happy words
- busy words
- quiet words
- noisy words
- fantasy words

As the children name the words, list them on the board. Encourage the children to explain why a word holds a particular connotation for them.

METHOD OF EVALUATION:
Observe the children's performance. It is suggested that an anecdotal record of each child's performance be kept, based on your observations.

RECEPTIVE LANGUAGE

PURPOSE:
To increase descriptive vocabulary

AREA OF LANGUAGE STRESSED:
Semantic understanding of vocabulary—Expanding vocabulary

DURATION OF LESSON:
Fifteen minutes

LESSON FORMAT:
Individual

LESSON 92: DESCRIBING OBJECTS

MATERIALS/EQUIPMENT/PHYSICAL LAYOUT:
Common objects such as a fork, a pencil, a piece of velvet, or a piece of satin

DESCRIPTION OF THE LESSON:
Place the objects on the table. Introduce the lesson by saying, "I have some things I want you to look at. I will describe one of the objects, and you will have to guess which one I am talking about." The following questions are asked:

- Which one is shiny and sharp? (the fork)
- Which one is soft? (the piece of velvet)
- Which one is smooth and silky? (the piece of satin)
- Which one is long and sharp? (the pencil)

To determine the correct item, the children must understand the descriptive words.

METHOD OF EVALUATION:
Determine the child's knowledge of descriptive words by observing whether the child selects the correct object. A percentage of correct responses may be obtained by dividing the number of correct responses made by the total number of responses possible.

$$\frac{\text{Correct responses}}{\text{Total responses}} = \text{Percentage correct}$$

RECEPTIVE LANGUAGE

PURPOSE:
To demonstrate an understanding of descriptive words

AREA OF LANGUAGE STRESSED:
Semantic understanding of vocabulary—Expanding vocabulary

DURATION OF LESSON:
Twenty minutes

little

LESSON FORMAT:
Group or individual

LESSON 93: SHAPE A WORD

MATERIALS/EQUIPMENT/PHYSICAL LAYOUT:
A list of words that depict feelings or are descriptive words

DESCRIPTION OF THE LESSON:
Give each child a list of words that evoke different feelings or images, such as sad, happy, shaky, terrified, shy, noisy, excited, strong, and little. Instruct the child to write the word in such a way that its shape will denote the feeling of the word. For example:

METHOD OF EVALUATION:
Determine if the child understands the concept that the words represent by the manner in which the child illustrates each word. It is suggested that an anecdotal record of each child's performance be kept, based on your observations.

RECEPTIVE LANGUAGE

PURPOSE:
To increase descriptive vocabulary

AREA OF LANGUAGE STRESSED:
Semantic understanding of vocabulary—Expanding vocabulary

DURATION OF LESSON:
Fifteen minutes

LESSON FORMAT:
Group or individual

LESSON 94: DESCRIBING WORDS

MATERIALS/EQUIPMENT/PHYSICAL LAYOUT:
Picture cards of familiar foods, such as ice cream, popcorn, a lemon, a piece of candy, hot chocolate, potato chips, a jar of honey, and so on.

DESCRIPTION OF THE LESSON:
Place the group of food pictures on the chalk tray or on a pocket chart. Then say to the child, ''Some words describe or tell about different foods. I'm going to say a word and I want you to find the picture of the food that I am describing.'' Then present a word, such as ''salty.'' The child must find the food that could be described as salty. Other descriptive words for foods are:

- sweet (candy)
- sour (lemon)
- sticky (honey)
- hot (hot chocolate)
- cold (ice cream)
- crunchy (potato chips)

METHOD OF EVALUATION:
Note whether the child selects the appropriate food to go with the descriptive word. A percentage of correct responses may be obtained by dividing the number of correct responses made by the total number of responses possible.

$$\frac{\text{Correct responses}}{\text{Total responses}} = \text{Percentage correct}$$

RECEPTIVE LANGUAGE

PURPOSE:
To increase descriptive vocabulary

AREA OF LANGUAGE STRESSED:
Semantic understanding of vocabulary—Expanding vocabulary

DURATION OF LESSON:
Fifteen to twenty minutes

LESSON FORMAT:
Group

LESSON 95: MOOD MAKERS

MATERIALS/EQUIPMENT/PHYSICAL LAYOUT:
Index cards, 3″ × 5″, containing mood words

DESCRIPTION OF THE LESSON:
After making a set of cards containing mood words, explain to the children that each one will have an opportunity to "act out" or portray a different mood. Each child picks a card and, without telling the others what the word is, uses facial expressions to depict the mood it conveys. The other children try to guess the word. The following mood words may be portrayed:

- lonesome
- happy
- scared
- sad
- excited
- morose
- angry
- worried
- anxious

For children whose primary language is not English, these words may be paired with their equivalents in the child's primary language.

METHOD OF EVALUATION:
Observe the child's ability to demonstrate appropriate facial expressions. It is suggested that an anecdotal record of the child's performance be kept, based on your observations.

RECEPTIVE LANGUAGE

PURPOSE:
To develop an understanding of synonyms

AREA OF LANGUAGE STRESSED:
Semantic understanding of vocabulary—Expanding vocabulary

LESSON 96: THE THESAURUS

MATERIALS/EQUIPMENT/PHYSICAL LAYOUT:
Construction paper, pencils, writing paper, and dictionaries

DESCRIPTION OF THE LESSON:
Say to the group of children, "Sometimes when we write stories, we use the same words again and again. We need to change our words so that our writing is more varied. For example, how can we change the word *said* to sound different?" The children may think of the following alternatives for the word *said:*

```
                            Said
    exclaimed                       whimpered

    stated                          pronounced

    declared                        recited

    uttered                         growled

    cried                           ordered
```

DURATION OF LESSON:
Thirty to forty-five minutes

Discuss the alternatives and how they represent slightly different meanings. Encourage the children to begin a class thesaurus, each child selecting a common word and thinking of a variety of synonyms to alternate for use in writing. Dictionaries may be needed for inquiries.

METHOD OF EVALUATION:
Evaluate each child's ability to think of different alternatives by counting the number of synonyms the child produces.

LESSON FORMAT:
Group

RECEPTIVE LANGUAGE

PURPOSE:
To develop and expand vocabulary

AREA OF LANGUAGE STRESSED:
Semantic understanding of vocabulary—Expanding vocabulary

DURATION OF LESSON:
Twenty minutes

LESSON FORMAT:
Individual

LESSON 97: HOMONYM HUNT

MATERIALS/EQUIPMENT/PHYSICAL LAYOUT:
Dictionaries and 3'' × 5'' index cards

DESCRIPTION OF THE LESSON:
Prepare a set of cards containing the following homonyms with identical spellings:

- grade—grade
- wave—wave
- fast—fast
- bark—bark
- pool—pool

The child's task is to select a card from the set of homonyms. Using the dictionary, the child identifies two or more different meanings for the same word. The child may wish to make a book and illustrate each homonym with a picture:

 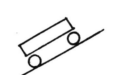

I'm in 3rd grade.   A steep grade

METHOD OF EVALUATION:
Observe the child's performance. It is suggested that an anecdotal record of the child's acquisition of vocabulary be kept, based on your observations.

RECEPTIVE LANGUAGE

PURPOSE:
To develop the ability to identify compound words

AREA OF LANGUAGE STRESSED:
Semantic understanding of vocabulary—Expanding vocabulary

DURATION OF LESSON:
Twenty minutes

LESSON FORMAT:
Group or individual

LESSON 98: COMPOUND CAPERS

MATERIALS/EQUIPMENT/PHYSICAL LAYOUT:
Magazines, glue, scissors, and 9″ × 12″ tagboard

DESCRIPTION OF THE LESSON:
After discussing compound words as two or more words combined, have the children look through old magazines and select pictures. Encourage the children to create nonsensical compound words by cutting apart the pictures to make unusual picture combinations. For example, a bubblehead may be created with a picture of bubbles on top of a person's body. A tomatohead may consist of a picture of a tomato on top of a person's shoulder. A buttonbird may be made by gluing buttons on a bird's body. The composite pictures may be glued on tagboard and labeled.

METHOD OF EVALUATION:
Observe each child's ability to develop novel compound words.

RECEPTIVE LANGUAGE

PURPOSE:
To increase vocabulary of action words

AREA OF LANGUAGE STRESSED:
Semantic understanding of vocabulary—Expanding vocabulary

DURATION OF LESSON:
To be completed over several class periods

LESSON FORMAT:
Group

LESSON 99: LET'S GO GROCERY SHOPPING

MATERIALS/EQUIPMENT/PHYSICAL LAYOUT:
Cookbooks

DESCRIPTION OF THE LESSON:
Tell the children that they are going to plan a meal. They are to use cookbooks to select an entree, a vegetable, a salad, and a dessert. A natural grouping procedure would be to divide the children into four task-oriented groups, one for each part of the meal. Each group selects its recipe and picks out words its members do not know. These words may need explanation and require the use of a dictionary. Following are some difficult words:

sauté	drain	reserve
brown	garnish	simmer
blend	coat	blanch
flute	shred	parboil

After the children have selected their recipes, have them make shopping lists for their ingredients. Next, encourage the children to read grocery advertisements in the local newspaper to find the best buys. The children may share their recipes with the class.

METHOD OF EVALUATION:
New vocabulary words may be tested orally or in a written format.

RECEPTIVE LANGUAGE

PURPOSE:
To supply vocabulary commonly associated with a group of words

AREA OF LANGUAGE STRESSED:
Semantic understanding of vocabulary—Learning common phrases

DURATION OF LESSON:
Twenty minutes

LESSON FORMAT:
Individual

LESSON 100: ASSOCIATION PHRASES

MATERIALS/EQUIPMENT/PHYSICAL LAYOUT:
Picture cards depicting the following:

- loaf of bread
- glass of liquid
- bowl of ice cream
- spoon
- pair of pants or shoes
- package of gum

DESCRIPTION OF THE LESSON:
Hold up a picture card and say, "This is a pair of _____." The child must complete the sentence, supplying the appropriate noun associated with the picture. After the child has mastered this task, a game may be played in which the child must supply the missing word without the visual stimulus. The child may use any appropriate nouns associated with the phrases modeled by the teacher, such as:

- a pack of _____
- a pail of _____
- a pocketful of _____
- a bag of _____
- a vase of _____
- a box of _____
- a can of _____
- a cup of _____
- a plateful of _____
- a couple of _____

METHOD OF EVALUATION:
Obtain a percentage of correct responses by dividing the number of correct responses the child made by the total number of responses possible.

$$\frac{\text{Correct responses}}{\text{Total responses}} = \text{Percentage correct}$$

RECEPTIVE LANGUAGE

PURPOSE:
To develop understanding of common phrases

AREA OF LANGUAGE STRESSED:
Semantic understanding of vocabulary—Learning common phrases

DURATION OF LESSON:
Forty-five minutes

LESSON FORMAT:
Group

LESSON 101: ANIMAL GROUPS

MATERIALS/EQUIPMENT/PHYSICAL LAYOUT:
Magazines, dictionaries, and word cards containing the words: *flock, herd, pack, school, litter,* and *pride*

DESCRIPTION OF THE LESSON:
Ask the children to look through magazines to find pictures of animals in groups. Explain to the children that, when animals gather in groups, their group name may be distinctive for that species. After they review the word cards orally, encourage the children to look up the words' meanings in the dictionaries provided. Finally, the children must match the correct word card with the pictures of the animal groups found previously:

- a school of fish
- a flock of geese
- a litter of puppies or kittens
- a pack of wolves
- a pride of lions

METHOD OF EVALUATION:
At a later date, determine if the children have retained the new vocabulary by reviewing the picture cards and counting correct responses. A percentage of correct responses may be obtained by dividing the number of correct responses made by the total number of responses possible.

$$\frac{\text{Correct responses}}{\text{Total responses}} = \text{Percentage correct}$$

RECEPTIVE LANGUAGE

PURPOSE:
To develop an understanding of idioms

AREA OF LANGUAGE STRESSED:
Semantic understanding of vocabulary—Learning common phrases

DURATION OF LESSON:
Twenty to thirty minutes

LESSON FORMAT:
Group

LESSON 102: UNDERSTANDING IDIOMS

MATERIALS/EQUIPMENT/PHYSICAL LAYOUT:
Prepare a list of commonly used idioms. The children will need crayons and paper.

DESCRIPTION OF THE LESSON:
Say to the children, ''Sometimes we say things that do not really mean what we said. For example, if I say it rained cats and dogs, it doesn't really mean that cats and dogs came out of the sky. It means that it rained hard. Let's see if you can figure out what these phrases really mean'':

- I was *under the weather*.
- She had *two left feet*.
- He was *on pins and needles*.
- The man was *all thumbs*.
- She was *down in the dumps*.
- He had a *green thumb*.
- He *weighed his words*.
- You *hit the nail on the head*.
- The *tables are turned*.
- It's *on the tip of my tongue*.
- She was *at the end of her rope*.

Have the children demonstrate these idioms in literal illustrations. For example:

He weighed his words.

METHOD OF EVALUATION:
Observe the children's performance. It is suggested that an anecdotal record of each child's acquisition of vocabulary be maintained, based on your observations.

Chapter 6

Lessons for Teaching Expressive Language Skills

USER'S GUIDE

EXPRESSIVE LANGUAGE

PURPOSE:
To develop the ability to identify words with the same initial sound

AREA OF LANGUAGE STRESSED:
Expressive phonology—Using alliteration

DURATION OF LESSON:
Fifteen minutes

LESSON FORMAT:
Small group

LESSON 103: ALLITERATION GAME

MATERIALS/EQUIPMENT/PHYSICAL LAYOUT:
None

DESCRIPTION OF THE LESSON:
Initiate the lesson by having the children think of one or two words to finish several alliterative sentences. For example:

- Boy baboons bake _____. (banana bread, Boston baked beans)
- Sammy Snake sneaks _____. (seven sneakers, six snacks)
- Peter Panda pats _____. (pretty posies, pink possums)

When each child has mastered this skill, ask the children to make up alliterative sentences of their own. For example, select the sound *m*, or have each child select the sound to be used. For more advanced students, this activity may assume a written format, with the children writing their own alliterative sentences.

METHOD OF EVALUATION:
Observe the child's use of alliteration. To obtain a percentage of correct responses, divide the number of correct responses made by the total number of responses possible.

$$\frac{\text{Correct responses}}{\text{Total responses}} = \text{Percentage correct}$$

EXPRESSIVE LANGUAGE

PURPOSE:
To use alliteration in identifying words

AREA OF LANGUAGE STRESSED:
Expressive phonology—Using alliteration

DURATION OF LESSON:
Twenty minutes

LESSON FORMAT:
Group

LESSON 104: A TRIP TO THE MOON

MATERIALS/EQUIPMENT/PHYSICAL LAYOUT:
None

DESCRIPTION OF THE LESSON:
The purpose of this exercise is to name objects beginning with the same consonant. Start the lesson by saying, "I'm going on a trip to the *m*oon and I'm going to take along a *m*onkey." The children in turn must also think of things beginning with the sound *m* that they will take to the moon. The game may be varied by changing the destination of the trip, such as, "I'm going on a trip to *T*angiers, and I'm going to take a *t*urtle." The children must think of words beginning with *t* to continue the game.

METHOD OF EVALUATION:
From each child's responses, determine if the child understands alliteration. Obtain a percentage of correct responses by dividing the number of correct responses made by the total number of responses possible.

$$\frac{\text{Correct responses}}{\text{Total responses}} = \text{Percentage correct}$$

EXPRESSIVE LANGUAGE

PURPOSE:
To develop complete sentences in oral expression

AREA OF LANGUAGE STRESSED:
Developing appropriate syntax—Developing complete kernel sentences

DURATION OF LESSON:
Twenty minutes

LESSON FORMAT:
Group or individual

LESSON 105: MAKE A SENTENCE

MATERIALS/EQUIPMENT/PHYSICAL LAYOUT:
None

DESCRIPTION OF THE LESSON:
Supply the child with three words. The child must think of a sentence that uses all three words. For example:

- girl—baked—burned: The girl baked cookies, but she burned them.
- fish—jump—water: I saw a fish jump out of the water.

METHOD OF EVALUATION:
Does the child's sentence meet all the requirements of adult syntax?

Give the child the opportunity to make complete sentences in several trials. Determine the percentage of correct responses by dividing the number of correct responses made by the total number of responses possible.

$$\frac{\text{Correct responses}}{\text{Total responses}} = \text{Percentage correct}$$

EXPRESSIVE LANGUAGE

PURPOSE:
To develop complete sentences in oral expression

AREA OF LANGUAGE STRESSED:
Developing appropriate syntax—Developing complete kernel sentences

DURATION OF LESSON:
Twenty minutes

LESSON FORMAT:
Individual

MATERIALS/EQUIPMENT/PHYSICAL LAYOUT:
Index cards, 3″ × 5″

LESSON 106: MAKE A NEW SENTENCE

DESCRIPTION OF THE LESSON:
Prepare three sets of index cards: a set of nouns, a set of verbs, and a set of adverbs.

Nouns	Verbs	Adverbs
boy	runs	quietly
girl	eats	loudly
cat	hops	rapidly
witch	dances	slowly
elephant	sings	quickly
tree	flies	softly

The child's task is to select one word card from each set and form a novel sentence, such as:

- The boy eats rapidly.
- The cat hops quietly.

METHOD OF EVALUATION:
In repeated trials, observe the child's ability to use syntax in forming new sentences. Obtain a percentage of correct responses by dividing the number of correct responses made by the total number of responses possible.

$$\frac{\text{Correct responses}}{\text{Total responses}} = \text{Percentage correct}$$

EXPRESSIVE LANGUAGE

PURPOSE:
To develop the ability to use correct word order

AREA OF LANGUAGE STRESSED:
Developing appropriate syntax—Developing correct word order

DURATION OF LESSON:
Fifteen to twenty minutes

LESSON FORMAT:
Group or individual

LESSON 107: SILLY SENTENCES

MATERIALS/EQUIPMENT/PHYSICAL LAYOUT:
A list of sentences whose word order is modeled incorrectly

DESCRIPTION OF THE LESSON:
Say, "I'm going to say a silly, mixed-up sentence. You have to say it the right way, using only the words I use."

- Dog has a boy the.
- Popcorn the I ate.
- Walked I to town.
- It say you.
- Elephant I the see.
- Home girl the ran.

METHOD OF EVALUATION:
A percentage of correct responses may be obtained by dividing the number of correct responses the child made by the total number of responses possible.

$$\frac{\text{Correct responses}}{\text{Total responses}} = \text{Percentage correct}$$

EXPRESSIVE LANGUAGE

PURPOSE:
To develop the ability to determine correct word order in sentences

AREA OF LANGUAGE STRESSED:
Developing appropriate syntax—Developing correct word order

LESSON 108: SENTENCE STOPPERS

MATERIALS/EQUIPMENT/PHYSICAL LAYOUT:
Envelopes and small word cards

DESCRIPTION OF THE LESSON:
Make sentence puzzles by printing one word on each card. Then place the cards for each sentence in an envelope. The child's task is to select an envelope and arrange the cards in order so that the sentence contains the words in the proper order. Here are some sample word-card sentences:

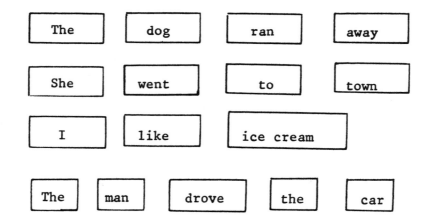

DURATION OF LESSON:
Fifteen to twenty minutes

LESSON FORMAT:
Individual

METHOD OF EVALUATION:
Obtain the percentage of correct responses by dividing the number of correct responses the child made by the total number of responses possible.

$$\frac{\text{Correct responses}}{\text{Total responses}} = \text{Percentage correct}$$

EXPRESSIVE LANGUAGE

PURPOSE:
To develop sentences with correct word order

AREA OF LANGUAGE STRESSED:
Developing appropriate syntax—Developing correct word order

DURATION OF LESSON:
Twenty minutes

LESSON FORMAT:
Group or individual

LESSON 109: SOUND WORDS

MATERIALS/EQUIPMENT/PHYSICAL LAYOUT:
A list of ''sound'' words, such as crunch, slurp, swish, and shhh

DESCRIPTION OF THE LESSON:
Supply the child with a sound word, such as crunch. Say, ''Let's see if we can use this sound word to build a sentence.'' For example:

- Crunch: Bob ate a potato chip, and it went *crunch*.
- Shhh: ''*Shhh*,'' said the girl as they tiptoed down the hall.

METHOD OF EVALUATION:
Determine if the child uses correct word order in sentences. Obtain a percentage of correct responses by dividing the number of correct responses made by the total number of responses possible.

$$\frac{\text{Correct responses}}{\text{Total responses}} = \text{Percentage Correct}$$

EXPRESSIVE LANGUAGE

PURPOSE:
To identify words within a specific word class

AREA OF LANGUAGE STRESSED:
Developing appropriate syntax—Word classes

DURATION OF LESSON:
Fifteen minutes

LESSON FORMAT:
Individual

LESSON 110: SENTENCE FRAMES

MATERIALS/EQUIPMENT/PHYSICAL LAYOUT:
Sentence frames written on tagboard strips

DESCRIPTION OF THE LESSON:
Introduce the lesson by saying, ''We are going to make our sentences longer by choosing cards that finish our sentences. See if you can finish my sentence by choosing a card that makes sense.''

Sample Sentences	*Sample Completion Cards*
Jane ate _____.	play ball
Bill went _____.	bananas and oranges
The girl ran _____.	to her friend's house
Boys and girls like to _____.	to the movie

METHOD OF EVALUATION:
Determine each child's ability to form sentences correctly with appropriate word cards. A percentage of correct responses may be obtained by dividing the number of correct responses made by the total number of responses possible.

$$\frac{\text{Correct responses}}{\text{Total responses}} = \text{Percentage correct}$$

EXPRESSIVE LANGUAGE

PURPOSE:
To identify words within a specific word class

AREA OF LANGUAGE STRESSED:
Developing appropriate syntax—Word classes

DURATION OF LESSON:
Fifteen minutes

LESSON FORMAT:
Individual

LESSON 111: COMPLETE A SENTENCE

MATERIALS/EQUIPMENT/PHYSICAL LAYOUT:
None

DESCRIPTION OF THE LESSON:
Verbally supply the child with a sentence frame. The child then completes the sentence with an appropriate word or phrase.

- I like ＿＿＿.
- The boy ＿＿＿.
- See the girl ＿＿＿.
- The ball was ＿＿＿.
- ＿＿＿ ate the cookie.
- The boy ＿＿＿ away.
- The girl ran ＿＿＿.
- Where did the boy ＿＿＿?
- I saw him ＿＿＿.
- Did you know that ＿＿＿?

METHOD OF EVALUATION:
Determine the percentage of correct responses by dividing the number of correct responses the child made by the total number of responses possible.

$$\frac{\text{Correct responses}}{\text{Total responses}} = \text{Percentage correct}$$

EXPRESSIVE LANGUAGE

PURPOSE:
To describe visual stimuli

AREA OF LANGUAGE STRESSED:
Recalling detail and describing objects and events—Describing visual detail

DURATION OF LESSON:
Twenty minutes

LESSON FORMAT:
Group

LESSON 112: A Point of VIEW

MATERIALS/EQUIPMENT/PHYSICAL LAYOUT:
Three blindfolds and some large objects for the children to identify—a doll, a stuffed animal, a tricycle, and a wagon

DESCRIPTION OF THE LESSON:
Blindfold three children. Placing an object on the floor or table, ask each child to touch the object and describe it. Place the children's hands on the object so that each child is touching a different part of the object. The children must work together to utilize the information provided by each child's description to name the object.

METHOD OF EVALUATION:
Observe the children's performance to determine the accuracy of their descriptions. It is suggested that an anecdotal record of each child's performance be kept, based on your observations.

EXPRESSIVE LANGUAGE

PURPOSE:
To develop the ability to describe visual detail

AREA OF LANGUAGE STRESSED:
Recalling details and describing objects and events—Describing visual stimuli

DURATION OF LESSON:
Twenty minutes

LESSON FORMAT:
Group

LESSON 113: NAME THE PICTURE

MATERIALS/EQUIPMENT/PHYSICAL LAYOUT:
Several large pictures mounted on construction paper

DESCRIPTION OF THE LESSON:
Place the pictures on a pocket chart or chalkboard tray. Select one child to begin the activity. The child mentally selects a picture, but does not reveal to the others which picture was chosen. The child then describes the selected picture. The other children try to guess which picture has been described. The child who guesses correctly has the next opportunity to describe a picture.

METHOD OF EVALUATION:
Observe to determine the accuracy of the children's descriptions. It is suggested that an anecdotal record of each child's performance be kept, based on your observations.

EXPRESSIVE LANGUAGE

PURPOSE:
To develop the ability to obtain the main idea from a picture stimulus

AREA OF LANGUAGE STRESSED:
Recalling details and describing objects and events—Describing visual stimuli

DURATION OF LESSON:
Thirty minutes

LESSON FORMAT:
Individual

LESSON 114: BOOK JACKETS

MATERIALS/EQUIPMENT/PHYSICAL LAYOUT:
Illustrated book jackets, glue, and 9″ × 12″ tagboard

DESCRIPTION OF THE LESSON:
After a number of interesting book jackets have been collected, each child chooses one that is appealing. The jacket is then glued to a piece of tagboard. Using the jacket picture, the child tells a story orally or writes a story on the tagboard.

METHOD OF EVALUATION:
As the child tells the story, determine whether it matches the picture. Alternatively, evaluate the expressive language in the story with the checklist of expressive language in Appendix A.

EXPRESSIVE LANGUAGE

PURPOSE:
To recall visual detail from a movie

AREA OF LANGUAGE STRESSED:
Recalling details and describing objects and events—Describing visual stimuli

DURATION OF LESSON:
Forty-five minutes

LESSON FORMAT:
Group

LESSON 115: PLAY IT AGAIN, SAM

MATERIALS/EQUIPMENT/PHYSICAL LAYOUT:
A short 11-minute 16 mm. film

DESCRIPTION OF THE LESSON:
Explain to the children that they will see a film without sound and that they must remember as many details as they can. The film is then played without sound. After it is over, list on the board the details that the children remember. The film is played again, this time with sound. The children then compare their list with the second showing of the film.

METHOD OF EVALUATION:
Observe the children's performance in recalling details in this activity. If a child appears to be having difficulty with the task, further development of the skill may be necessary.

EXPRESSIVE LANGUAGE

PURPOSE:
To develop the ability to use descriptive clues in riddles

AREA OF LANGUAGE STRESSED:
Recalling details and describing objects and events—Describing visual stimuli

DURATION OF LESSON:
Thirty minutes

LESSON FORMAT:
Group or individual

LESSON 116: PICTURE MY RIDDLE

DESCRIPTION OF THE LESSON:
Have each child search through magazines to find a colorful object or picture. The child glues the picture onto a piece of tagboard. Using the second sheet of tagboard, the child cuts a small hole so that only a portion of the picture shows through. The second piece of tagboard is then fastened by staple or glue at the top. On the top piece of tagboard, the child writes a riddle, giving clues through descriptive words as to what the picture is. After each child has completed this task, the children may exchange their riddles. Each child must read a classmate's riddle and try to guess what it is. To check the answer, the top piece of tagboard may be lifted to reveal the picture underneath.

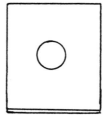

MATERIALS/EQUIPMENT/PHYSICAL LAYOUT:
Magazines; 9″ × 12″ tagboard, two sheets per child; glue; and scissors

METHOD OF EVALUATION:
Observe the children's use of descriptive words in the riddle. It is suggested that an anecdotal record of each child's performance be kept, based on your observations.

EXPRESSIVE LANGUAGE

PURPOSE:
To develop the ability to describe objects

AREA OF LANGUAGE STRESSED:
Recalling details and describing objects—Describing visual stimuli

DURATION OF LESSON:
Forty-five minutes

LESSON FORMAT:
Group or individual

LESSON 117: MACHINE FANTASY

MATERIALS/EQUIPMENT/PHYSICAL LAYOUT:
White construction paper and crayons or colored pencils

DESCRIPTION OF THE LESSON:
Encourage the children to draw a new machine that performs an unusual task, such as a machine that changes rocks into gold, a cat-spanking machine, a machine that fixes meals, and so on. Each child draws and colors a picture of the new machine on white construction paper. The child shows the picture to the class and explains how it functions.

METHOD OF EVALUATION:
Evaluate the child's expressive language with the checklist of expressive language in Appendix A.

EXPRESSIVE LANGUAGE

PURPOSE:
To develop the ability to describe visual stimuli

AREA OF LANGUAGE STRESSED:
Recalling details and describing objects and events—Describing visual detail

DURATION OF LESSON:
Forty-five minutes

LESSON FORMAT:
Group

LESSON 118: FASHION FUN

MATERIALS/EQUIPMENT/PHYSICAL LAYOUT:
Articles of clothing

DESCRIPTION OF THE LESSON:
Ask the children to wear their favorite articles of clothing to school. Tell them that the clothing will be entered in a class fashion show. Each child takes a turn as the narrator of the fashion show, describing another child's outfit. Present the following ideas to the children to structure their narration:

- Describe the color and fabric of the clothing.
- Describe the design, shape, or style of the clothing.
- Describe places the article of clothing could be worn.

METHOD OF EVALUATION:
Evaluate the child's expressive language skills with the checklist of expressive language in Appendix A.

EXPRESSIVE LANGUAGE

PURPOSE:
  To develop the ability to describe objects

AREA OF LANGUAGE STRESSED:
  Recalling details and describing objects and events—Describing visual stimuli

DURATION OF LESSON:
  Forty-five minutes

LESSON FORMAT:
  Group

LESSON 119: WOULD YOU BELIEVE IT?

MATERIALS/EQUIPMENT/PHYSICAL LAYOUT:
  Wood scraps, string, cardboard, paper, and glue

DESCRIPTION OF THE LESSON:
  Have the children construct an object out of the materials. After it is completed, divide the children into groups. Encourage each group to create a commercial to sell the object. They may perform their commercials in a variety of formats (spoken, sung, or dramatized). Have each group give their commercial to the other class members.

METHOD OF EVALUATION:
  It is difficult to evaluate individual expressive language in this lesson, due to the group format of the activity. However, it is suggested that an anecdotal record of each child's performance be kept, based on your observations.

EXPRESSIVE LANGUAGE

PURPOSE:
  To develop the ability to describe visual stimuli

AREA OF LANGUAGE STRESSED:
  Recalling details and describing objects and events—Describing visual stimuli

DURATION OF LESSON:
  Forty-five minutes

LESSON FORMAT:
  Group or individual

LESSON 120: THEME COLLAGES

MATERIALS/EQUIPMENT/PHYSICAL LAYOUT:
  Old magazines, scissors, construction paper, and glue

DESCRIPTION OF THE LESSON:
  Select a theme such as *My Family, My Pet,* or *Me.* Using the magazines, the child selects and cuts out pictures that best characterize the theme. The child glues them into a collage and describes the pictures to the other class members.

METHOD OF EVALUATION:
  Evaluate the children's expressive language skills with the checklist of expressive language in Appendix A.

EXPRESSIVE LANGUAGE

PURPOSE:
To develop the ability to describe the function of common objects

AREA OF LANGUAGE STRESSED:
Recalling details and describing objects and events—Describing visual stimuli

DURATION OF LESSON:
Twenty minutes

LESSON FORMAT:
Group or individual

LESSON 121: WHAT'S IT FOR?

MATERIALS/EQUIPMENT/PHYSICAL LAYOUT:
Common objects found in the home and at school, such as:

tweezers	eggbeater	spatula
thermometer	hole punch	kitchen tongs
shoehorn	rubber band	doorstop
screwdriver	scale	paperweight

DESCRIPTION OF THE LESSON:
Hold up an object and ask, ''What do we use this for? Who might use this tool? Show me how to use it. Tell us about it.'' Select one child to describe the uses of the object. In a variation of this task, have the children think of new ways of using the objects.

METHOD OF EVALUATION:
Determine the accuracy of the child's description and evaluate the child's use of expressive language with the checklist of expressive language in Appendix A.

EXPRESSIVE LANGUAGE

PURPOSE:
To develop the ability to describe visual stimuli

AREA OF LANGUAGE STRESSED:
Recalling details and describing objects and events—Describing visual stimuli

DURATION OF LESSON:
Fifteen to twenty minutes

LESSON FORMAT:
Individual

LESSON 122: VIEWMASTER STORY

MATERIALS/EQUIPMENT/PHYSICAL LAYOUT:
A viewmaster and several story discs

DESCRIPTION OF THE LESSON:
As the child views the story in the viewmaster, encourage the child to describe what is seen in each frame.

METHOD OF EVALUATION:
Evaluate the child's use of expressive language with the checklist of expressive language in Appendix A.

EXPRESSIVE LANGUAGE

PURPOSE:
  To develop the ability to describe visual stimuli

AREA OF LANGUAGE STRESSED:
  Recalling details and describing objects and events—Describing visual stimuli

DURATION OF LESSON:
  Fifteen minutes per picture

LESSON FORMAT:
  Individual

LESSON 123: PICTURES, PLEASE

MATERIALS/EQUIPMENT/PHYSICAL LAYOUT:
  Instant developing camera and film

DESCRIPTION OF THE LESSON:
  Give the child the camera. Go with the child on a walk around the school or school grounds. Find an interesting activity that is taking place, such as a class project, a game, or workmen performing a job. Have the child take a picture of the event. Upon returning to the classroom, the child must describe the picture to the rest of the class.

METHOD OF EVALUATION:
  During the child's description of the picture, evaluate the child's oral language skills with the checklist of expressive language in Appendix A.

EXPRESSIVE LANGUAGE

PURPOSE:
  To develop the ability to describe visual stimuli

AREA OF LANGUAGE STRESSED:
  Recalling details and describing objects and events—Describing visual stimuli

DURATION OF LESSON:
  Fifteen to twenty minutes

LESSON FORMAT:
  Group or individual

LESSON 124: THE PICTURE CUBE

MATERIALS/EQUIPMENT/PHYSICAL LAYOUT:
  A small cardboard box, colored butcher paper, six interesting pictures (one for each side of the box), and glue

DESCRIPTION OF THE LESSON:
  In preparation for this lesson, cover the cardboard box with butcher paper and glue one picture on each of the six sides of the box. Place the box on the table, and direct one child to select a favorite picture. Ask, ''Why do you like this picture? What does it remind you of? Tell us about it.'' The child then holds the box and describes the picture, pointing out various parts to illustrate the verbal description.

METHOD OF EVALUATION:
  Evaluate the child's spontaneous language skill with the checklist of expressive language in Appendix A.

EXPRESSIVE LANGUAGE

PURPOSE:
To develop the ability to describe objects

AREA OF LANGUAGE STRESSED:
Recalling details and describing objects and events—Describing visual stimuli

DURATION OF LESSON:
Fifteen to twenty minutes

LESSON FORMAT:
Group

LESSON 125: THE FOOD BOX

MATERIALS/EQUIPMENT/PHYSICAL LAYOUT:
A small metal box containing index cards (3″ × 5″), on each of which is a picture of a different food, such as a sandwich, a slice of watermelon, or a piece of pizza.

DESCRIPTION OF THE LESSON:
Ask the child to choose a card without telling the other children what it is. Tell the child to describe the food. Use the following questions as prompts:

- Would you tell us about it?
- What does it look like?
- What color is it?
- What shape does it have?
- How big is it?
- How does it taste?

As the child describes the food, have the other children try to guess the food being described. To expand this activity to include cultural considerations, pictures of different ethnic foods may be used.

METHOD OF EVALUATION:
Evaluate the level of the child's oral language skill with the checklist of expressive language in Appendix A.

EXPRESSIVE LANGUAGE

PURPOSE:
To develop the ability to describe objects

AREA OF LANGUAGE STRESSED:
Recalling details and describing objects and events—Describing visual stimuli

DURATION OF LESSON:
To be completed over several class periods

LESSON FORMAT:
Individual and then group

LESSON 126: THE PEEKBOX

MATERIALS/EQUIPMENT/PHYSICAL LAYOUT:
A tape recorder, a blank cassette tape, and a shoebox containing a dioramic scene with a small hole for individual viewing

DESCRIPTION OF THE LESSON:
Place the peekbox and the tape recorder on a table in the classroom. During free time, the children may examine the peekbox. Encourage each child to view the scene and tell a story about it. Tape-record the story for later use. When all of the children have recorded their stories, the tape may be played for the class and the stories compared.

METHOD OF EVALUATION:
The tape recording, containing a sample of each child's use of expressive language, may be analyzed with any of several standarized evaluation instruments or with the checklist of expressive language in Appendix A.

EXPRESSIVE LANGUAGE

PURPOSE:
To develop the ability to describe events

AREA OF LANGUAGE STRESSED:
Recalling details and describing objects and events—Describing events

DURATION OF LESSON:
Twenty to thirty minutes

LESSON FORMAT:
Group or individual

LESSON 127: IMAGINE THAT . . .

MATERIALS/EQUIPMENT/PHYSICAL LAYOUT:
None

DESCRIPTION OF THE LESSON:
Initiate a group discussion, using the following story starters and probes as introductions:

- Imagine you are invisible. Where would you go?
- Run fast. Here comes . . .
- I get scared when . . .
- Imagine you are an animal. Which one would you like to be? Why?
- If you were the teacher, what would you do?
- We have been visited by a creature from outer space. Tell us about the creature.
- You were just given a lot of money. What will you do with it?
- Imagine you are a famous person. Who would you like to be? Why?
- Something funny happened on the way to school . . .
- I saw a strange light in the house . . .
- Imagine you can fly. Tell us about it.
- Crack! The noise was so loud it hurt my ears . . .
- I had such a bad day you wouldn't believe it! First . . .
- Something shining on the ground caught my eye. It was . . .
- I found a magic rock . . .
- I heard them fighting on the playground . . .
- Imagine you are the president of the United States. How would you run the country?
- Today, my dog . . .
- The neatest thing that ever happened to me was . . .
- Imagine you are an inventor. What would you invent?

METHOD OF EVALUATION:
Observe whether a child uses a particular language construction in spontaneous conversation. Evaluate with the generalization check in Appendix E. Alternatively, evaluate the content of the child's expressive language using the checklist of expressive language in Appendix A.

EXPRESSIVE LANGUAGE

PURPOSE:
To develop the ability to describe events

AREA OF LANGUAGE STRESSED:
Recalling details and describing objects and events—Describing events

DURATION OF LESSON:
Fifteen to twenty minutes

LESSON FORMAT:
Group or individual

LESSON 128: ANIMAL STORIES

MATERIALS/EQUIPMENT/PHYSICAL LAYOUT:
Cards with an animal picture on one side and factual information on the other

DESCRIPTION OF THE LESSON:
Hold up an animal card and say, "I'm going to tell you some interesting things about this animal. Then you may tell a story about the animal." Read the information to the children. Ask one of the children to tell a story about the animal, using some of the details read previously.

METHOD OF EVALUATION:
Determine if the child has incorporated the presented information into the story about the animal. The content of the child's expressive language may be evaluated with the checklist of expressive language in Appendix A.

EXPRESSIVE LANGUAGE

PURPOSE:
To develop the ability to use phrases to describe events

AREA OF LANGUAGE STRESSED:
Recalling details and describing objects and events—Describing events

DURATION OF LESSON:
Thirty minutes

LESSON FORMAT:
Group

LESSON 129: WHAT IS A PET?

MATERIALS/EQUIPMENT/PHYSICAL LAYOUT:
Butcher paper or a chart tablet

DESCRIPTION OF THE LESSON:
Ask the children to use phrases in describing a specific topic. For example, ask, "What is a pet?" The children may answer, "A pet is . . .

- a pal on Saturday."
- a fantastic frisbee partner."
- someone to share your hot dog with."
- a hungry, bottomless pit."
- nowhere to be found on bath day."

As the children dictate their phrases, write them on a chart. They may be illustrated by the children at a later date. Similar topics that may be used in this lesson are:

- What is a house?
- What is a mother?
- What is a friend?
- What is a flower?

METHOD OF EVALUATION:
Determine if the children's phrases are appropriate to the topic. It is suggested that an anecdotal record of each child's performance be kept, based on your observations.

EXPRESSIVE LANGUAGE

PURPOSE:
To develop the ability to describe events

AREA OF LANGUAGE STRESSED:
Recalling details and describing objects and events—Describing events

DURATION OF LESSON:
Twenty to thirty minutes

LESSON FORMAT:
Group of six children

LESSON 130: FOLDER STORIES

MATERIALS/EQUIPMENT/PHYSICAL LAYOUT:
Six manila folders, each containing a picture

DESCRIPTION OF THE LESSON:
Give one folder to each of the children and instruct them not to open them. Then begin to tell a story. After a few sentences, point to a child who, after looking in a folder, continues the story. The child's story must be related to the picture in the folder. This process is continued until all the children have had an opportunity to add to the story. The last child finishes the story.

To expand this activity to include cultural awareness, the folders may contain pictures about various ethnic legends, fables, or historical events.

METHOD OF EVALUATION:
Evaluate the child's oral language skill with the checklist of expressive language in Appendix A.

EXPRESSIVE LANGUAGE

PURPOSE:
To develop the ability to describe events

AREA OF LANGUAGE STRESSED:
Recalling details and describing objects and events—Describing events

DURATION OF LESSON:
Thirty minutes

LESSON FORMAT:
Group or individual

LESSON 131: WHAT IF?

MATERIALS/EQUIPMENT/PHYSICAL LAYOUT:
A tape recorder and a blank cassette tape

DESCRIPTION OF THE LESSON:
Sometimes all that children need in order to express themselves is a provocative topic. Say to the children, "Today we are going to use our imaginations to think of what things would be like if the impossible were to happen. For example, what if . . .

- dogs could talk?"
- you were invisible?"
- we didn't have telephones?"
- you were locked in a time warp in the year 1850?"
- you had a machine that made money?"

Tape record each child's answers.

METHOD OF EVALUATION:
Evaluate the tape-recorded samples of each child's expressive language with the checklist of expressive language in Appendix A.

EXPRESSIVE LANGUAGE

PURPOSE:
To develop the ability to describe events

AREA OF LANGUAGE STRESSED:
Recalling details and describing objects and events—Describing events

DURATION OF LESSON:
Thirty minutes

LESSON FORMAT:
Group

LESSON 132: SPORTS EYE NEWS

MATERIALS/EQUIPMENT/PHYSICAL LAYOUT:
Have the children make a mock microphone out of common objects found in the classroom.

DESCRIPTION OF THE LESSON:
Using one of the children's favorite team sports, divide the children into two teams. The number of team players need not be the exact number used in regulation play. Choose one child to be the sports announcer. Have the two teams participate in a pretend game, performing all actions in slow motion. The task of the sports announcer is to give a play-by-play description of the game to the viewing audience.

METHOD OF EVALUATION:
Evaluate the announcer's ability to describe events with the checklist of expressive language in Appendix A.

EXPRESSIVE LANGUAGE

PURPOSE:
To develop the ability to describe events

AREA OF LANGUAGE STRESSED:
Recalling details and describing objects and events—Describing events

DURATION OF LESSON:
Fifteen to twenty minutes

LESSON FORMAT:
Group

LESSON 133: LOST AND FOUND

MATERIALS/EQUIPMENT/PHYSICAL LAYOUT:
Lost and found advertisements from a local newspaper

DESCRIPTION OF THE LESSON:
Ask the children to think of what objects people are inclined to lose and how one would go about trying to get them back. Choose an ad from the lost and found column of the local newspaper. For example, "Lost: one black and brown shepherd dog in vicinity of Mulberry Street. Answers to name of Topper. If found, call 247-1035." Ask the children to create a story about how the dog was lost.

METHOD OF EVALUATION:
Evaluate each child's oral language skill with the checklist of expressive language in Appendix A.

EXPRESSIVE LANGUAGE

PURPOSE:
To develop the ability to describe events

AREA OF LANGUAGE STRESSED:
Recalling details and describing objects and events—Describing events

DURATION OF LESSON:
To be continued over several class periods

LESSON FORMAT:
Group

LESSON 134: SILHOUETTES ON THE WALL

MATERIALS/EQUIPMENT/PHYSICAL LAYOUT:
The following materials are needed:

- construction paper
- scissors
- pencil
- paper
- magazines
- bright lamp or light
- glue

DESCRIPTION OF THE LESSON:
Using a bright lamp to cast a shadow, draw a silhouette of each child. Have the child cut out the silhouette. Next, ask the children to find pictures to demonstrate personal hobbies and interests. These pictures should be selected and cut out from the magazines provided to the children. The children then glue their pictures onto their silhouettes and are given an opportunity to describe their interests and hobbies to the class.

METHOD OF EVALUATION:
Evaluate each child's oral language skill with the checklist of expressive language in Appendix A.

EXPRESSIVE LANGUAGE

PURPOSE:
To develop the ability to describe events

AREA OF LANGUAGE STRESSED:
Recalling details and describing objects and events—Describing events

DURATION OF LESSON:
Fifteen minutes

LESSON FORMAT:
Group or inidividual

LESSON 135: STORY STARTERS

MATERIALS/EQUIPMENT/PHYSICAL LAYOUT:
None

DESCRIPTION OF THE LESSON:
Say, "I am going to start a story and I want you to finish it. Last night I heard a strange sound. It . . ." Encourage each child to tell a short story based on the starter sentence. Other story starters are:

- It was dark . . .
- The man was laughing hard . . .
- I went to town with a friend and . . .
- Yesterday I found $100 . . .

METHOD OF EVALUATION:
Use the checklist of expressive language in Appendix A to evaluate the child's oral language skill.

EXPRESSIVE LANGUAGE

PURPOSE:
To develop the ability to narrate a story

AREA OF LANGUAGE STRESSED:
Recalling details and describing objects and events—Describing events

DURATION OF LESSON:
Fifteen to twenty minutes

LESSON FORMAT:
Group

LESSON 136: HEADLINE HUNTING

MATERIALS/EQUIPMENT/PHYSICAL LAYOUT:
Headlines of human interest stories chosen from the local newspaper, such as, "Girl Meets Bear" or "Trio Makes Narrow Escape."

DESCRIPTION OF THE LESSON:
Read a newspaper headline to the children and ask, "What do you think this story is about? What might have happened in this story?" Encourage the children to discuss possible story events together and to create the sequence of events that might have taken place. Ask one of the children to retell the story. If the children possess reading skills, allow them to hunt through newspapers to select their own headlines.

METHOD OF EVALUATION:
Evaluate each child's ability to narrate a story, using the checklist of expressive language in Appendix A.

EXPRESSIVE LANGUAGE

PURPOSE:
To develop the ability to predict outcomes

AREA OF LANGUAGE STRESSED:
Recalling details and describing objects and events—Describing events

DURATION OF LESSON:
Twenty minutes

LESSON FORMAT:
Group

LESSON 137: THE SOOTHSAYER

MATERIALS/EQUIPMENT/PHYSICAL LAYOUT:
None

DESCRIPTION OF THE LESSON:
To develop the children's ability to predict outcomes, use open-ended questions to stimulate creative thinking. For example: What will the world be like in the year 2050? What will people be like? What kinds of schools will we have? What foods will we eat?

In a variation of the lesson, have the children select from a travel magazine a picture depicting life in a foreign country. Ask the children to imagine they are going to live in this new country. Ask them, "What will you eat? Where will you work? What will your life be like?"

METHOD OF EVALUATION:
Assess expressive language in the child's verbal description with the checklist of expressive language in Appendix A.

EXPRESSIVE LANGUAGE

PURPOSE:
To describe events in an exaggerated fashion

AREA OF LANGUAGE STRESSED:
Recalling details and describing objects and events—Describing events

DURATION OF LESSON:
Twenty minutes

LESSON FORMAT:
Group

LESSON 138: TELL A WHOPPER!

MATERIALS/EQUIPMENT/PHYSICAL LAYOUT:
A small plastic whale or a tagboard cutout of a whale

DESCRIPTION OF THE LESSON:
Explain that a whopper is a tall tale or a big lie. Explain that the whale is also considered a whopper of a mammal. The task of each child is to hold the whale and tell the biggest whopper possible. The child passes the whale to another child who tells another whopper of a story.

METHOD OF EVALUATION:
Each child's expressive language in telling a whopper may be evaluated with the checklist of expressive language in Appendix A.

EXPRESSIVE LANGUAGE

PURPOSE:
To develop the ability to give oral directions

AREA OF LANGUAGE STRESSED:
Recalling details and describing objects and events—Giving verbal directions

DURATION OF LESSON:
Twenty minutes

LESSON FORMAT:
Group

LESSON 139: TEACH THE CLASS

MATERIALS/EQUIPMENT/PHYSICAL LAYOUT:
Variable

DESCRIPTION OF THE LESSON:
Identify a special talent or interest of each child. For example, one child may be particularly adept at making paper airplanes. Encourage the child to teach the class how to perform the task. The other children must follow the child's directions in making the object. This activity may be expanded by having the children describe games of different cultures represented in the class.

METHOD OF EVALUATION:
Observe the children's directions to determine if they were clear and concise. It is suggested that an anecdotal record of each child's performance be kept, based on your observations.

EXPRESSIVE LANGUAGE

PURPOSE:
To develop the ability to give verbal directions

AREA OF LANGUAGE STRESSED:
Recalling details and describing objects and events—Giving verbal directions

DURATION OF LESSON:
Two or three 20-minute periods

LESSON FORMAT:
Group or individual

LESSON 140: PLAN A PARTY

MATERIALS/EQUIPMENT/PHYSICAL LAYOUT:
Reference books on children's party games

DESCRIPTION OF THE LESSON:
Explain to the children that a party is being planned and that one or more of them is responsible for planning the games. The children must write down the materials or equipment needed and describe to the rest of the class how to play the game. This activity may be extended to include important cultural celebrations observed by the children in the class. For example, a Christmas piñata party may be described.

METHOD OF EVALUATION:
Observe the children's ability to describe directions to the game accurately. It is suggested that an anecdotal record of each child's performance be kept, based on your observations.

EXPRESSIVE LANGUAGE

PURPOSE:
To develop the ability to give verbal directions

AREA OF LANGUAGE STRESSED:
Recalling details and describing objects and events—Giving verbal directions

DURATION OF LESSON:
Thirty to forty-five minutes

LESSON FORMAT:
Group or individual

LESSON 141: MAP READING

MATERIALS/EQUIPMENT/PHYSICAL LAYOUT:
Paper and rulers

DESCRIPTION OF THE LESSON:
Instruct the children to draw a neighborhood map, including their houses, the houses of neighbors, and familiar neighborhood landmarks, such as churches, stores, and schools. Have the children draw the route to commonly visited places, such as a friend's house or a store. Each child must then describe the route to the other class members.

METHOD OF EVALUATION:
Observe the child's accuracy in describing the route correctly. It is suggested that an anecdotal record of each child's performance be kept, based on your observations.

EXPRESSIVE LANGUAGE

PURPOSE:
To develop the ability to obtain and report factual information

AREA OF LANGUAGE STRESSED:
Recalling details and describing objects and events—Reporting factual information

DURATION OF LESSON:
To be completed in two 30-minute periods

LESSON FORMAT:
Group

LESSON 142: WHO'S THE FAMOUS PERSON?

MATERIALS/EQUIPMENT/PHYSICAL LAYOUT:
Biographies of famous persons, suited to the reading level of the children who should have access to library resources

DESCRIPTION OF THE LESSON:
Ask the children to choose a famous person they would like to learn more about. The children may utilize library resources to obtain biographical information. In a group discussion format, each child orally describes the famous character chosen, keeping the identity of the person a secret from the group. The child should be encouraged to use the following information as clues to the person's identity:

- where the person lived or was born
- when the person lived
- what important deed the famous person performed

After the child describes the person, the other members of the group must guess the identity of the person described. This activity may be varied to observe cultural considerations by allowing the children to choose a famous person within their ethnic or cultural heritage.

METHOD OF EVALUATION:
Through informal observation, evaluate the children's ability to report factual information. It is suggested that an anecdotal record of each child's performance be kept, based on your observations.

EXPRESSIVE LANGUAGE

PURPOSE:
To describe cause-and-effect relationships

AREA OF LANGUAGE STRESSED:
Recalling details and describing objects and events—Determining cause and effect

DURATION OF LESSON:
Fifteen to twenty minutes

LESSON FORMAT:
Individual

LESSON 143: IF, THEN

MATERIALS/EQUIPMENT/PHYSICAL LAYOUT:
None

DESCRIPTION OF THE LESSON:
Pose ''What if'' questions, asking the child to relate the effect. Examples of ''What if'' questions are:

- What if there were no traffic signs?
- What happens if you don't feed a pet?
- What can happen if you play with matches?
- What if you left a window open on a rainy day?
- What if you dropped a cookie on the floor in front of your dog?

METHOD OF EVALUATION:
Observe the child's ability to state cause-and-effect relationships. To determine the percentage of correct responses, divide the number of correct responses made by the total number of responses possible.

$$\frac{\text{Correct responses}}{\text{Total responses}} = \text{Percentage correct}$$

EXPRESSIVE LANGUAGE

PURPOSE:
To identify objects and their component parts

AREA OF LANGUAGE STRESSED:
Developing expressive vocabulary—Naming persons and objects (nouns)

DURATION OF LESSON:
Twenty minutes

LESSON FORMAT:
Group or individual

LESSON 144: IDENTIFYING PARTS

MATERIALS/EQUIPMENT/PHYSICAL LAYOUT:
Common objects or pictures of objects found within the classroom

DESCRIPTION OF THE LESSON:
Say to the children, "This is a chair. A chair has different parts. Let's see if we can name the parts: back, seat, legs, and arms. Now let's find out the names for the parts of other objects." The children learn the names of the parts pointed out. For example:

- for a book: cover, pages, spine
- for a shirt: cuffs, collar, sleeves, pockets, buttons, buttonholes
- for a house: door, window, chimney, stairs, steps, different rooms
- for a bike: handlebars, seat, tires, spokes, pedals, brake

METHOD OF EVALUATION:
Determine if new vocabulary is learned by making periodic checks to see if the child can correctly point to a named part and can correctly name the part when you point to it. A percentage of correct responses may be obtained by dividing the number of correct responses made by the total number of responses possible.

$$\frac{\text{Correct responses}}{\text{Total responses}} = \text{Percentage correct}$$

EXPRESSIVE LANGUAGE

PURPOSE:
To expand expressive vocabulary when discussing objects

AREA OF LANGUAGE STRESSED:
Developing expressive vocabulary—Naming persons and objects (nouns)

DURATION OF LESSON:
Fifteen to twenty minutes

LESSON FORMAT:
Group

LESSON 145: SELL-A-THON

MATERIALS/EQUIPMENT/PHYSICAL LAYOUT:
Objects or pictures of objects that can be sold, such as an orange, a popsicle, a car, a toy, a glass of lemonade, or a hamburger

DESCRIPTION OF THE LESSON:
Introduce the activity by bringing in some sample advertisements. After reading two or three to the group, explain that each child will have the opportunity to sell something, to persuade the others to buy the product. A child is then assigned five nouns to be used in giving the "sales pitch." The child stands in front of the class with an object and gives an advertisement, using the five nouns within that context. The children then evaluate whether the salesperson was convincing enough to make them want to buy the product, and why.

METHOD OF EVALUATION:
Determine if each child used the five nouns appropriately within the context of the commercial.

EXPRESSIVE LANGUAGE

PURPOSE:
To develop the ability to identify objects

AREA OF LANGUAGE STRESSED:
Developing expressive vocabulary—Naming persons and objects (nouns)

DURATION OF LESSON:
Fifteen to twenty minutes

LESSON FORMAT:
Individual

LESSON 146: OCCUPATIONS AROUND US

MATERIALS/EQUIPMENT/PHYSICAL LAYOUT:
A flannelboard, felt cutouts representing persons in different occupations, tools or instruments of the occupations, and some clothing worn by persons in the occupations

DESCRIPTION OF THE LESSON:
Ask the child to select a career or occupation, such as police work, firefighting, dentistry, and so on. Using the felt cutouts, the child must select the appropriate clothing for the occupation and the tools or instruments needed to engage in the occupation. While doing this, the child must name the items. If the child has difficulty, supply the correct term or label for the item.

METHOD OF EVALUATION:
Determining correct and incorrect responses may not be feasible in the initial phases of learning new vocabulary. However, in subsequent lessons using the same felt cutouts, a percentage of correct responses may be obtained by dividing the number of correct responses the child made by the total number of responses possible.

$$\frac{\text{Correct responses}}{\text{Total responses}} = \text{Percentage correct}$$

EXPRESSIVE LANGUAGE

PURPOSE:
  To develop the ability to identify objects

AREA OF LANGUAGE STRESSED:
  Developing expressive vocabulary—Naming persons and objects (nouns)

DURATION OF LESSON:
  Fifteen to twenty minutes

LESSON FORMAT:
  Group or individual

LESSON 147: CATALOG CAPERS

MATERIALS/EQUIPMENT/PHYSICAL LAYOUT:
  A mail order catalog and a blindfold

DESCRIPTION OF THE LESSON:
  Blindfold the child and give the child a catalog. The child places the catalog with the spine on the table and lets it fall open. Next, the child places a finger on a picture on the exposed pages. Remove the blindfold and have the child name the object. The following questions may be used: What is it? What would you use it for? Who would use it?

METHOD OF EVALUATION:
  Determine the child's ability to identify nouns. A percentage of correct responses may be obtained by dividing the number of correct responses made by the total number of responses possible.

$$\frac{\text{Correct responses}}{\text{Total responses}} = \text{Percentage correct}$$

EXPRESSIVE LANGUAGE

PURPOSE:
  To develop alternative labels for persons and objects

AREA OF LANGUAGE STRESSED:
  Developing expressive vocabulary—Naming persons and objects (nouns)

DURATION OF LESSON:
  Twenty minutes

LESSON FORMAT:
  Group

LESSON 148: LOTS OF LABELS

MATERIALS/EQUIPMENT/PHYSICAL LAYOUT:
  Pictures of objects and persons cut from magazines

DESCRIPTION OF THE LESSON:
  Explain that people and objects may be called different things in different settings. For example, a female teacher may also be called a woman, lady, mother, housewife, or grandmother, depending upon such things as age and circumstances. With the use of picture stimuli, encourage the children to name alternative labels for different persons and objects, for example, for a man (father, grandfather, uncle, brother, worker) or a dog (puppy, mutt, hound, canine).

METHOD OF EVALUATION:
  Determine by observation the children's ability to name alternative words for objects and persons. It is suggested that an anecdotal record of each child's performance in increasing vocabulary be kept, based on your observations.

EXPRESSIVE LANGUAGE

PURPOSE:
To increase vocabulary of action words

AREA OF LANGUAGE STRESSED:
Developing expressive vocabulary—Using action words (verbs)

DURATION OF LESSON:
Twenty minutes

LESSON FORMAT:
Group

LESSON 149: WHAT'S YOUR FAVORITE SOUND?

MATERIALS/EQUIPMENT/PHYSICAL LAYOUT:
None

DESCRIPTION OF THE LESSON:
Ask the class to name some very pleasant sounds, such as gurgling water, a crackling fire, or a calliope, and then to list several unpleasant sounds, such as a baby's cry or a fingernail scratching on the chalkboard. Next, ask the children to describe their own favorite sounds to the class without divulging what makes the sound. For example, one favorite sound goes "ping-ping, pop-pop" (popcorn). The other children must guess what makes the sound.

METHOD OF EVALUATION:
Determine through observation whether the children can describe favorite sounds using action words. It is suggested that an anecdotal record of each child's performance be kept, based on your observations.

EXPRESSIVE LANGUAGE

PURPOSE:
To develop an expressive vocabulary of action words

AREA OF LANGUAGE STRESSED:
Developing expressive vocabulary—Using action words (verbs)

DURATION OF LESSON:
Fifteen to twenty minutes

LESSON FORMAT:
Group

MATERIALS/EQUIPMENT/PHYSICAL LAYOUT:
A list of words that represent noises

LESSON 150: NOISY WORDS

DESCRIPTION OF THE LESSON:
Say to the children, "Some words describe funny sounds. What do you think of when you hear these words?"

crunch	pop	howl
clang	whistle	creak
ring	fizz	jingle
bang	boom	chirp
thump	purr	buzz
sizzle	crack	beep

Continue by asking, for example, "Can you make a sentence using the word creak?" Encourage the children to attempt to make the sounds described.

In a variation of this lesson, ask the children to think of words that tell what sound the following objects make:

- motorcycle
- rain
- car
- bell
- dog
- telephone
- bird
- airplane
- cat

METHOD OF EVALUATION:
Observe the children's language in successive sessions to determine their ability to carry over vocabulary into spontaneous language (see the generalization check in Appendix B).

EXPRESSIVE LANGUAGE

PURPOSE:
To describe objects according to their texture

AREA OF LANGUAGE STRESSED:
Developing expressive vocabulary—Using descriptive words (adjectives and adverbs)

DURATION OF LESSON:
Fifteen to twenty minutes

LESSON FORMAT:
Individual

LESSON 151: THE TOUCHING BOARD

MATERIALS/EQUIPMENT/PHYSICAL LAYOUT:
A blindfold and two sets of textured materials, such as macaroni, cotton, velvet, or sandpaper, with one set glued to 3″ × 5″ tagboard cards and the other to a large piece of cardboard

DESCRIPTION OF THE LESSON:
Blindfold the child and present a small card containing one of the textured materials. Then ask the child, "How does this feel? Is it smooth? Is it bumpy? Can you find one on the big board just like it?" The child then matches the card with the corresponding texture on the cardboard. After the child has matched all the cards, hold up the cardboard and ask the child to describe it. Some vocabulary words that may be developed are:

- rough
- soft
- smooth
- squishy
- scratchy
- sharp
- silky
- bumpy

METHOD OF EVALUATION:
At a later date, check the child's retention of vocabulary words using the same cards. Determine the child's percentage of correct responses by dividing the number of correct responses made by the total number of responses possible.

$$\frac{\text{Correct responses}}{\text{Total responses}} = \text{Percentage correct}$$

EXPRESSIVE LANGUAGE

PURPOSE:
To develop and expand vocabulary of descriptive words

AREA OF LANGUAGE STRESSED:
Developing expressive vocabulary—Using descriptive words (adjectives and adverbs)

DURATION OF LESSON:
Twenty minutes

LESSON FORMAT:
Group or individual

LESSON 152: WORD TRIANGLES

MATERIALS/EQUIPMENT/PHYSICAL LAYOUT:
Marking pens and tagboard, cut into equilateral triangles, one for each child

DESCRIPTION OF THE LESSON:
Discuss with the children how some words evoke visual images. Ask the children to identify all the words they imagine when they hear the word *desert*. They may respond by saying, "parched, thirsty, barren, scorched, prickly, sparse, dry, or hot." Write the word *desert* on one of the triangles and add the children's descriptive words as they say them:

Next, give each child a triangle with another word written on it, for example:

- circus
- Christmas
- mountain
- cloud
- forest
- sea

After the children have had an opportunity to repeat this procedure independently on their own word triangles, have them read their descriptors to the group to see if the other children can guess the key word. This lesson may be expanded to include bilingual children who can be encouraged to make word triangles in their native language.

METHOD OF EVALUATION:
Observe the children's ability to choose appropriate descriptor words. It is suggested that an anecdotal record of each child's performance be kept, based on your observations.

EXPRESSIVE LANGUAGE

PURPOSE:
To describe objects according to taste

AREA OF LANGUAGE STRESSED:
Developing expressive vocabulary—Using descriptive words (adjectives and adverbs)

DURATION OF LESSON:
Fifteen to twenty minutes

LESSON FORMAT:
Group or individual

LESSON 153: THE TASTE TEST

MATERIALS/EQUIPMENT/PHYSICAL LAYOUT:
A blindfold and small jars containing these foods:

- jelly
- peanut butter
- popcorn
- lemon juice
- carrot bits
- tart citrus candy
- potato chips
- mild chili
- unseasoned spaghetti

DESCRIPTION OF THE LESSON:
Blindfold a child and say, "Taste this. What does it taste like? Is it sweet or salty? Is it hot? Describe it and try to guess what it is." Stress the following vocabulary:

- bitter
- hot
- sweet
- sour
- salty
- crunchy
- tart
- bland
- spicy

This lesson may be expanded culturally to include ethnic or native foods in the taste experience.

METHOD OF EVALUATION:
In subsequent activities, use picture cards to determine the extent to which vocabulary words are carried over. A percentage of correct responses may be obtained by dividing the number of correct responses a child made by the total number of responses possible.

$$\frac{\text{Correct responses}}{\text{Total responses}} = \text{Percentage correct}$$

EXPRESSIVE LANGUAGE

PURPOSE:
To develop a vocabulary of descriptive words

AREA OF LANGUAGE STRESSED:
Developing expressive vocabulary—Using descriptive words (adjectives and adverbs)

DURATION OF LESSON:
Fifteen to twenty minutes

LESSON FORMAT:
Group or individual

LESSON 154: FUN WITH ADJECTIVES

MATERIALS/EQUIPMENT/PHYSICAL LAYOUT:
A list of adjectives

DESCRIPTION OF THE LESSON:
Using the list of adjectives, ask the children to identify objects that reflect each characteristic. Say, for example, "Name all the objects you can think of that are cold." Appropriate answers might be ice cream, snow, icicles, or a popsicle. The following descriptive words may be used:

cold	ugly	noisy
soft	dirty	quiet
smooth	clean	sour
rough	fat	slow
hot	sticky	fast
sharp	large	fattening
dry	tiny	crowded
red	pretty	expensive
blue	bumpy	beautiful
hard	bright	high

METHOD OF EVALUATION:
Determine the child's understanding of the descriptive words by observing if the named words exhibit the appropriate characteristic.

EXPRESSIVE LANGUAGE

PURPOSE:
To develop a vocabulary of words that describe feelings

AREA OF LANGUAGE STRESSED:
Developing expressive vocabulary—Using descriptive words (adjectives and adverbs)

DURATION OF LESSON:
Twenty minutes

LESSON FORMAT:
Group

LESSON 155: HAPPY, SAD, TIRED, AND GLAD

MATERIALS/EQUIPMENT/PHYSICAL LAYOUT:
Pictures of faces with different expressions, such as sad, happy, afraid, disappointed, and angry

DESCRIPTION OF THE LESSON:
Hold up a picture of one of the faces. Ask a child to describe how the person in the picture is feeling. Introduce words such as sad, happy, and embarrassed. Then ask the children to guess why the person in the picture might feel that way. Encourage the children to relate events that made them react in a similar manner.

METHOD OF EVALUATION:
At a later date, use picture cards to determine the extent to which the vocabulary words have been generalized. A percentage of correct responses may be obtained by dividing the number of correct responses a child made by the total number of responses possible.

$$\frac{\text{Correct responses}}{\text{Total responses}} = \text{Percentage correct}$$

EXPRESSIVE LANGUAGE

PURPOSE:
To develop the ability to use words to describe a person

AREA OF LANGUAGE STRESSED:
Developing expressive vocabulary—Using descriptive words (adjectives and adverbs)

DURATION OF LESSON:
Fifteen to twenty minutes

LESSON FORMAT:
Individual

LESSON 156: WHAT'S IN A NAME?

MATERIALS/EQUIPMENT/PHYSICAL LAYOUT:
Dictionaries

DESCRIPTION OF THE LESSON:
In this lesson the children use their own names to create a personal image. They choose a descriptive word for each letter in their names, trying as best as possible to choose words that fit their personalities, for example: *Sarah—silly—artistic relaxed—angelic—honest* or *David—appealing—vigorous—idealistic—debater.*

The children may also use their friends' name letters to find descriptive words for them.

METHOD OF EVALUATION:
Check each child's name words to determine if they appropriately describe the child. The child may also be checked for retention of the meanings of new vocabulary words.

EXPRESSIVE LANGUAGE

PURPOSE:
To identify adverb phrases in sentences

AREA OF LANGUAGE STRESSED:
Developing expressive vocabulary—Using descriptive words (adjectives and adverbs)

DURATION OF LESSON:
Fifteen to twenty minutes

LESSON FORMAT:
Group or individual

LESSON 157: WORD DETECTIVES

MATERIALS/EQUIPMENT/PHYSICAL LAYOUT:
Prewritten list of sentences containing adverb phrases (for teacher use only)

DESCRIPTION OF THE LESSON:
Say to the children, "Some words tell us when things happen. Listen to the following sentences to find the words that tell when":

- Last night I ate some cake. (last night)
- I will go to town tomorrow. (tomorrow)
- During the movie I got thirsty. (during the movie)
- I will do it before dinner. (before dinner)
- Early in the morning I eat breakfast. (early in the morning)

After the children can correctly select the adverb phrase indicating the time of an event, repeat the process for adverb phrases that tell where an event takes place. For example:

- He digs in the garden. (in the garden)
- Mother cooks in the kitchen. (in the kitchen)
- She played by the house. (by the house)
- The boy sat beside the stream. (beside the stream)

Continue by saying, "Sometimes words and phrases tell us how something was done. Listen for the how phrases in these sentences:"

- The boy ate hungrily. (hungrily)
- The girl ran quickly down the hall. (quickly)
- The elephant walked slowly. (slowly)

METHOD OF EVALUATION:
Observe each child's accuracy in identifying adverb phrases in sentences. To obtain a percentage of correct responses, divide the number of correct responses made by the total number of responses possible.

$$\frac{\text{Correct responses}}{\text{Total responses}} = \text{Percentage correct}$$

EXPRESSIVE LANGUAGE

PURPOSE:
To develop the ability to use vocabulary in a unique manner

AREA OF LANGUAGE STRESSED:
Developing expressive vocabulary—Creating new words

DURATION OF LESSON:
Thirty minutes

LESSON FORMAT:
Group or individual

LESSON 158: NAME THAT OBJECT

MATERIALS/EQUIPMENT/PHYSICAL LAYOUT:
Magazines, glue, and scissors

DESCRIPTION OF THE LESSON:
Give each child a magazine and ask the child to find pictures of animals, buildings, plants, and people. Using two pictures, the child then combines them, making an unusual object or person. For example, a person's head may be placed on a plant and named with a humorous or absurd title.

METHOD OF EVALUATION:
Determine if the children are able to create novel vocabulary words. It is suggested that an anecdotal record of each child's performance be maintained, based on your observations.

EXPRESSIVE LANGUAGE

PURPOSE:
To develop the ability to create unique vocabulary

AREA OF LANGUAGE STRESSED:
Developing expressive vocabulary—Creating new words

DURATION OF LESSON:
Thirty minutes

LESSON FORMAT:
Group

LESSON 159: SNURDLY TUFFS

MATERIALS/EQUIPMENT/PHYSICAL LAYOUT:
Paper, pencil, chalk, and chalkboard

DESCRIPTION OF THE LESSON:
Gather the group at the table and write an imaginary word on the chalkboard, such as "snurdly tuffs." Say to the children, "I ate some snurdly tuffs for breakfast. What did you have?" Encourage the children to create new words by recombining parts of words and letters. When a child has created a new word, it may be written on the board. Then ask the child, "Can you eat it? Can you wear it? Is it something to play?" Encourage the child to use the new word in a sentence to give the other children a hint as to what it is. Other imaginary words that may be presented to the children to spur their imaginations to build new words are:

- blaggers
- gribbling
- crumpkins
- trifting meese
- muckled
- wirled grumpator

METHOD OF EVALUATION:
Observe to determine if the children are able to create unique words. It is suggested that an anecdotal record for each child be kept, based on your observations.

EXPRESSIVE LANGUAGE

PURPOSE:
  To develop a vocabulary of compound words

AREA OF LANGUAGE STRESSED:
  Developing expressive vocabulary—Compound words

DURATION OF LESSON:
  Twenty minutes

LESSON FORMAT:
  Group or individual

LESSON 160: COMPOUND WORDS I

MATERIALS/EQUIPMENT/PHYSICAL LAYOUT:
  Pictures of parts of rebuses (pictures depicting words) that illustrate compound words

DESCRIPTION OF THE LESSON:
  Place on the table a set of eight to ten pictures of parts of rebuses that illustrate compound words, such as firetruck, schoolbus, blackbird, and snowball. Each child must find a pair of pictures that go together to make a rebus of this type of compound word.

METHOD OF EVALUATION:
  Determine the percentage of correct matches by dividing the number of correct responses the child made by the total number of responses possible.

$$\frac{\text{Correct responses}}{\text{Total responses}} = \text{Percentage correct}$$

EXPRESSIVE LANGUAGE

PURPOSE:
  To develop a vocabulary of compound words

AREA OF LANGUAGE STRESSED:
  Developing expressive vocabulary—Compound words

DURATION OF LESSON:
  Ten minutes

LESSON FORMAT:
  Group or individual

LESSON 161: COMPOUND WORDS II

MATERIALS/EQUIPMENT/PHYSICAL LAYOUT:
  None

DESCRIPTION OF THE LESSON:
  Provide the children with a word that can be used to create several compound words. Ask the children to think of as many compound words as they can, using the core word provided, such as:

- book—bookcase, bookcover, bookstore, bookmark, bookend, bookshelf
- school—schoolbus, schoolhouse, schoolyard, schoolwork
- tree—treetop, treehouse

METHOD OF EVALUATION:
  Count the correct responses of each child. To obtain a percentage of correct responses, divide the number of correct responses made by the total number of responses possible.

$$\frac{\text{Correct responses}}{\text{Total responses}} = \text{Percentage correct}$$

EXPRESSIVE LANGUAGE

PURPOSE:
To develop the ability to use compound words

AREA OF LANGUAGE STRESSED:
Developing expressive vocabulary—Compound words

DURATION OF LESSON:
Fifteen to twenty minutes

LESSON FORMAT:
Individual

LESSON 162: COMPOUND CONCEPTS

MATERIALS/EQUIPMENT/PHYSICAL LAYOUT:
Tagboard cards, 9″ × 12″, each with a word printed at the top that can be made a part of several compound words

DESCRIPTION OF THE LESSON:
Explain that compound words are two or more words combined; then have the child select a tagboard card. Using the word printed at the top, the child must think of all the possible ways to form new compound words and then list them on the card.

```
Snow

snowball

snowmobile

snowsuit
```

After the list is completed, encourage the child to develop sentences using each compound word.

METHOD OF EVALUATION:
Determine the percentage of correct responses by dividing the number of correct responses the child made by the total number of responses possible.

$$\frac{\text{Correct responses}}{\text{Total responses}} = \text{Percentage correct}$$

EXPRESSIVE LANGUAGE

PURPOSE:
To develop the ability to identify synonyms

AREA OF LANGUAGE STRESSED:
Developing expressive vocabulary—Synonyms

DURATION OF LESSON:
Fifteen minutes

LESSON FORMAT:
Individual

LESSON 163: Synonym Sets

MATERIALS/EQUIPMENT/PHYSICAL LAYOUT:
Envelopes, each containing three word cards: two with words that represent synonyms, the third with an unrelated word

DESCRIPTION OF THE LESSON:
Say to the child, ''In this envelope are three words. Two of them mean the same thing. Find the pair that matches.'' Here are some sample sets:

- big, large, red
- tiny, tired, small
- hat, cap, rat
- car, ship, boat
- jump, leap, run
- fast, quick, glad
- happy, joyous, sorry
- bad, terrible, slow

For children who are nonreaders, picture cards instead of word cards may be used.

METHOD OF EVALUATION:
Obtain the percentage of correct responses by dividing the number of correct responses the child made by the total number of responses possible.

$$\frac{\text{Correct responses}}{\text{Total responses}} = \text{Percentage correct}$$

EXPRESSIVE LANGUAGE

PURPOSE:
To develop the ability to identify synonyms

AREA OF LANGUAGE STRESSED:
Developing expressive vocabulary—Synonyms

DURATION OF LESSON:
Fifteen to twenty minutes

LESSON FORMAT:
Group or individual

MATERIALS/EQUIPMENT/PHYSICAL LAYOUT:
Prewritten sentences

LESSON 164: Synonym Sentences

DESCRIPTION OF THE LESSON:
Produce a model sentence, repeating a word for which a synonym must be identified. For example, say, ''The boy ran *fast*. Fast.'' Then ask the children, ''Can you think of all the words that mean the same thing as fast?'' The children must respond with alternative words (synonyms) that make the sentence mean the same, such as, ''The boy ran quickly. The boy ran rapidly.'' Other sentences that may be used are:

- The girl was *ill*. (sick, ailing)
- The boy *shouted*. (yelled, shrieked, screamed)
- The ice cream was *good*. (tasty, delicious)

METHOD OF EVALUATION:
Determine the percentage of correct responses by dividing the number of correct responses the child made by the total number of responses possible.

$$\frac{\text{Correct responses}}{\text{Total responses}} = \text{Percentage correct}$$

EXPRESSIVE LANGUAGE

PURPOSE:
To identify synonyms for color words

AREA OF LANGUAGE STRESSED:
Developing expressive vocabulary—Synonyms

DURATION OF LESSON:
Thirty minutes

LESSON FORMAT:
Group

LESSON 165: COLOR WORDS

MATERIALS/EQUIPMENT/PHYSICAL LAYOUT:
Mail order catalogs

DESCRIPTION OF THE LESSON:
Indicate to the children that there are many words to describe different shades and hues of color. Distribute the catalogs and ask the children to read the descriptions of the different clothing items and to identify alternatives for the word *blue*. The children may respond with these synonyms: teal, azure, turquoise, sky blue, royal blue, navy blue, aquamarine, cobalt blue, and peacock blue. Each child is then assigned a color and looks independently for all the synonyms associated with that color.

METHOD OF EVALUATION:
Observe the number of variations each child correctly identifies. It is suggested that an anecdotal record of each child's performance be maintained.

EXPRESSIVE LANGUAGE

PURPOSE:
To develop the ability to identify antonyms

AREA OF LANGUAGE STRESSED:
Developing expressive vocabulary—Antonyms

DURATION OF LESSON:
Fifteen to twenty minutes

LESSON FORMAT:
Group (two teams)

LESSON 166: THE OPPOSITE GAME

MATERIALS/EQUIPMENT/PHYSICAL LAYOUT:
Paper and pencils

DESCRIPTION OF THE LESSON:
After a discussion of opposites, the group is divided into two teams and asked to make a list of antonym pairs. A member of Team 1 presents a word on its list, *night,* for example. A member of Team 2 must then give the word that is opposite of night, or *day.* If the member of Team 2 gives the right word, that team receives a point. The game continues, this time with team roles reversed. The team with the most points wins. Examples of opposite pairs are:

- day—night
- big—little
- broken—fixed
- heavy—light
- fast—slow
- in—out
- happy—sad
- fat—skinny

METHOD OF EVALUATION:
By observing and recording their responses, identify the children who have difficulty with the task.

EXPRESSIVE LANGUAGE

PURPOSE:
To develop a vocabulary of word opposites

AREA OF LANGUAGE STRESSED:
Developing expressive vocabulary—Antonyms

DURATION OF LESSON:
Fifteen minutes

LESSON FORMAT:
Group or individual

LESSON 167: FUN WITH OPPOSITES

MATERIALS/EQUIPMENT/PHYSICAL LAYOUT:
Picture cards depicting opposite relationships

DESCRIPTION OF THE LESSON:
In a preliminary lesson, ask the child to practice naming opposites. Give the child two opposite cards (sad and happy) and ask the child to name what is seen in the pictures. In a second task, ask the child to select a card and match it to its opposite. Finally, the child may act out opposite feelings. Say the word *sad* and ask the child to dramatize its opposite, *happy*.

METHOD OF EVALUATION:
Determine the percentage of correct responses in the matching task by dividing the number of correct responses the child made by the total number of responses possible.

$$\frac{\text{Correct responses}}{\text{Total responses}} = \text{Percentage correct}$$

EXPRESSIVE LANGUAGE

PURPOSE:
To develop the ability to recognize word patterns

AREA OF LANGUAGE STRESSED:
Developing expressive vocabulary—Palindromes

DURATION OF LESSON:
Twenty minutes

LESSON FORMAT:
Group or individual

LESSON 168: PLAYING WITH PALINDROMES

MATERIALS/EQUIPMENT/PHYSICAL LAYOUT:
Dictionaries and 3″ × 5″ index cards

DESCRIPTION OF THE LESSON:
Explain that palindromes are words that read the same whether read forward or backward. Encourage the children to:

- name as many palindromes as they can.
- use the dictionary to find more.
- write one palindrome on each index card.

If the children do not know the meaning of the word, they may write a definition on the back of the index card. Common palindromes are otto, bib, ewe, sees, deed, mom, dad, peep, toot, pop, and tot.

METHOD OF EVALUATION:
Evaluate the child's ability to identify palindromes by counting and recording the number of palindromes listed by each child.

EXPRESSIVE LANGUAGE

PURPOSE:
To develop the ability to identify singular and plural forms of objects

AREA OF LANGUAGE STRESSED:
Morphology—Plurals

DURATION OF LESSON:
Fifteen to twenty minutes

LESSON FORMAT:
Individual

LESSON 169: SINGULAR AND PLURAL

MATERIALS/EQUIPMENT/PHYSICAL LAYOUT:
Procure or make a cardboard wheel such as the type used for pizza. Place pictures of objects, both singular and plural, around the perimeter of the wheel. Place a spinner in the center.

DESCRIPTION OF THE LESSON:
The child spins the arrow. If it lands on a singular object, the child must name its plural form. If it lands on a plural object, the child must identify its singular form. Irregular plurals, such as *children* and *men,* may be included to increase the difficulty.

METHOD OF EVALUATION:
Determine the percentage of correct responses by dividing the number of correct responses the child made by the total number of responses possible.

$$\frac{\text{Correct responses}}{\text{Total responses}} = \text{Percentage correct}$$

EXPRESSIVE LANGUAGE

PURPOSE:
To develop the ability to create new words with suffixes

AREA OF LANGUAGE STRESSED:
Morphology—Suffixes

DURATION OF LESSON:
Twenty minutes

LESSON FORMAT:
Individual

LESSON 170: END-A-WORD

MATERIALS/EQUIPMENT/PHYSICAL LAYOUT:
Prepare two sets of cards, one with root words, the other with commonly used suffixes. For example:

Sample root words	Sample suffixes
help	ing
paint	er
eat	ful
run	less
cry	ly
care	ness
happy	fully

A dictionary will also be needed.

DESCRIPTION OF THE LESSON:
Explain to the child how different word endings, or suffixes, can change and expand the meaning of words. Ask the child to choose a card with a root word. Using the suffixes, the child must then select suffix cards to make variations of the word. For example, for the word *care* the child may create the words *careful, careless, caring,* and *carefully.* Encourage the child to use the dictionary to ensure that the words are real words. Discuss with the child the meaning of each suffix and the child's new words.

METHOD OF EVALUATION:
Determine the percentage of correct responses in using suffixes to form new words by dividing the number of correct responses the child made by the total number of responses possible.

$$\frac{\text{Correct responses}}{\text{Total responses}} = \text{Percentage correct}$$

EXPRESSIVE LANGUAGE

PURPOSE:
To develop appropriate use of future, present, and past tense verbs

AREA OF LANGUAGE STRESSED:
Morphology—Verb tenses

DURATION OF LESSON:
Twenty minutes

LESSON FORMAT:
Individual

LESSON 171: VERB TENSES

MATERIALS/EQUIPMENT/PHYSICAL LAYOUT:
Picture cards depicting three phases of an event: before it happens, as it is happening, and after it has happened

DESCRIPTION OF THE LESSON:
Present the three cards to the child. Ask the child to put the cards in order of future, present, and past events. Then ask the child to describe each picture using the proper verb tense, for example, the boy will eat, the boy is eating, the boy ate.

METHOD OF EVALUATION:
It may be advisable to use separate charting procedures to determine the percentage of correct responses for regular and irregular future verbs, present progressive verbs, and past tense verbs. For each verb tense, divide the number of correct responses the child made by the total number of responses possible.

$$\frac{\text{Correct responses}}{\text{Total responses}} = \text{Percentage correct}$$

EXPRESSIVE LANGUAGE

PURPOSE:
To develop correct usage of verb tenses

AREA OF LANGUAGE STRESSED:
Morphology—Verb tenses

DURATION OF LESSON:
Fifteen minutes

LESSON FORMAT:
Individual

LESSON 172: THE VERB WHEEL

MATERIALS/EQUIPMENT/PHYSICAL LAYOUT:
Procure or make a cardboard wheel such as the type used for pizza. Fasten pictures around the perimeter of the wheel, each picture showing a person performing such actions as eating, playing, sleeping, and driving. Place a spinner arrow in the center of the wheel.

DESCRIPTION OF THE LESSON:
The child must spin the arrow. When it lands on an action picture, the child must identify the present progressive form of the verb that indicates the action (for example, eating) and then give its past tense form (ate).

METHOD OF EVALUATION:
Determine the percentage of correct responses by dividing the number of correct responses the child made by the total number of responses possible.

$$\frac{\text{Correct responses}}{\text{Total responses}} = \text{Percentage correct}$$

EXPRESSIVE LANGUAGE

PURPOSE:
To develop correct usage of pronouns

AREA OF LANGUAGE STRESSED:
Morphology—Pronouns

DURATION OF LESSON:
Fifteen minutes

LESSON FORMAT:
Individual

LESSON 173: PRONOUN, PLEASE

MATERIALS/EQUIPMENT/PHYSICAL LAYOUT:
Pictures of a male and a female or male and female dolls and several small toys, such as cars, blocks, or plastic zoo and farm animals

DESCRIPTION OF THE LESSON:
Introduce the picture characters. Instruct the child to give the objects to the characters. Elicit pronouns with the following directions as the child manipulates the characters and objects:

- Give him the car. Whose car is it?
- Give her the block. Whose block is it?
- Give me the horse. Whose horse is it?
- You hold the cow. Whose cow is it?

The child must respond with the appropriate pronoun: his, her, my, your, hers, mine, or yours.

METHOD OF EVALUATION:
Obtain the percentage of correct responses in pronoun usage by dividing the number of correct responses the child made by the total number of responses possible.

$$\frac{\text{Correct responses}}{\text{Total responses}} = \text{Percentage correct}$$

EXPRESSIVE LANGUAGE

PURPOSE:
To respond appropriately to Wh questions

AREA OF LANGUAGE STRESSED:
Making changes in the basic sentence—Questions

DURATION OF LESSON:
Twenty minutes

LESSON FORMAT:
Individual or small group

LESSON 174: WHO'S IN THE KITCHEN?

MATERIALS/EQUIPMENT/PHYSICAL LAYOUT:
A doll house and plastic dolls representing a mother, father, baby, boy, girl, and family dog

DESCRIPTION OF THE LESSON:
Place one of the plastic figures in a room of the doll house. Then ask questions such as:

- Who is in the kitchen?
- Where is father?
- What is the girl doing in the bedroom?
- Who is in the bathroom?
- Where is the dog?
- What is the dog doing?

Vary the location of the figures in the doll house and continue the questioning.

METHOD OF EVALUATION:
Observe the child's ability to answer Wh questions appropriately. Obtain the percentage of correct responses by dividing the number of correct responses made by the total number of responses possible.

$$\frac{\text{Correct responses}}{\text{Total responses}} = \text{Percentage correct}$$

EXPRESSIVE LANGUAGE

PURPOSE:

To develop the ability to use Wh questions appropriately

LESSON 175: WH QUESTION GAME

MATERIALS/EQUIPMENT/PHYSICAL LAYOUT:

A circular game board with a spinner and with the words *who, where, what, why, how much,* and *when* around the perimeter:

AREA OF LANGUAGE STRESSED:

Making changes in the basic sentence—Questions

DURATION OF LESSON:

Twenty minutes

DESCRIPTION OF THE LESSON:

Ask the child to spin the spinner. When it stops on a word, ask a question beginning with that word. The child must respond in a complete sentence. Use questions like:

- Who cooks dinner at your house?
- How much do you weigh?
- When does your family eat dinner?
- Where is your book?
- Why do people need food?
- What do you do when you get home from school?

Then the child spins the spinner again. This time, the child must ask a question, appropriately using a wh word. You or another child must respond.

METHOD OF EVALUATION:

Observe whether the child responds to and asks Wh questions appropriately and obtain a percentage of correct responses by dividing the number of correct responses made by the total number of responses possible.

$$\frac{\text{Correct responses}}{\text{Total responses}} = \text{Percentage correct}$$

LESSON FORMAT:

Group or individual

EXPRESSIVE LANGUAGE

PURPOSE:
To obtain information by asking appropriate yes/no-response questions

AREA OF LANGUAGE STRESSED:
Making changes in the basic sentence—Questions

DURATION OF LESSON:
Twenty minutes

LESSON FORMAT:
Individual

LESSON 176: 20 QUESTIONS

MATERIALS/EQUIPMENT/PHYSICAL LAYOUT:
None

DESCRIPTION OF THE LESSON:
Explain that the child will have to guess the identity of an animal, a person, book, movie, or other object by asking appropriate questions. The questions must be worded in such a way that they may be answered by a yes or no response. The child has 20 questions in which to arrive at the answer. Questions such as the following would be appropriate:

- Is it living?
- Is it a person?
- Is it an animal?
- Does it have four legs?
- Does it have fur?

METHOD OF EVALUATION:
Observe whether the child uses appropriate syntax in the questions. Determine the percentage of correct responses by dividing the number of correct responses made by the total number of responses possible.

$$\frac{\text{Correct responses}}{\text{Total responses}} = \text{Percentage correct}$$

EXPRESSIVE LANGUAGE

PURPOSE:
To develop the ability to transform statements into questions

AREA OF LANGUAGE STRESSED:
Making changes in the basic sentence—Questions

DURATION OF LESSON:
Fifteen minutes

LESSON FORMAT:
Group or individual

LESSON 177: QUESTIONS, QUESTIONS

MATERIALS/EQUIPMENT/PHYSICAL LAYOUT:
A set of cards that make sentences, with one word on each card:

The	boy	is	happy

DESCRIPTION OF THE LESSON:
Using the word cards, explain that in sentences that are declarative or tell something, usually the subject comes first. Demonstrate how changing the helping word to the initial place in the sentence transforms the sentence into a question that asks something. Present orally a declarative statement, such as, ''The girl is walking,'' and ask a child to transform it into a question. Other examples are:

- Statement: Sue is eating.
  Question: Is Sue eating?
- Statement: The boy is sad.
  Question: Is the boy sad?
- Statement: He was driving.
  Question: Was he driving?
- Statement: She can sing.
  Question: Can she sing?

The lesson may be varied for children who have reading skills. Place the set of word cards on the table, forming a declarative statement. Ask the child to rearrange the cards to form a question.

METHOD OF EVALUATION:
The percentage of correct responses may be obtained by dividing the number of correct responses the child made by the total number of responses possible.

$$\frac{\text{Correct responses}}{\text{Total responses}} = \text{Percentage correct}$$

EXPRESSIVE LANGUAGE

PURPOSE:
To develop the ability to ask Wh questions

AREA OF LANGUAGE STRESSED:
Making changes in the basic sentence—Questions

DURATION OF LESSON:
To be completed outside of class

LESSON FORMAT:
Individual

LESSON 178: DAYS OF LONG AGO

MATERIALS/EQUIPMENT/PHYSICAL LAYOUT:
Tape recorder and blank cassette tape

DESCRIPTION OF THE LESSON:
The child's task is to interview parents, grandparents, or a senior citizen about the ways in which their lives were different from those of younger people of contemporary times. Encourage the child to use questions that are appropriate in content and syntax. For example:

- What were the houses like?
- What did children do for fun?
- How was clothing different?
- What was school like then?
- What inventions do we have now that did not exist then?

Instruct the child to tape record the interview and play it for the class.

METHOD OF EVALUATION:
Determine from the tape recording whether the child asked appropriate questions. It is suggested that an anecdotal record of each child's performance be maintained.

EXPRESSIVE LANGUAGE

PURPOSE:
To develop the ability to use questions appropriately

AREA OF LANGUAGE STRESSED:
Making changes in the basic sentence—Questions

DURATION OF LESSON:
To be completed over a period of days

LESSON FORMAT:
Individual

LESSON 179: CAREER INTERVIEWS

MATERIALS/EQUIPMENT/PHYSICAL LAYOUT:
Tape recorder and blank cassette tape

DESCRIPTION OF THE LESSON:
The child's task is to conduct an interview with an adult working in the school setting, such as the school nurse, principal, librarian, or cook. The child uses questions in the interview to gain information about the person, for example, the person's job responsibilities and personal characteristics. These questions may be suggested to the child for use in the interview:

- What are your duties?
- What kind of training did you have to get the job?
- Why do/don't you like your work?
- When do you work?
- What are your hobbies?

The child tape-records the interview, which may be shared with the class.

METHOD OF EVALUATION:
Analyze the tape to determine whether the child's questions were correctly stated. It is suggested that an anecdotal record of the child's performance be maintained.

EXPRESSIVE LANGUAGE

PURPOSE:
To develop the ability to ask questions

AREA OF LANGUAGE STRESSED:
Making changes in the basic sentence—Questions

DURATION OF LESSON:
Thirty to forty-five minutes

LESSON FORMAT:
A small group of children divided into pairs

LESSON 180: EYE WITNESS NEWS

MATERIALS/EQUIPMENT/PHYSICAL LAYOUT:
A short story or newspaper article

DESCRIPTION OF THE LESSON:
Introduce the lesson by saying, "I am going to read a story. After I finish, you are going to pretend you are a news reporter who is trying to find out more information. You may ask who, what, where, and why questions to find out." Read the story and then pair the children. One child in each pair acts as the news reporter and asks the questions. The other child answers the questions, following the details of the story. This process may be repeated with the children reversing roles.

METHOD OF EVALUATION:
Observe whether the child is forming questions appropriately. It is suggested that an anecdotal record for each child be kept, based on your observations.

EXPRESSIVE LANGUAGE

PURPOSE:
To develop the ability to combine sentences using possessives

AREA OF LANGUAGE STRESSED:
Making changes in the basic sentence—Combining sentences

DURATION OF LESSON:
Thirty minutes

LESSON FORMAT:
Group or individual

LESSON 181: TWO FOR ONE

MATERIALS/EQUIPMENT/PHYSICAL LAYOUT:
None

DESCRIPTION OF THE LESSON:
Explain that a possessive means that something belongs to a person or object. Give the child an opportunity to use possessives by restating sentences such as the following:

- The girl has a horse.
  Possessive: The girl's horse
- The dog has a bone.
  Possessive: The dog's bone
- The man has a car.
  Possessive: The man's car

After the child has mastered this task, ask the child to combine two sentences together, using a possessive. For example:

- The boy has a dog. The dog is brown.
  Possessive: The boy's dog is brown.
- The girl has a new dress. The dress is yellow.
  Possessive: The girl's new dress is yellow.

METHOD OF EVALUATION:
Determine the child's accuracy in combining sentences using possessives. Obtain the percentage of correct responses by dividing the number of correct responses made by the total number of responses possible.

$$\frac{\text{Correct responses}}{\text{Total responses}} = \text{Percentage correct}$$

EXPRESSIVE LANGUAGE

PURPOSE:
To develop the ability to combine sentences with the appropriate use of clauses

AREA OF LANGUAGE STRESSED:
Making changes in the basic sentence—Combining sentences

DURATION OF LESSON:
Thirty minutes

LESSON FORMAT:
Group or individual

LESSON 182: SENTENCE COMBINATIONS I

MATERIALS/EQUIPMENT/PHYSICAL LAYOUT:
A piece of tagboard, 9″ × 12″

DESCRIPTION OF THE LESSON:
Explain that there are ways of combining sentences without relying upon "and" or "because" as conjunctions. Give the children three sentences, either orally or written on the tagboard. For example:

- The girl walked to town.
- The girl is named Janet.
- The girl wore a yellow dress.

The children's task is to combine the three thoughts into a single sentence, such as, "Janet, who wore a yellow dress, walked to town."

An example of combining sentences with the use of clauses can be illustrated as follows:

I see a dog.
The dog is brown.
The dog is jumping.   Combination: I see a brown dog jumping.

METHOD OF EVALUATION:
Observe each child's ability to combine sentences. Obtain a percentage of correct responses by dividing the number of correct responses made by the total number of responses possible.

$$\frac{\text{Correct responses}}{\text{Total responses}} = \text{Percentage correct}$$

EXPRESSIVE LANGUAGE

PURPOSE:
To develop the ability to combine sentences with conjunctions

AREA OF LANGUAGE STRESSED:
Making changes in the basic sentence—Combining sentences

DURATION OF LESSON:
Thirty minutes

LESSON FORMAT:
Group or individual

LESSON 183: SENTENCE COMBINATIONS II

MATERIALS/EQUIPMENT/PHYSICAL LAYOUT:
A piece of tagboard, 9″ × 12″

DESCRIPTION OF THE LESSON:
Explain that conjunctions such as ''and'' may be used to expand sentences. On the tagboard, write two sentences that may be joined by expanding the subject phrase, the verb phrase, or the direct object phrase of sentences. For example:

- *Expanding the subject phrase:*
  Bob ate. Jane ate.
  Expansion: Bob and Jane ate.
  Mary swims. Ted swims.
  Expansion: Mary and Ted swim.

- *Expanding the verb phrase:*
  Joe runs. Joe jumps.
  Expansion: Joe runs and jumps.
  Bob reads. Bob writes.
  Expansion: Bob reads and writes.

- *Expanding the direct object phrase:*
  Joan likes apples. Joan likes peaches.
  Expansion: Joan likes apples and peaches.
  Bill plays chess. Bill plays checkers.
  Expansion: Bill plays chess and checkers.

The task of the child is to join the sentences in the three cases with ''and,'' either orally or in a written format on the tagboard.

METHOD OF EVALUATION:
Observe the child's ability to join sentences with the conjunction *and*. Obtain a percentage of correct responses by dividing the number of correct responses made by the total number of responses possible.

$$\frac{\text{Correct responses}}{\text{Total responses}} = \text{Percentage correct}$$

EXPRESSIVE LANGUAGE

PURPOSE:
To join phrases with the conjunction *because*

AREA OF LANGUAGE STRESSED:
Making changes in the basic sentence—Expanding sentences

DURATION OF LESSON:
Twenty minutes

LESSON FORMAT:
Group or individual

LESSON 184: WHY? BECAUSE

MATERIALS/EQUIPMENT/PHYSICAL LAYOUT:
Why? Because Cards (Learning Development Aids, Park Works, Norwich Road, Wisbech, Cambs, England) or absurd pictures found in magazines

DESCRIPTION OF THE LESSON:
Using either the commercially made cards depicting cause and effect relationships or pictures of absurdities, show the child a picture and ask, "Why did this happen?" or, "Why is this a silly picture?" The child must answer in a complete sentence, such as, "The boy is jumping in the water because he's going to save the girl," or, "That's silly because people don't have green hair."

METHOD OF EVALUATION:
Observe each child's ability to join phrases correctly with the conjunction *because*. Obtain a percentage of correct responses by dividing the number of correct responses made by the total number of responses possible.

$$\frac{\text{Correct responses}}{\text{Total responses}} = \text{Percentage correct}$$

EXPRESSIVE LANGUAGE

PURPOSE:
To develop the ability to expand sentences by adding words and phrases

AREA OF LANGUAGE STRESSED:
Making changes in the basic sentence—Expanding sentences

DURATION OF LESSON:
Twenty minutes

LESSON FORMAT:
Group or individual

LESSON 185: SENTENCE ADDITION

MATERIALS/EQUIPMENT/PHYSICAL LAYOUT:
A piece of tagboard, 9″ × 12″

DESCRIPTION OF THE LESSON:
In preparation, write a basic declarative sentence at the top of a piece of tagboard. Say, "Let's see if we can tell more about our sentence by adding some words." Following are examples of the process:

- The boy ate. The boy ate a hamburger. The boy ate until everything was gone. The boy ate his breakfast and went to school.

Other basic sentences to be expanded include:

- The girl ran.
- The dog jumped.
- The man walked.
- The boy wished.

The child's task is to expand the basic sentence into several modified sentences.

METHOD OF EVALUATION:
Determine the child's ability to expand sentences by counting the number of correct sentence modifications. Obtain a percentage of correct responses by dividing the number of correct responses made by the total number of responses possible.

$$\frac{\text{Correct responses}}{\text{Total responses}} = \text{Percentage correct}$$

EXPRESSIVE LANGUAGE

PURPOSE:
To develop the ability to expand sentences

AREA OF LANGUAGE STRESSED:
Making changes in the basic sentence—Expanding sentences

DURATION OF LESSON:
Fifteen minutes

LESSON FORMAT:
Group or individual

LESSON 186: BUILDING SENTENCES

MATERIALS/EQUIPMENT/PHYSICAL LAYOUT:
None

DESCRIPTION OF THE LESSON:
In eliciting longer sentences orally from children, use selective questions to obtain descriptions of a movie or television program. The following format is suggested. The child's initial statement, ''I saw a movie,'' can be preserved in these expanded sentences:

Teacher's question: What kind of movie was it?
Child's expansion: I saw a _____
movie. (science fiction)

Teacher's question: Where did you go to see it?
Child's expansion: I saw a movie _____.
(at the theater)

Teacher's question: What was the movie about?
Child's expansion: I saw a movie about _____.
(space travel)

Teacher's question: When did you go to see it?
Child's expansion: I saw a movie _____.
(on Saturday)

Teacher's question: Who did you go with?
Child's expansion: I saw a movie _____.
(with my friend)

The child's task is to expand the basic sentence by adding words and phrases, keeping the core sentence intact in its expanded content. After the child has expanded several separate sentences, encourage the use of compound sentences by combining two or more thoughts, for example, On Saturday I went to the movie with my friend. This exercise may be modified by allowing the child to expand sentences independently in a written format.

METHOD OF EVALUATION:
Determine the number of correct expansions. Obtain the percentage of correct responses by dividing the number of correct responses made by the total number of responses possible.

$$\frac{\text{Correct responses}}{\text{Total responses}} = \text{Percentage correct}$$

EXPRESSIVE LANGUAGE

PURPOSE:
To develop the ability to vary stress in the voice

AREA OF LANGUAGE STRESSED:
Voice control—Stress

DURATION OF LESSON:
Fifteen minutes

LESSON FORMAT:
Individual

LESSON 187: COPY CAT

MATERIALS/EQUIPMENT/PHYSICAL LAYOUT:
None

DESCRIPTION OF THE LESSON:
Model a short sentence, stressing a certain word in the sentence. The child must imitate the sentence, placing stress on the same word. In the following sentences, for example, the underlined words are to be emphasized:

- She *likes* you.
- The *boy* likes candy.
- Eat *all* of it.
- The boy *walked*.
- *I* can't do it.

METHOD OF EVALUATION:
Determine the number of correct responses by keeping a tally of which sentences the child could imitate using correct stress. Obtain a percentage of correct responses by dividing the number of correct responses made by the total number of responses possible.

$$\frac{\text{Correct responses}}{\text{Total responses}} = \text{Percentage correct}$$

EXPRESSIVE LANGUAGE

PURPOSE:
To develop the ability to use intonation appropriately in the voice

AREA OF LANGUAGE STRESSED:
Voice control—Intonation

DURATION OF LESSON:
Fifteen minutes

LESSON FORMAT:
Group

MATERIALS/EQUIPMENT/PHYSICAL LAYOUT:
A set of tagboard strips, 2″ × 12″, with common expressive phrases written on them

LESSON 188: EXPRESSING FEELINGS

DESCRIPTION OF THE LESSON:
Introduce the lesson by explaining that the manner in which things are expressed influences their meaning and that different intonation and stress in a person's voice may change the meaning of a statement. Each child chooses a phrase card and uses one manner of intonation to express the feeling of the phrase. A second child may be given the opportunity to say it in another way to change its meaning. Examples of common phrases are:

- Stop it.
- Please don't do that.
- Do you know who?
- That's great.
- Look at him go.
- I'm embarrassed.
- Didn't you know?

METHOD OF EVALUATION:
Observe the child's ability to vary intonation. It is suggested that an anecdotal record of the child's use of voice control be kept, based on your observations.

EXPRESSIVE LANGUAGE

PURPOSE:
To recognize variations in voice pitch and volume

AREA OF LANGUAGE STRESSED:
Voice control—Pitch and volume

DURATION OF LESSON:
Fifteen minutes

LESSON FORMAT:
Group or individual

LESSON 189: FUNNY VOICES

MATERIALS/EQUIPMENT/PHYSICAL LAYOUT:
None

DESCRIPTION OF THE LESSON:
Say to the child, ''I am going to say something in a funny voice. Let's see if you can say it the same way.'' Then present orally the following sentences:

- My house is white. (softly whispering)
- I said, no. (loudly)
- I like ice cream. (low voice)
- I can play baseball. (high voice)

Continue with several more modeled sentences. The child must repeat the sentences using the same volume or pitch.

METHOD OF EVALUATION:
Observe if the sentences are correctly imitated. It is suggested that an anecdotal record of the child's use of pitch and volume be maintained.

EXPRESSIVE LANGUAGE

PURPOSE:
To develop the use of common social phrases in conversation

AREA OF LANGUAGE STRESSED:
Social communication—Using appropriate phrases in conversation

DURATION OF LESSON:
Twenty minutes

LESSON FORMAT:
Group

MATERIALS/EQUIPMENT/PHYSICAL LAYOUT:
None

LESSON 190: POLITE PEOPLE

DESCRIPTION OF THE LESSON:
Introduce the lesson by saying, ''Sometimes we say things to be courteous to others. When would you use these words?''

- Thank you.
- Please.
- I'm sorry.
- Excuse me.
- No thank you.
- May I?
- You're welcome.
- Pardon me.

Then have the children dramatize situations in which these phrases may be used. The following are examples of role-playing situations:

- one child helping another with a task
- offering children in the class a snack
- one child accidentally bumping another
- a person asking for a favor
- asking your mother for a cookie
- receiving a present from someone

METHOD OF EVALUATION:
Determine through observation if the child uses the phrases appropriately. It is suggested that an anecdotal record of the child's use of social language be maintained.

EXPRESSIVE LANGUAGE

PURPOSE:
To use appropriate language in a social setting

AREA OF LANGUAGE STRESSED:
Social communication—Using appropriate phrases in conversation

DURATION OF LESSON:
Thirty minutes

LESSON FORMAT:
Group

LESSON 191: DINING OUT

MATERIALS/EQUIPMENT/PHYSICAL LAYOUT:
Menus obtained from a local restaurant, one per child

DESCRIPTION OF THE LESSON:
Explain to the children that they are to pretend they are eating out in a restaurant. They will be given a specified amount of money, and they are to stay within that amount when deciding what to order. They must decide what items they would choose, and what the total cost of their meals will be. One child is selected to be the waiter or waitress. The children must order their own meals, using appropriate social manners when ordering or requesting items.

METHOD OF EVALUATION:
Determine through observation the absence or presence of appropriate social language, such as the child's ability to describe what item is wanted, and terms of courtesy, such as please, thank you, excuse me, and so on. It is suggested that an anecdotal record of the child's use of social language be maintained.

EXPRESSIVE LANGUAGE

PURPOSE:
To develop the use of common phrases in conversation

AREA OF LANGUAGE STRESSED:
Social communication—Using appropriate phrases in conversation

DURATION OF LESSON:
Twenty minutes

LESSON FORMAT:
Small group or pairs

LESSON 192: INTRODUCING FRIENDS

MATERIALS/EQUIPMENT/PHYSICAL LAYOUT:
None

DESCRIPTION OF THE LESSON:
Model appropriate ways of introducing people. Have the children practice several different types of introductions.

- introducing themselves to another person
- introducing one person to another
- introducing peers
- introducing their parents to another person
- introducing their teacher to another person

METHOD OF EVALUATION:
Determine if the introductions are made correctly. It is suggested that an anecdotal record of the child's social language be maintained.

EXPRESSIVE LANGUAGE

PURPOSE:
To develop social language appropriate for telephone use

AREA OF LANGUAGE STRESSED:
Social communication—Using appropriate phrases in conversation

DURATION OF LESSON:
Thirty minutes

LESSON FORMAT:
Small group or pairs

LESSON 193: TELEPHONE TALK I

MATERIALS/EQUIPMENT/PHYSICAL LAYOUT:
Two simulator telephones

DESCRIPTION OF THE LESSON:
Pair the children up. Assign one child to be the caller, the other child to receive the telephone call. Stress appropriate language. For example:

Caller: May I please speak to Jane? Or, Is Jane there?
Respondent: Hello. Yes. Just a minute please. Or, No, she isn't home right now. May I tell her who called? Or, May I take a message?
Caller: Please tell her to call me back at 423-7701.

METHOD OF EVALUATION:
Observe whether the child uses correct telephone language. It is suggested that an anecdotal record of the child's performance be kept, based on your observations.

EXPRESSIVE LANGUAGE

PURPOSE:
To develop social language appropriate for telephone use

AREA OF LANGUAGE STRESSED:
Social communication—Using appropriate phrases in conversation

DURATION OF LESSON:
Thirty minutes

LESSON FORMAT:
Group

MATERIALS/EQUIPMENT/PHYSICAL LAYOUT:
Two simulator telephones

LESSON 194: TELEPHONE TALK II

DESCRIPTION OF THE LESSON:
Instruct pairs of children to role play various telephone conversations:

- calling the police to report a burglary or accident
- calling the fire department to report a fire
- calling a friend to invite to a party
- a parent calling school with a message for the child
- the teacher calling a parent to relay a message
- calling the doctor for an appointment
- calling the next-door neighbors to tell them their dog is loose
- calling a movie theater to find out the time of the main feature
- calling a toy store to see if it carries a particular toy
- calling a friend to play

METHOD OF EVALUATION:
Observe the appropriateness of the child's language and make suggestions for alternative ways of expressing thoughts. It is suggested that an anecdotal record of the child's performance be kept, based on your observations.

EXPRESSIVE LANGUAGE

PURPOSE:
To develop social language in communicating feelings

AREA OF LANGUAGE STRESSED:
Social communication—Communicating feelings

DURATION OF LESSON:
To be continued over a period of days

LESSON FORMAT:
Each individual may participate, one or two at a time

LESSON 195: THE VIP

MATERIALS/EQUIPMENT/PHYSICAL LAYOUT:
A camera, film, and 9″ × 12″ tagboard

DESCRIPTION OF THE LESSON:
The children may borrow a camera or use one belonging to one of their family. In turn, they take pictures of their family members in home activities. After developing the film, one child in the class is named the Very Important Person (VIP) of the day or week. The child shows the class pictures of his or her family members, pets, home furnishings, hobbies, family member occupations, and other home activities. The children may make books about themselves, gluing their photographs onto tagboard and binding them. These books can be used repeatedly in oral language activities. As the child shares family and personal pictures, encourage the child to use expressive language in sharing interests and ideas as well.

METHOD OF EVALUATION:
Evaluate the child's oral language with the checklist of expressive language in Appendix A. Also, observe the child's other social communication skills, such as confidence in speaking before others, the ability to speak in a well-modulated voice, and the ability to discuss and explain in a natural fashion. It is suggested that an anecdotal record of the child's performance be kept, based on your observations.

EXPRESSIVE LANGUAGE

PURPOSE:
To develop the ability to produce direct quotations

AREA OF LANGUAGE STRESSED:
Social communication—Communicating feelings

DURATION OF LESSON:
Thirty minutes

LESSON FORMAT:
Group or individual

LESSON 196: QUOTABLE QUOTES

MATERIALS/EQUIPMENT/PHYSICAL LAYOUT:
Magazines, scissors, glue, and 9″ × 12″ construction paper or tagboard

DESCRIPTION OF THE LESSON:
Distribute the magazines and direct the children to find pictures that show a person in conversation with another person or performing an activity independently. The pictures are then glued to construction paper or tagboard. Ask the children, "What is this person thinking right now? What do you think this person is saying?" Using the cartoon balloon method of illustrating conversation, ask the child to produce a direct quote, which may be either humorous or serious.

METHOD OF EVALUATION:
Determine through observation if the child captures the meaning of the picture in the quotation. It is suggested that an anecdotal record of the child's ability to communicate feelings be kept, based on your observations.

EXPRESSIVE LANGUAGE

PURPOSE:
To develop the ability to reach group consensus

AREA OF LANGUAGE STRESSED:
Social communication—Group consensus

DURATION OF LESSON:
Thirty minutes

LESSON FORMAT:
Group

LESSON 197: GROUP DECISIONS

MATERIALS/EQUIPMENT/PHYSICAL LAYOUT:
Chalkboard and chalk

DESCRIPTION OF THE LESSON:
Appoint a chairperson for the group. The chairperson leads the group in planning a class party, deciding on refreshments, games, preparation, and cleanup. The children must reach a group consensus on these details and assign duties to class members. Act, or have one of the children act, as a recorder, writing the lists of responsibilities on the chalkboard.

METHOD OF EVALUATION:
Determine through observation how the group works together in making decisions and reaching a consensus.

Chapter 7

Lessons for Enriching the Language Environment

USER'S GUIDE

LANGUAGE ENRICHMENT

PURPOSE:
To develop an awareness of rhyming words

AREA OF LANGUAGE STRESSED:
Poetry—Rhyming words

DURATION OF LESSON:
Thirty minutes

LESSON FORMAT:
Group

LESSON 198: NURSERY RHYME PANTOMIMES

MATERIALS/EQUIPMENT/PHYSICAL LAYOUT:
Familiar nursery rhymes

DESCRIPTION OF THE LESSON:
Explain to the children that you will read a nursery rhyme to them twice. As it is read the second time, the children will pantomime the actions. The following nursery rhymes lend themselves to pantomime:

- Little Miss Muffet
- Humpty Dumpty
- Jack and Jill
- Little Bo Peep
- Old Mother Hubbard

Following the dramatic interpretation of the rhyme, read the rhyme a third time, but this time omit the rhyming words. The child must apply the appropriate rhyming word. For example:

> Little Miss Muffet
> Sat on a _____ (tuffet),
> Eating her curds and whey.
> Along came a spider
> Who sat down _____ (beside her)
> And frightened Miss Muffet _____ (away).

METHOD OF EVALUATION:
By observing if the child can supply the appropriate rhyming word, determine the child's awareness of rhyming words.

LANGUAGE ENRICHMENT

PURPOSE:
To create a rhyming answer to a riddle

AREA OF LANGUAGE STRESSED:
Poetry—Rhyming words

DURATION OF LESSON:
Twenty minutes

LESSON FORMAT:
Group or individual

LESSON 199: WHERE IS IT?

MATERIALS/EQUIPMENT/PHYSICAL LAYOUT:
None

DESCRIPTION OF THE LESSON:
Explain to the children that they will have to answer a riddle to help find an object and that the answer must rhyme with the teacher's question. Give the following examples to familiarize the children with the format:

Question: Oh my goodness. Where is my book?
Answer: On your desk. Go take a look.

Question: Oh my, oh me. Where is the bee?
Answer: Flying around the honey tree.

Question: Please tell me now. Where is the cow?
Answer: With the farmer, next to the plow.

METHOD OF EVALUATION:
Determine each child's percentage of correct responses in selecting appropriate rhyming words by dividing the number of correct responses made by the total number of responses possible.

$$\frac{\text{Correct responses}}{\text{Total responses}} = \text{Percentage correct}$$

LANGUAGE ENRICHMENT

PURPOSE:
To develop the ability to rhyme words

AREA OF LANGUAGE STRESSED:
Poetry—Rhyming words

DURATION OF LESSON:
Twenty minutes

LESSON FORMAT:
Group

LESSON 200: RHYME ALONG WITH ME

MATERIALS/EQUIPMENT/PHYSICAL LAYOUT:
Chalkboard and chalk

DESCRIPTION OF THE LESSON:
Divide the group into two teams. A member of Team A provides a word, such as "man." A member of Team B must respond with a word that rhymes with man, such as "fan" or "ran." If the word rhymes, Team B receives a point. If not, Team A receives the point. The team exchange turns until the time limit is up. The team with the most points is the winner.

METHOD OF EVALUATION:
Observe to determine each child's accuracy in creating rhyming words. It is suggested that an anecdotal record of each child's performance be kept, based on your observations.

LANGUAGE ENRICHMENT

PURPOSE:
   To develop the ability to supply a rhyming word

AREA OF LANGUAGE STRESSED:
   Poetry—Rhyming words

DURATION OF LESSON:
   Fifteen minutes

LESSON FORMAT:
   Group

LESSON 201: FILL IN RHYMES

MATERIALS/EQUIPMENT/PHYSICAL LAYOUT:
   A list of two-line poems

DESCRIPTION OF THE LESSON:
   After explaining what rhyming words are and how rhyming words sound alike, provide a two-line poem, but omit the last word. The child must insert the rhyming word to complete the poem.

- I saw a bee
  Up in a _____. (tree)
- Look at the dog,
  Sitting on a _____. (log)
- There is an otter
  Under the _____. (water)

- There goes a man
  Driving a _____. (van)
- The little boy
  Wants a _____. (toy)
- We're in the sun
  Having _____. (fun)

METHOD OF EVALUATION:
   Observe to determine if the child can supply the rhyming word. Obtain a percentage of correct responses by dividing the number of correct responses made by the total number of responses possible.

$$\frac{\text{Correct responses}}{\text{Total responses}} = \text{Percentage correct}$$

LANGUAGE ENRICHMENT

PURPOSE:
   To develop the ability to rhyme words

AREA OF LANGUAGE STRESSED:
   Poetry—Rhyming words

DURATION OF LESSON:
   Twenty minutes

LESSON FORMAT:
   Group or individual

LESSON 202: RHYMING PAIRS

MATERIALS/EQUIPMENT/PHYSICAL LAYOUT:
   Pairs of rhyming pictures, such as fan—man, toy—boy, rain—train, and dish—fish

DESCRIPTION OF THE LESSON:
   Place one set of the pictures of rhyming pairs along the chalk tray. Hold up a picture card from the second set and name the object. The child must select the rhyming picture from the cards on the chalk tray.

METHOD OF EVALUATION:
   Observe each child's ability to match rhyming pictures. Obtain a percentage of correct responses by dividing the number of correct responses made by the total number of responses possible.

$$\frac{\text{Correct responses}}{\text{Total responses}} = \text{Percentage correct}$$

LANGUAGE ENRICHMENT

PURPOSE:
To develop the ability to rhyme words

AREA OF LANGUAGE STRESSED:
Poetry—Rhyming words

DURATION OF LESSON:
Fifteen minutes

LESSON FORMAT:
Group or individual

LESSON 203: BOX OF RHYMES

MATERIALS/EQUIPMENT/PHYSICAL LAYOUT:
A cardboard box with a lid and several small objects representing rhyming pairs, such as hat—cat, jar—car, soap—rope, and ring—string

DESCRIPTION OF THE LESSON:
Place the objects inside the box. Ask the child to select a rhyming pair from the objects in the box.

METHOD OF EVALUATION:
Observe whether the child can match rhyming objects. Obtain a percentage of correct responses by dividing the number of correct responses made by the total number of responses possible.

$$\frac{\text{Correct responses}}{\text{Total responses}} = \text{Percentage correct}$$

LANGUAGE ENRICHMENT

PURPOSE:
To develop the ability to produce rhyming words

| I can eat | | I can hide |

AREA OF LANGUAGE STRESSED:
Poetry—Rhyming words

DURATION OF LESSON:
Twenty minutes

LESSON FORMAT:
Group or individual

LESSON 204: RHYME TIME

MATERIALS/EQUIPMENT/PHYSICAL LAYOUT:
Index cards, 3″ × 5″, with an action phrase printed on each, for example:

| I can walk | | I can hop |

DESCRIPTION OF THE LESSON:
The child selects an index card. On a separate piece of paper, the child writes the same phrase that is on the card. For example, a card may say, "I can ride." The child must think of an action word that rhymes with ride and develop a phrase using that rhyming word. For example: I can ride. You can slide. Other rhyming phrases can be used to familiarize the child with the format for rhyming:

- I can drive. You can _____. (dive)
- I can see. You can _____. (ski)

METHOD OF EVALUATION:
Examine the child's rhymes and obtain a percentage of correct responses by dividing the number of correct responses made by the total number of responses possible.

$$\frac{\text{Correct responses}}{\text{Total responses}} = \text{Percentage correct}$$

LANGUAGE ENRICHMENT

PURPOSE:
To develop the ability to rhyme words

AREA OF LANGUAGE STRESSED:
Poetry—Rhyming words

DURATION OF LESSON:
Twenty minutes

LESSON FORMAT:
Group (two teams)

LESSON 205: RHYMING WITH BEANBAGS

MATERIALS/EQUIPMENT/PHYSICAL LAYOUT:
One beanbag

DESCRIPTION OF THE LESSON:
Divide the class into two equal teams facing each other in rows. One child on Team A says a word, such as dog, and throws the beanbag to a child on Team B. The child on Team B receiving the beanbag must think of a word to rhyme with dog, such as log. If the word rhymes, the child on Team B who received the toss thinks of a new word, such as cat. The beanbag is now thrown to the second child on Team A, who has to supply the rhyming word. The game continues until all the children have had an opportunity to play.

METHOD OF EVALUATION:
Observe whether a child is having difficulty rhyming words and, if necessary, provide more practice with rhyming activities in succeeding lessons. It is suggested that an anecdotal record of each child's performance be kept, based on your observations.

LANGUAGE ENRICHMENT

PURPOSE:
To develop the ability to rhyme words

AREA OF LANGUAGE STRESSED:
Poetry—Rhyming words

DURATION OF LESSON:
Fifteen minutes

LESSON FORMAT:
Group or individual

MATERIALS/EQUIPMENT/PHYSICAL LAYOUT:
None

LESSON 206: NAME POETRY

DESCRIPTION OF THE LESSON:
Children enjoy using their own names to create a rhyme. Provide the first part of the rhyme, and ask the child to supply the missing word.

- Jean, Jean,
  Ate a ___.
- Jim, Jim,
  Went for a ___.
- Mike, Mike,
  Rode a ___.
- Sam, Sam,
  Ate some ___.
- Randy, Randy,
  Ate some ___.
- Mark, Mark,
  Caught a ___.

Give each child repeated trials by providing other names for creating rhymes.

METHOD OF EVALUATION:
Observe the child's ability to rhyme words. Obtain a percentage of correct responses by dividing the number of correct responses made by the total number of responses possible.

$$\frac{\text{Correct responses}}{\text{Total responses}} = \text{Percentage correct}$$

LANGUAGE ENRICHMENT

PURPOSE:
To develop the ability to write poetry

AREA OF LANGUAGE STRESSED:
Poetry—Writing poetry

DURATION OF LESSON:
Twenty minutes

LESSON FORMAT:
Group or individual

LESSON 207: ROSES ARE RED

MATERIALS/EQUIPMENT/PHYSICAL LAYOUT:
Paper, pencil, chalk, and a chalkboard

DESCRIPTION OF THE LESSON:
This lesson emphasizes the creative use of new phrases in a familiar poem. It will enable a child to imitate or reproduce rhythmic patterns. Have the child create new versions of the poem "Roses are Red" by changing two or more lines. For example:

Roses are red,	Roses are red,
Violets are blue,	Grass is green.
I am hungry,	You're the nicest person
How about you?	I've ever seen!

METHOD OF EVALUATION:
Determine through observation if the child correctly follows the format in creating a new poem. It is suggested that an anecdotal record for each child be kept, based on your observations.

LANGUAGE ENRICHMENT

PURPOSE:
To recognize and identify the pattern in a quatrain (four-line poem)

AREA OF LANGUAGE STRESSED:
Poetry—Writing poetry

DURATION OF LESSON:
Twenty minutes

LESSON FORMAT:
Group

MATERIALS/EQUIPMENT/PHYSICAL LAYOUT:
Several four-line poems, or quatrains (usually rhyming in an abab, abba, or aabb format), which may be found in a book of Mother Goose rhymes.

LESSON 208: QUICK QUATRAINS

DESCRIPTION OF THE LESSON:
After the children listen to and read a quatrain, ask them to identify its format. Use the following example:

Old King Cole was a merry old *soul,* (a)
And a merry old soul was *he.* (b)
He called for his pipe and he called for his *bowl,* (a)
And he called for his fiddlers *three.* (b)

By determining which words rhyme, the children can identify this as an abab format. Similarly, the following quatrain, "Twinkle, Twinkle Little Star," will be found to have an aabb format:

Twinkle, twinkle little *star,* (a)
How I wonder what you *are.* (a)
Up above the world so *high,* (b)
Like a diamond in the *sky.* (b)

METHOD OF EVALUATION:
Determine each child's ability to recognize a quatrain pattern by observing if the child can correctly identify the format. It is suggested that an anecdotal record of the child's performance be kept, based on your observations.

LANGUAGE ENRICHMENT

PURPOSE:
    To create a poem using descriptive adjectives

AREA OF LANGUAGE STRESSED:
    Poetry—Writing poetry

DURATION OF LESSON:
    Thirty minutes

LESSON FORMAT:
    Group or individual

LESSON 209: DESCRIPTIVE POETRY

MATERIALS/EQUIPMENT/PHYSICAL LAYOUT:
    Pencil and paper

DESCRIPTION OF THE LESSON:
    Ask the children to think of an object they would like to write about. Ask them to find an alternative or synonym for the object that means approximately the same thing, for example, dog—puppy, canary—bird. Then ask them to think of six words (adjectives) that describe the object. They can now arrange a poem in the following format:

Dog	*Soda*
licking chewing playing	sticky sweet fizzy
cuddly furry sleepy	burping slurping tickling
puppy	pop

METHOD OF EVALUATION:
    Observe to determine the child's ability to think of six modifiers for the object and the child's ability to use them in a poem.

LANGUAGE ENRICHMENT

PURPOSE:
To write a short poem

AREA OF LANGUAGE STRESSED:
Poetry—Writing poetry

DURATION OF LESSON:
Thirty minutes

LESSON 210: SHAPE-A-POEM

MATERIALS/EQUIPMENT/PHYSICAL LAYOUT:
Paper and pencil

DESCRIPTION OF THE LESSON:
Ask the children to think of a three- or four-line poem about a simple concrete object, such as an ice cream cone, a hat, a kite, or a balloon. After the child has written the poem, demonstrate how to write the poem in the shape of the object. For example:

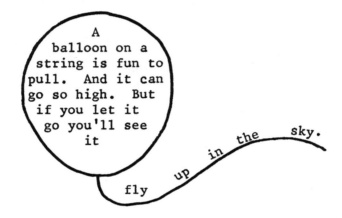

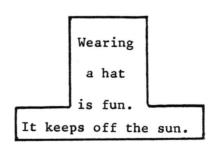

LESSON FORMAT:
Group or individual

METHOD OF EVALUATION:
Observe whether the child can develop a short poem. It is suggested that an anecdotal record of the child's performance be kept, based on your observations.

LANGUAGE ENRICHMENT

PURPOSE:
To develop a three-line poem

AREA OF LANGUAGE STRESSED:
Poetry—Writing poetry

DURATION OF LESSON:
Thirty minutes

LESSON FORMAT:
Group or individual

LESSON 211: POETRY TRIANGLES

MATERIALS/EQUIPMENT/PHYSICAL LAYOUT:
A chalkboard, chalk, a coat hanger, pencils or marking pens, and a 5″ × 5″ × 5″ tagboard triangle for each child

DESCRIPTION OF THE LESSON:
Draw a triangle on the board and say, "We are going to make up a poem to fit this triangle. The poem will have three lines, just as this triangle has three sides. We will be able to read the poem starting at any place on the triangle." Present one line of the poem to start the children thinking: "Summer is neat." Ask the children to think of two more lines to complete the poem. For example:

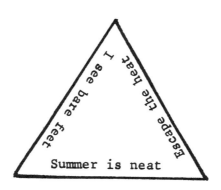

Once the children can do this as a group, give each child a tagboard triangle to use for a poem. Ask each child to complete a three-line poem independently. After all the triangle poems have been completed, they may be shared with the class and then attached to a coat hanger and hung from the ceiling as a mobile.

METHOD OF EVALUATION:
Observe to determine the children's ability to develop a three-line poem. It is suggested that an anecdotal record of each child's performance be kept, based on your observations.

LANGUAGE ENRICHMENT

PURPOSE:
To develop the ability to write haiku

AREA OF LANGUAGE STRESSED:
Poetry—Writing poetry

DURATION OF LESSON:
Thirty minutes

LESSON FORMAT:
Group or individual

MATERIALS/EQUIPMENT/PHYSICAL LAYOUT:
Paper and pencil

LESSON 212: HAIKU

DESCRIPTION OF THE LESSON:
Explain that a haiku is a three-line poem that expresses a single idea in nature. Each haiku has a standard number of syllables in each line:

- line one—five syllables
- line two—seven syllables
- line three—five syllables

Have the children list a number of topics to use in writing haiku, for example, water, sunflowers, the beach, or birds. Model a haiku to demonstrate its format.

> *The Sunflower*
> Yellow petals shine
> A flower reaching for sun
> Lighting up the day.

The children may create a poem together, or each child may create a haiku independently.

METHOD OF EVALUATION:
Determine whether the child can create a haiku. It is suggested that an anecdotal record of the child's skills in writing haiku be maintained.

LANGUAGE ENRICHMENT

PURPOSE:
To develop the ability to reproduce a rhythmic pattern

AREA OF LANGUAGE STRESSED:
Music—Rhythmic patterns

DURATION OF LESSON:
Twenty minutes

LESSON FORMAT:
Group or individual

LESSON 213: I'VE GOT RHYTHM

MATERIALS/EQUIPMENT/PHYSICAL LAYOUT:
Several different rhythm instruments, including wooden sticks, sandpaper blocks, a drum, and a tambourine

DESCRIPTION OF THE LESSON:
Say to the child, "I'm going to beat these sticks in a rhythm. Listen and see if you can make the same rhythm." Vary the rhythm by emphasizing certain beats. In one rhythm, the first beat may be stressed; in another, the fourth beat may be emphasized. The child's task is to reproduce the rhythm in precisely the same manner.

METHOD OF EVALUATION:
Determine the percentage of correct responses in reproducing rhythmic patterns by dividing the number of correct responses the child made by the total number of responses possible.

$$\frac{\text{Correct responses}}{\text{Total responses}} = \text{Percentage correct}$$

LANGUAGE ENRICHMENT

PURPOSE:
　To identify high and low sounds

AREA OF LANGUAGE STRESSED:
　Music—Learning musical vocabulary

DURATION OF LESSON:
　Fifteen minutes

LESSON FORMAT:
　Group or individual

LESSON 214: RESONATOR BELLS

MATERIALS/EQUIPMENT/PHYSICAL LAYOUT:
　Two resonator bell blocks and a mallet

DESCRIPTION OF THE LESSON:
　Say to the child, "We are going to listen to some bells." Strike each bell and ask, "Which one is the high sound? Which one is the low sound?" If the child succeeds in selecting the right sounds with two bells, the lesson may be varied by giving the child three or four bells to arrange according to a scale of sounds. As the lesson is conducted, stress the vocabulary words *high* and *low*.

METHOD OF EVALUATION:
　Observe the child's ability to identify tones correctly by stating whether the tone was high or low. It is suggested that an anecdotal record of the child's ability to use musical vocabulary be maintained.

LANGUAGE ENRICHMENT

PURPOSE:
　To develop vocabulary associated with music

AREA OF LANGUAGE STRESSED:
　Music—Learning musical vocabulary

DURATION OF LESSON:
　Fifteen minutes

LESSON FORMAT:
　Group

MATERIALS/EQUIPMENT/PHYSICAL LAYOUT:
　A kazoo, a recorder, a guitar, and an autoharp or piano

LESSON 215: FAST—SLOW AND HIGH—LOW

DESCRIPTION OF THE LESSON:
　Using one of the musical instruments, strike, or have a child strike, a note or series of notes. The children must identify whether the note was:

- high or low
- soft or loud
- fast or slow
- near or far

For variation, extend the activity by recording the following home and school sounds and have the children use the specified vocabulary in discussing the sounds:

- telephone ringing
- dog barking
- electric drill or saw
- doorbell
- mixer
- ringing school bell
- hair dryer
- hammer pounding

METHOD OF EVALUATION:
　Evaluate the child's use of vocabulary with the generalization check in Appendix B.

LANGUAGE ENRICHMENT

PURPOSE:
To develop poetic verse in song

AREA OF LANGUAGE STRESSED:
Music—Developing poetic verse in song

DURATION OF LESSON:
Thirty minutes

LESSON FORMAT:
Group or individual

LESSON 216: CHANGE A SONG

MATERIALS/EQUIPMENT/PHYSICAL LAYOUT:
Chalk and chalkboard

DESCRIPTION OF THE LESSON:
Explain that the class will create new words to an already popular song. Lead the class in singing "Twinkle Twinkle Little Star." Write the song on the board. Then ask the children to choose what they would like to write about, a cat for example. Ask them to think of words that might describe a cat or its actions. Start the first part of the song as the children continue to create new lines for it.

> Furry, furry little cat,
> How I wonder where you're at.
> Are you underneath the chair?
> Are you hiding here or there?
> Furry, furry little cat,
> How I wonder where you're at.

Encourage the children to write their own verses independently.

METHOD OF EVALUATION:
Determine from observation if the child can use different words in a familiar song. It is suggested that an anecdotal record be kept of the child's ability to develop verse in song.

LANGUAGE ENRICHMENT

PURPOSE:
To develop a singing commercial for a favorite product

AREA OF LANGUAGE STRESSED:
Music—Developing poetic verse in song

DURATION OF LESSON:
Thirty minutes

LESSON FORMAT:
Groups of four or five

LESSON 217: SINGING COMMERCIALS

MATERIALS/EQUIPMENT/PHYSICAL LAYOUT:
Tape-recorded samples of popular commercials for soft drinks, soaps, or cars

DESCRIPTION OF THE LESSON:
Have the children divide into groups and select a new product to sell. Using the tape-recorded music as the tune for the commercial, have each group create a song for its new product. Ask each group to demonstrate its commercial song.

METHOD OF EVALUATION:
Estimate by observation each child's contribution to the group process.

LANGUAGE ENRICHMENT

PURPOSE:
   To identify music typical of different countries or states

AREA OF LANGUAGE STRESSED:
   Music—Cultural considerations in music

DURATION OF LESSON:
   To be completed over several lessons

LESSON FORMAT:
   Group

LESSON 218: MUSIC AROUND THE WORLD

MATERIALS/EQUIPMENT/PHYSICAL LAYOUT:
   Instrumental records depicting music of different countries and books about those countries

DESCRIPTION OF THE LESSON:
   Instruct the children to use the school's library resources to identify the types of instruments used to produce cultural music typical of a country or state. Ask them to listen to records that depict a distinct style of music. The styles chosen should depend upon the cultural makeup of the class. The following examples may be used to begin the activity:

- Mexican brass band
- Venezuelan cuatro/harpa
- Caribbean steel drum
- traditional American Indian chants
- Hawaiian guitar music for hula dancing

METHOD OF EVALUATION:
   Determine from observation the child's ability to identify the country or state associated with the music style.

LANGUAGE ENRICHMENT

PURPOSE:
   To identify dances typical of specific cultures

AREA OF LANGUAGE STRESSED:
   Music—Cultural considerations in music

DURATION OF LESSON:
   To be completed over several sessions

LESSON FORMAT:
   Group

LESSON 219: CULTURAL DANCES

MATERIALS/EQUIPMENT/PHYSICAL LAYOUT:
   Music of different cultures

DESCRIPTION OF THE LESSON:
   Depending on the cultural makeup of the class, select several dances common in specific cultural groups. Ask persons in the community to act as resources in demonstrating various cultural dances, or select some of the children to demonstrate the dances. In this way, the children learn to identify the culture associated with the dance. The following dances may be demonstrated:

- Mexican hat dance
- Hawaiian hula
- American Indian dances

METHOD OF EVALUATION:
   Observe whether the children identify the cultures associated with different dances.

LANGUAGE ENRICHMENT

PURPOSE:
To demonstrate ease in speaking before others

AREA OF LANGUAGE STRESSED:
Dramatics—Puppetry

DURATION OF LESSON:
Twenty minutes

LESSON FORMAT:
Group

LESSON 220: PUPPET FRIEND

MATERIALS/EQUIPMENT/PHYSICAL LAYOUT:
Puppet

DESCRIPTION OF THE LESSON:
Speaking as the puppet, say to the children, "Hi, kids. My name is Mister Happy. I live here at school. I like to play games. Jump rope is my favorite. I'd like to know more about you. Can you tell me something about yourself?" The children then take turns sharing information about themselves, such as details about their interests, hobbies, and families.

METHOD OF EVALUATION:
Observe the child's ease in speaking before others. It is suggested that an anecdotal record of the child's performance be kept, based on your observations.

LANGUAGE ENRICHMENT

PURPOSE:
To develop appropriate expressive language through the use of puppets

AREA OF LANGUAGE STRESSED:
Dramatics—Puppetry

DURATION OF LESSON:
Thirty minutes

LESSON FORMAT:
Group

LESSON 221: THE PUPPET FAMILY

MATERIALS/EQUIPMENT/PHYSICAL LAYOUT:
A set of family puppets consisting of a mother, father, and two or three children

DESCRIPTION OF THE LESSON:
Give the children a hypothetical situation to act out with the puppets. For example, have them pretend that one child in the family is late for dinner. Assign the children parts and ask them to dramatize the scene. Continue by varying the situations and allowing different children to participate.

METHOD OF EVALUATION:
Determine the level of each child's language functioning with the checklist of expressive language in Appendix A.

LANGUAGE ENRICHMENT

PURPOSE:
To dramatize a sequence of events

AREA OF LANGUAGE STRESSED:
Dramatics—Puppetry

DURATION OF LESSON:
Forty-five minutes

LESSON FORMAT:
Group

LESSON 222: COMIC STRIP PUPPETS

MATERIALS/EQUIPMENT/PHYSICAL LAYOUT:
Paper bags, comic strip stories, crayons, scissors, glue, and construction paper

DESCRIPTION OF THE LESSON:
Read several comic strip stories to the children. Then divide the children into groups. Each group makes its own paper bag puppets, decorating them with construction paper and crayon. A puppet is made for each comic strip character. The children then dramatize the comic strip stories.

METHOD OF EVALUATION:
Observe each child's ability to dramatize the comic strip stories. It is suggested that an anecdotal record of each child's performance be kept, based on your observations.

LANGUAGE ENRICHMENT

PURPOSE:
To develop the ability to create new endings to familiar fairy tales

AREA OF LANGUAGE STRESSED:
Dramatics—Dramatizing stories

DURATION OF LESSON:
Thirty minutes

LESSON FORMAT:
Small groups

LESSON 223: FRACTURED FAIRY TALES

MATERIALS/EQUIPMENT/PHYSICAL LAYOUT:
None

DESCRIPTION OF THE LESSON:
Begin the lesson by saying, "Today we are going to act out new endings for some familiar stories." Then present one of the following statements:

- Let's pretend Hansel and Gretel meet a friendly giant in the woods. What happens next?
- Let's pretend the three bears are at home when Goldilocks visits. What do the bears do?
- Suppose the three little pigs meet the seven dwarfs instead of the big, bad wolf.
- What if Cinderella didn't meet the fairy godmother? How would she get to the ball?

Give the children five to ten minutes of planning time, then have them act out their alternative endings.

METHOD OF EVALUATION:
Observe the dramatic skills of each child and how each group works together in dramatizing an alternative ending.

LANGUAGE ENRICHMENT

PURPOSE:
To develop the ability to sequence stories correctly

AREA OF LANGUAGE STRESSED:
Dramatics—Dramatizing stories

DURATION OF LESSON:
Forty-five minutes

LESSON FORMAT:
Group

LESSON 224: STICK PUPPET STORIES

MATERIALS/EQUIPMENT/PHYSICAL LAYOUT:
A familiar story or fairy tale, tongue depressors, cardboard or tagboard, glue, crayons, and scissors

DESCRIPTION OF THE LESSON:
Read a familiar story to the children and ask the following questions:

- How does the story begin?
- Who are the main characters of the story?
- How many puppets will you need to make?
- What will the puppets say?
- How does the story end?

Assign each child a character. Have the children make stick puppets representing their characters by decorating the tongue depressors with tagboard or cardboard and coloring them with crayon. Tack or glue the puppets to the tongue depressors. Be sure the children are allowed time to practice the play before presenting it.

METHOD OF EVALUATION:
Observe the children's skills in dramatization. It is suggested that an anecdotal record of each child's performance be kept, based on your observations.

LANGUAGE ENRICHMENT

PURPOSE:
To develop the ability to predict outcomes

AREA OF LANGUAGE STRESSED:
Dramatics—Dramatizing stories

DURATION OF LESSON:
Forty-five minutes to one hour

LESSON FORMAT:
Group

LESSON 225: HAPPY ENDINGS

MATERIALS/EQUIPMENT/PHYSICAL LAYOUT:
A children's play or mystery story with the ending omitted

DESCRIPTION OF THE LESSON:
Read a play or story and divide the class into groups. Have each group write or orally describe an ending to the play. Assign characters and allow each group to dramatize its play for the rest of the class.

METHOD OF EVALUATION:
Observe each child's skills in dramatization. It is suggested that an anecdotal record of each child's performance be kept, based on your observations.

LANGUAGE ENRICHMENT

PURPOSE:
To develop a story plot from a last-line ending

AREA OF LANGUAGE STRESSED:
Dramatics—Dramatizing stories

DURATION OF LESSON:
Thirty minutes

LESSON FORMAT:
Group

MATERIALS/EQUIPMENT/PHYSICAL LAYOUT:
None

LESSON 226: NEVER TRUST A DONKEY

DESCRIPTION OF THE LESSON:
Explain to the children, "I am going to give you the last line of a story. You must make up the rest of the story by using the last line and then develop the story into a short play for the other children." Divide the class into groups of four or five and give each group a last line to be used in the story. Each group must gather together to discuss its line and create a plot to dramatize it. Following are some last-line endings that may be used:

- That's the last time I'll ever trust a donkey.
- Don't ever say I didn't warn you.
- And the monkey took a bow.
- Never leave a stone unturned.
- Always be true to your friends.

METHOD OF EVALUATION:
Since this is a group effort, each individual's contribution to plot development must be observed. Each child's ability to use expressive language may be evaluated with the checklist of expressive language in Appendix A. In addition, the child's use of specific language constructions may be evaluated with the generalization check in Appendix B.

LANGUAGE ENRICHMENT

PURPOSE:
To develop skills in social communication through dramatization

AREA OF LANGUAGE STRESSED:
Dramatics—Role playing

DURATION OF LESSON:
Thirty to forty-five minutes

LESSON FORMAT:
Small group

MATERIALS/EQUIPMENT/PHYSICAL LAYOUT:
None

LESSON 227: LET'S PRETEND

DESCRIPTION OF THE LESSON:
Introduce the lesson by saying, "It's fun to act out things that we see around us. And it's fun to pretend we are someone else. Let's see who can act out these situations." Following are several suggestions for situations and the number of children needed to dramatize each:

- fixing dinner (two children)
- playing with toys at Christmas time (three children)
- giving the dog a bath (two children)
- going to the store to buy bread and milk (two children)
- going to a circus (four children)
- buying a pair of shoes (two children)

METHOD OF EVALUATION:
Observe the children's ability to use role playing in social communication. It is suggested that an anecdotal record of each child's performance be kept, based on your observations.

LANGUAGE ENRICHMENT

PURPOSE:
   To develop skills in social communication through dramatization

AREA OF LANGUAGE STRESSED:
   Dramatics—Role playing

DURATION OF LESSON:
   Forty-five minutes

LESSON FORMAT:
   Group

LESSON 228: LET'S DRESS UP

MATERIALS/EQUIPMENT/PHYSICAL LAYOUT:
   Old clothing such as old gowns, beads, men's suits, costumes, feathers, high-heeled shoes, and hats

DESCRIPTION OF THE LESSON:
   Give the children repeated opportunities to dramatize home and family situations, using costumes and adult clothing. Divide the children into groups to decide which situations they wish to dramatize and who will portray specific characters. Each group dramatizes its short play for the other children in the class. This activity may be extended to include the role playing of different ethnic or family customs.

METHOD OF EVALUATION:
   Observe the children's ability to use role playing in social communication. It is suggested that an anecdotal record of each child's performance be kept, based on your observations.

LANGUAGE ENRICHMENT

PURPOSE:
   To develop skills in social communication through dramatization

AREA OF LANGUAGE STRESSED:
   Dramatics—Role playing

DURATION OF LESSON:
   Thirty minutes

LESSON FORMAT:
   Group

LESSON 229: ROLE PLAYING PLOTS

MATERIALS/EQUIPMENT/PHYSICAL LAYOUT:
   None

DESCRIPTION OF THE LESSON:
   Assign the children to groups to role play various situations. The following are suggestions for structuring the role playing:

- Pretend you are climbing a mountain and you're almost to the top.
- Pretend you are a teacher trying to teach something.
- Pretend you are a waitress or waiter and are waiting on a family.
- Pretend you are on a riverboat trip.
- Pretend you are on vacation.
- Pretend you are in a rodeo lassoing a calf.
- Pretend you are at the beach.

METHOD OF EVALUATION:
   Determine the effectiveness of each group in depicting the situation and observe each child's skills in social communication. It is suggested that an anecdotal record of each child's performance be kept, based on your observations.

LANGUAGE ENRICHMENT

PURPOSE:
To develop skills in social communication through dramatization

AREA OF LANGUAGE STRESSED:
Dramatics—Role playing

DURATION OF LESSON:
Thirty minutes

LESSON FORMAT:
Small group

LESSON 230: ROLE PLAYING SCHOOL SITUATIONS

MATERIALS/EQUIPMENT/PHYSICAL LAYOUT:
None

DESCRIPTION OF THE LESSON:
Say to the children, "Today we are going to role play things that happen at school." Following are several suggestions for role-playing situations and the number of children needed to dramatize each:

- Pretend you are going to show a new girl around the school. How would you introduce her to your friends? (two children)
- Suppose you and a friend have an argument on the playground and a teacher comes over to find out what happened. (three children)
- Pretend your group has been assigned to plan a party for your class. How would you go about it? (four children)

METHOD OF EVALUATION:
Observe the children's ability to communicate socially with their peers. It is suggested that an anecdotal record of each child's performance be kept, based on your observations.

LANGUAGE ENRICHMENT

PURPOSE:
To develop skills in social communication through dramatization

AREA OF LANGUAGE STRESSED:
Dramatics—Role playing

DURATION OF LESSON:
Twenty minutes

LESSON FORMAT:
Group

LESSON 231: TOY TALK

MATERIALS/EQUIPMENT/PHYSICAL LAYOUT:
Pictures of two animals, two toys, and two other objects

DESCRIPTION OF THE LESSON:
Say to the children, "We are going to pretend that we are toys or animals and talk to each other the way we think they would talk." Show the class pictures of two toys. Assign a pair of children to pretend they are the two toys talking to each other. Say to the children, "Tell what you look like. Explain what you like to do. How do you feel?" Have the children role play the two toys in conversation. Continue the lesson, giving other children opportunities to portray characters.

METHOD OF EVALUATION:
Observe the children's ability to use role playing in social communication. It is suggested that an anecdotal record of each child's performance be kept, based on your observations.

LANGUAGE ENRICHMENT

PURPOSE:
  To develop skills in social communication through dramatization

AREA OF LANGUAGE STRESSED:
  Dramatics—Role playing

DURATION OF LESSON:
  Thirty minutes

LESSON FORMAT:
  Group

LESSON 232: PLAYGROUND PROBLEMS

MATERIALS/EQUIPMENT/PHYSICAL LAYOUT:
  None

DESCRIPTION OF THE LESSON:
  Present a hypothetical playground situation to the children. Have different groups role play solutions. Compare alternative endings through discussion. The following situations may be used for dramatization:

  • Two friends are walking together. Another person comes up and begins to tease one.
  • Three children are playing ball. Another child comes up and kicks the ball away.
  • Teams are being chosen for a game. One child is left out.
  • One child runs up to the teacher and begins to tell on another.

METHOD OF EVALUATION:
  Observe the children's ability to use role playing in social communication. It is suggested that an anecdotal record of each child's performance be kept, based on your observations.

LANGUAGE ENRICHMENT

PURPOSE:
  To develop skills in social communication through dramatization

AREA OF LANGUAGE STRESSED:
  Dramatics—Role playing

DURATION OF LESSON:
  Thirty minutes

LESSON FORMAT:
  Group

LESSON 233: RESTAURANT TALK

MATERIALS/EQUIPMENT/PHYSICAL LAYOUT:
  None

DESCRIPTION OF THE LESSON:
  Discuss appropriate ways of ordering food when dining out. Give the children an opportunity to role play going to a restaurant to eat. Emphasize the following:

  • use of polite phrases
  • use of table manners when eating
  • appropriate dinner conversation
  • communication with restaurant workers

METHOD OF EVALUATION:
  Observe the children's ability to use role playing in social communication. It is suggested that an anecdotal record of each child's performance be kept, based on your observations.

LANGUAGE ENRICHMENT

PURPOSE:
 To develop skills in social communication through dramatization

AREA OF LANGUAGE STRESSED:
 Dramatics—Role playing

DURATION OF LESSON:
 Twenty minutes

LESSON FORMAT:
 Group

LESSON 234: THE TOY SHOP

MATERIALS/EQUIPMENT/PHYSICAL LAYOUT:
 None

DESCRIPTION OF THE LESSON:
 Children love the magical idea of toys coming to life. Select four or five children to pretend they are toys in a toy shop. Everyone has gone home for the night. The toys are alone. What happens? Some toys that may come to life are:

- teddy bear
- rocking horse
- electric train
- toy airplane
- doll
- pair of roller skates

METHOD OF EVALUATION:
 Observe the children's ability to use role playing in social communication. It is suggested that an anecdotal record of each child's performance be kept, based on your observations.

LANGUAGE ENRICHMENT

PURPOSE:
 To develop skills in social communication through dramatization

AREA OF LANGUAGE STRESSED:
 Dramatics—Role playing

DURATION OF LESSON:
 Thirty minutes

LESSON FORMAT:
 Group

MATERIALS/EQUIPMENT/PHYSICAL LAYOUT:
 Common objects found around the home or school, such as a cup, blender, comb, shoe, belt, or desk

LESSON 235: HELLO, SHOE

DESCRIPTION OF THE LESSON:
 A child selects an object and pretends to be a television talk show host. The child begins to interview the object, asking questions pertinent to its function. Another child takes the role of the object and responds. For example, the following dialogue might be presented:

> *Question:* Hello, Mr. Shoe. So delighted to have you on our show. Tell me, where have you been today?
> *Answer:* Well, I've traveled far.
>
> *Question:* Oh? Where did you go?
> *Answer:* I've been to Alaska and back.
>
> *Question:* What did you do in Alaska?
> *Answer:* I went skiing and then walked the pipeline.

METHOD OF EVALUATION:
 Observe the children's skill in using role playing in social communication. It is suggested that an anecdotal record of each child's performance be kept, based on your observations.

LANGUAGE ENRICHMENT

PURPOSE:
   To develop skills in social communication through dramatization

AREA OF LANGUAGE STRESSED:
   Dramatics—Role playing

DURATION OF LESSON:
   Forty-five minutes

LESSON FORMAT:
   Group

LESSON 236: TV CELEBRITY

MATERIALS/EQUIPMENT/PHYSICAL LAYOUT:
   A large cardboard refrigerator box and either tempera and paintbrushes or colored butcher paper

DESCRIPTION OF THE LESSON:
   Cut a square opening the size of a television screen in the empty refrigerator carton. On the back side of the box, cut a door so that the children may enter and exit through the back opening. The word *television* may be painted on the box with tempera or it may be put on with pieces of colored butcher paper. One child is selected to be the interviewer. Another child portrays a famous celebrity, such as a movie star, famous sports figure, or politician. The interview is conducted inside the television box.

METHOD OF EVALUATION:
   Observe the children's ability to use role playing in social communication. It is suggested that a record of each child's performance be kept, based on your observations.

LANGUAGE ENRICHMENT

PURPOSE:
   To develop skills in social communication through dramatization

AREA OF LANGUAGE STRESSED:
   Dramatics—Role playing

DURATION OF LESSON:
   Thirty minutes

LESSON FORMAT:
   Group

LESSON 237: JOB HATS

MATERIALS/EQUIPMENT/PHYSICAL LAYOUT:
   Hats representing people in different occupations, such as a chef, police officer, fireman, armed services officer, football player, or nurse

DESCRIPTION OF THE LESSON:
   Have one child select a hat. Ask the child, "What do you do for a living? Tell us about your job. What is the hardest part of your job? Tell us what you like best about your occupation." Give the other children opportunities to role play different occupations.

METHOD OF EVALUATION:
   Observe the children's ability to use role playing in social communication. It is suggested that an anecdotal record of each child's performance be kept, based on your observations.

LANGUAGE ENRICHMENT

PURPOSE:
   To develop skills in social communication through dramatization

AREA OF LANGUAGE STRESSED
   Dramatics—Role playing

DURATION OF LESSON:
   Forty-five minutes

LESSON FORMAT:
   Group

LESSON 238: THE DAILY NEWS DRAMA

MATERIALS/EQUIPMENT/PHYSICAL LAYOUT:
   Newspapers

DESCRIPTION OF THE LESSON:
   Encourage the children to look for newspaper stories that lend themselves to dramatization, such as "Rescuers Save Four Fishermen," or "UFO? Not for Long." The children should be given time to plan and develop their characters and plot. They may embellish the plot by making up information that is not contained in the article, but the play must contain in some form the basic who, what, when, where, and why information commonly present in most newspaper articles. The children can then perform the play for other members of the class.

METHOD OF EVALUATION:
   Observe the children's ability to use role playing in social communication. It is suggested that an anecdotal record of each child's performance be kept, based on your observations.

LANGUAGE ENRICHMENT

PURPOSE:
   To develop skills in social communication through dramatization

AREA OF LANGUAGE STRESSED:
   Dramatics—Role playing

DURATION OF LESSON:
   Thirty minutes

LESSON FORMAT:
   Group

LESSON 239: ORDER IN THE COURT

MATERIALS/EQUIPMENT/PHYSICAL LAYOUT:
   None

DESCRIPTION OF THE LESSON:
   Using a hypothetical crime, such as a bank robbery or a civil suit in a property line dispute, have the children create a court scene. Appoint a judge, attorneys, jury, defendant, and plaintiff. Then have the children enact the court scene.

METHOD OF EVALUATION:
   Observe the children's ability to use role playing in social communication. It is suggested that an anecdotal record of each child's performance be kept, based on your observations.

LANGUAGE ENRICHMENT

PURPOSE:
To develop skills in social communication through dramatization

AREA OF LANGUAGE STRESSED:
Dramatics—Role playing

DURATION OF LESSON:
Thirty minutes

LESSON FORMAT:
Group

LESSON 240: BUY MY PRODUCT

MATERIALS/EQUIPMENT/PHYSICAL LAYOUT:
A number of props used to sell products, such as a tube of toothpaste, shampoo, a can of soup, soap, chewing gum, and hairspray

DESCRIPTION OF THE LESSON:
After discussing why particular products appeal to people and the variety of ways television advertisements try to influence viewers, give the children an opportunity to stand up and sell selected products to the other group members. Use the following example to illustrate what an advertisement is:

> Boys and girls, everybody likes gum. But the best flavored gum in the universe is Fresh Mint. Taste Fresh Mint and you'll discover the cool flavor that makes you feel good all over.

After several children have had turns selling the same product, discuss which presentation made the children want to buy the product and why.

METHOD OF EVALUATION:
Observe the children's ability to use role playing in social communication. It is suggested that an anecdotal record of each child's performance be kept, based on your observations.

LANGUAGE ENRICHMENT

PURPOSE:
To develop skills in social communication through dramatization

AREA OF LANGUAGE STRESSED:
Dramatics—Role playing

DURATION OF LESSON:
Thirty minutes

LESSON FORMAT:
Pairs of children

LESSON 241: NEW INVENTIONS

MATERIALS/EQUIPMENT/PHYSICAL LAYOUT:
Common objects found around the home and school, such as thread spools, rubber bands, paper clips, popsicle sticks, pipe cleaners, and wood scraps

DESCRIPTION OF THE LESSON:
After the children are divided into pairs, encourage them to think of a new invention and then make it, using the materials provided. After collaborating on the possible uses of their invention, the pairs of children may dramatize and/or describe its use to the other members of the class.

METHOD OF EVALUATION:
Observe the children's ability to use role playing in social communication. It is suggested that an anecdotal record of each child's performance be kept, based on your observations.

LANGUAGE ENRICHMENT

PURPOSE:
To develop skills in social communication through dramatization

AREA OF LANGUAGE STRESSED:
Dramatics—Role playing

DURATION OF LESSON:
Thirty minutes

LESSON FORMAT:
Groups of two or three

MATERIALS/EQUIPMENT/PHYSICAL LAYOUT:
None

LESSON 242: ANIMAL FRIENDS

DESCRIPTION OF THE LESSON:
Divide the children into pairs or groups of three. Ask each child to portray an animal character. The following animal scenes may be dramatized:

- a snake having tea with an elephant and a rooster
- a monkey and an octopus going grocery shopping
- a raccoon and a bear going fishing
- an eagle and a dog going for a hot-air balloon ride
- a sheepdog and a horse rounding up cattle
- a tiger and a mouse riding in an airplane
- a pig and a cat having dinner with a bird

Encourage the children to develop conversations among animal friends.

METHOD OF EVALUATION:
Observe the children's ability to use role playing in social communication. It is suggested that an anecdotal record of each child's performance be kept, based on your observations.

LANGUAGE ENRICHMENT

PURPOSE:
To communicate using nonverbal language

AREA OF LANGUAGE STRESSED:
Dramatics—Pantomime, mimicry, and story plays

DURATION OF LESSON:
Twenty minutes

LESSON FORMAT:
Group

MATERIALS/EQUIPMENT/PHYSICAL LAYOUT:
None

LESSON 243: NATURE MOVES

DESCRIPTION OF THE LESSON:
Explain that the children are to act out things that happen in nature. Ask them to close their eyes and picture certain images. Ask for volunteers to pantomime each of the following scenes:

- a wave crashing on the beach
- a flower opening on a vine
- a bee buzzing from flower to flower
- a flower wilting
- a tree bending in a windstorm
- a fish swimming in the lake

METHOD OF EVALUATION:
Observe the children's ability to use interpretive movement in social communication. It is suggested that an anecdotal record of each child's performance be kept, based on your observations.

LANGUAGE ENRICHMENT

PURPOSE:
To communicate using nonverbal language

AREA OF LANGUAGE STRESSED:
Dramatics—Pantomime, mimicry, and story plays

DURATION OF LESSON:
Twenty minutes

LESSON FORMAT:
Group

LESSON 244: A PANTOMIME PARTY

MATERIALS/EQUIPMENT/PHYSICAL LAYOUT:
None

DESCRIPTION OF THE LESSON:
The following are some ideas for mimetic activities:

- just waking up
- eating ice cream
- eating something you don't like
- making a bed
- making a sandwich
- blow drying your hair
- playing baseball—first as a pitcher, then as a batter
- going fishing and catching a big one!

METHOD OF EVALUATION:
Observe the children's ability to use interpretive movement in social communication. It is suggested that an anecdotal record of each child's performance be kept, based on your observations.

LANGUAGE ENRICHMENT

PURPOSE:
To communicate using nonverbal language

AREA OF LANGUAGE STRESSED:
Dramatics—Pantomime, mimicry, and story plays

DURATION OF LESSON:
Thirty minutes

LESSON FORMAT:
Pairs of children

MATERIALS/EQUIPMENT/PHYSICAL LAYOUT:
None

LESSON 245: PANTOMIMING PARTNERS

DESCRIPTION OF THE LESSON:
Say to the children, "I want you to act out these situations with your partner in pantomime, without talking":

- You and your sister are getting ready for school. You must get dressed, eat breakfast, and brush your teeth. Hurry! Here comes the bus!
- You and a friend are going to a movie. You pay the cashier, go into the theater, and get your popcorn and soda. Pretend you are watching a scary movie.
- You and a friend are going to the playground on a Saturday. First you play baseball. Your friend is up to bat. Next, you climb on the monkeybars. Oh, there's a tetherball. Why don't you play a game?

METHOD OF EVALUATION:
Observe the children's use of interpretive movement in social communication. It is suggested that an anecdotal record of each child's performance be kept, based on your observations.

LANGUAGE ENRICHMENT

PURPOSE:
   To communicate using nonverbal language

AREA OF LANGUAGE STRESSED:
   Dramatics—Pantomime, mimicry, and story plays

DURATION OF LESSON:
   Fifteen minutes

LESSON FORMAT:
   Pairs of children

LESSON 246: MIRROR MIME

MATERIALS/EQUIPMENT/PHYSICAL LAYOUT:
   Two children's chairs facing each other, about 24 inches apart

DESCRIPTION OF THE LESSON:
   Explain that the following activity will be similar to looking in a mirror. Assign two children to be partners. One child will lead, making facial motions, hand gestures, and body movements. The second child is to mimic the partner's actions and facial movements as closely as possible. The children then trade roles, and the second child has the opportunity of leading the first in pantomiming different actions.

METHOD OF EVALUATION:
   Observe the children's ability to use interpretive movement in social communication. It is suggested that an anecdotal record of each child's performance be kept, based on your observations.

LANGUAGE ENRICHMENT

PURPOSE:
   To communicate using nonverbal language

AREA OF LANGUAGE STRESSED:
   Dramatics—Pantomime, mimicry, and story plays

DURATION OF LESSON:
   Thirty minutes

LESSON FORMAT:
   Pairs of children

LESSON 247: MIMETIC MOVES

MATERIALS/EQUIPMENT/PHYSICAL LAYOUT:
   Action picture cards illustrating familiar sports, household routines, and school activities

DESCRIPTION OF THE LESSON:
   Give each pair of children a set of picture cards. Have one child in each pair select a card and then pantomime the action. The other child must guess the activity being demonstrated. Then have the children reverse roles.

METHOD OF EVALUATION:
   Observe the children's ability to use interpretive movement in social communication. It is suggested that an anecdotal record of each child's performance be kept, based on your observations.

LANGUAGE ENRICHMENT

PURPOSE:
To communicate using nonverbal language

AREA OF LANGUAGE STRESSED:
Dramatics—Pantomime, mimicry, and story plays

DURATION OF LESSON:
Twenty minutes

LESSON FORMAT:
Group

LESSON 248: FAIRY TALE STORY PLAYS

MATERIALS/EQUIPMENT/PHYSICAL LAYOUT:
Familiar fairy tales

DESCRIPTION OF THE LESSON:
Explain that story plays are mimes or movements performed without words in a story sequence. Read a familiar fairy tale and have the children pantomime the story. Fairy tales that lend themselves to this treatment include:

- Goldilocks and the Three Bears
- Cinderella
- Little Red Riding Hood
- Rumpelstiltskin
- Three Billy Goats Gruff

METHOD OF EVALUATION:
Observe the children's ability to use interpretive movements in social communication. It is suggested that an anecdotal record of each child's performance be kept, based on your observations.

LANGUAGE ENRICHMENT

PURPOSE:
To communicate using nonverbal language

AREA OF LANGUAGE STRESSED:
Dramatics—Pantomime, mimicry, and story plays

DURATION OF LESSON:
Fifteen minutes

LESSON FORMAT:
Group

LESSON 249: THE PICNIC

MATERIALS/EQUIPMENT/PHYSICAL LAYOUT:
None

DESCRIPTION OF THE LESSON:
Present the following story play and have the children pantomime the movements involved:

Teacher:	Let's go on a picnic! What shall we take? Let's take sandwiches, apples, and cake. We need to pack our food in the basket. Someone mix up the lemonade and put it in the thermos.
Children's pantomime:	Making sandwiches, wrapping cake, washing fruit, making lemonade, packing the basket, and getting the car ready.
Teacher:	Everyone in? Fasten your seatbelts. It's a long drive to the lake. Let's play a car game.
Children's pantomime:	Buckling up and playing games.
Teacher:	Here we are at the lake. Get the blanket. Let's spread out the food and then play.
Children's pantomime:	Getting out of the car, spreading out the blanket, and unpacking the food.
Teacher:	Look. Let's go wading in the pond. Let's sail our boats and swim.
Children's pantomime:	Wading, sailing, and swimming.
Teacher:	It's time to eat.
Children's pantomime:	Unwrapping sandwiches, pouring lemonade, drinking and eating.
Teacher:	Someone brought a bat and ball. Let's play baseball.
Children's pantomime:	Playing baseball.
Teacher:	It's time to go home.
Children's pantomime:	Packing up the car, getting in, and buckling up.
Teacher:	I'm so tired.
Children's pantomime:	Snoozing on the way home.

METHOD OF EVALUATION:
Observe the children's ability to use interpretive movement in social communication. It is suggested that an anecdotal record of each child's performance be kept, based on your observations.

LANGUAGE ENRICHMENT

PURPOSE:
To communicate using nonverbal language

AREA OF LANGUAGE STRESSED:
Dramatics—Pantomime, mimicry, and story plays

DURATION OF LESSON:
Fifteen minutes

LESSON FORMAT:
Group

MATERIALS/EQUIPMENT/PHYSICAL LAYOUT:
None

DESCRIPTION OF THE LESSON:
Present the following story play and have the children pantomime the movements involved:

Teacher:	A family went on a trip to the jungle in Africa. When the members of the family got off the plane, they rode in an old jeep on a bumpy road.
Children's pantomime:	Riding in a jeep, being jostled from side to side.
Teacher:	When they came to a clearing, they set up camp. Father set up the tent.
Children's pantomime:	Pounding in tent stakes.
Teacher:	Mother unpacked the suitcases.
Children's pantomime:	Opening suitcases and shaking out clothing.

LESSON 250: A TRIP TO THE JUNGLE

Teacher:	And the children went for a walk. Because the jungle was so quiet, the children tiptoed as they went.
Children's pantomime:	Tiptoeing.
Teacher:	Suddenly the children were frightened by a noise overhead.
Children's pantomime:	Looking upward with frightened faces.
Teacher:	Oh, it was only a silly monkey jumping from limb to limb in a tree.
Children's pantomime:	Pretending to jump here and there.
Teacher:	Then they heard a rustling in the grass. It was a snake slithering away.
Children's pantomime:	Crawling like a snake.
Teacher:	Then they heard an elephant slowly walking through the brush. The elephant stopped to scratch his back on a tree. He swayed as he walked deeper into the jungle.
Children's pantomime:	Walking like elephants with arms for trunks, gently swaying from side to side, scratching their backs by rubbing against something.
Teacher:	Then they heard a loud, scary CRACK! Oh, it was thunder. It started to rain hard, so the children ran as fast as they could back to the shelter of the tent.
Children's pantomime:	Running back to camp.
Teacher:	And the children told their parents all about the animals they saw in the jungle.
Children's pantomime:	Talking excitedly to the parents.

METHOD OF EVALUATION:
Observe the children's ability to use interpretive movement in social communication. It is suggested that an anecdotal record of each child's performance be kept, based on your observations.

Checklist of Expressive Language

The checklist of expressive language in Table A-1 is designed to assist the teacher in evaluating pupil progress on the lessons for teaching expressive language (in Chapter 6) and for enriching the language environment (in Chapter 7). The checklist is administered while the child is engaged in the prescribed language lesson. Prior to the beginning of the lesson, the teacher should enter in the appropriate section the children's names, the date, and the starting time of the observation. If not directly involved in the activity, it is best if the teacher remains seated unobtrusively, but close enough to observe and record the interactions of the children. If the teacher is involved in the activity, the checklist can be placed discreetly nearby, so that the appropriate language construction can be quickly recorded as it occurs.

While the checklist is designed to be used with a single child or small group of children, the amount of time needed to gain the necessary information will vary, depending upon the number of children to be observed. Through experience, it has been determined that the most effective way to use the checklist with a group is to observe one child at a time, following the activity of each child until all the appropriate items have been recorded. Then the performance of the next child is observed, until the language constructions of all of the children targeted for evaluation have been recorded.

A simple means of scoring is suggested: A plus (+) is placed in the appropriate box if the child exhibits the particular construction during the language activity. A minus (−) is recorded in the box if the construction is not exhibited.

After the checklist is completed, the teacher may use the information to help plan further evaluation of the child's language skills. The section entitled ''Tests to be Administered'' is available for the teacher who wishes to pinpoint formal assessment procedures for expressive language problems.

Table A-1 The Checklist of Expressive Language

Date(s) _____   + Construction Present
Time _____   − Construction Absent

Child's Name	Gestures	Uses a few recognizable words	Uses 2-3 word phrases	Uses simple, declarative sentences	Uses correct word order	Uses past and future tense verbs	Uses auxiliary verbs (is, are, was, were)	Uses plural nouns	Uses pronouns correctly	Uses subject-verb agreement	Uses articles (a, an, the)	Uses appropriate prepositions	Uses transformations (wh questions, negation, conjoining)	Tests to be Administered

Appendix B

The Generalization Check

The generalization check in Exhibit B-1 is designed to help the teacher determine if a construction learned in a language session has generalized to spontaneous language, and if the response has been maintained over time. The teacher first fills in the child's name and date of observation. Next, the specific language construction in question is listed, such as the child's ability to generalize the use of plural nouns. Then the particular setting is described in which the child is observed. For example, a particularly good time to check for language generalization is during free-play periods. The starting time and the termination time of the observation should also be noted. Correct and incorrect responses can easily be recorded in the appropriate section after each response. The correct and incorrect responses are then added together to give a total response figure. To determine the child's accuracy level, the correct responses the child made are divided by the total number of responses possible. This provides the teacher with a percentage of correct responses for that particular language construction.

Exhibit B-1 The Generalization Check

Date: _____ Student: _____
Construction: _____
_____
Setting: _____
_____
Observation time: _____
Correct responses: _____
Incorrect responses: _____
Total responses: _____

$$\frac{\text{Correct responses}}{\text{Total responses}} = \text{Percentage correct} = \underline{\hspace{2cm}}$$

Free and Inexpensive Materials to Enrich the Language Environment

A rich language environment in the special education classroom need not be expensive to create if the teacher learns to collect and store objects and materials commonly found around the home and school. The teacher may design and implement language lessons either by using common household items or by creatively fashioning materials from arts and crafts supplies.

The following lists include almost all of the items needed to conduct the lessons provided in this sourcebook for the teaching of language in the special education classroom.

Sources for Pictures

baseball cards
coloring books
comic books
magazines
mail-order catalogs
newspapers
workbooks

References

children's books
dictionaries
encyclopedias
fairy tales
nursery rhymes

Audiovisual Materials

autoharp
blank cassette tapes
felt objects
filmstrip projector
filmstrips
flannelboard or feltboard
guitar
instant developing camera and film
kazoo
listening center
piano
recorder (musical instrument)
resonator bells and mallet
rhythm instruments
tape recorder
viewmaster and discs

Miscellaneous Objects

artificial fruits and
  vegetables
beanbags
belt
blindfold
book jackets

bottle caps
can of soup
cans
cartons
chalk
clothespins

coat hangers
coins
colored blocks or
  one-inch cubes
comb
cookbooks

corks
costume beads
costumes
doll clothes
doll house
doorstep
eggbeater
eating utensils
envelopes
feathers
foods
greeting cards
gum
hats
hole punch
jars
kitchen tongs
lamp

magnets
mirror
newspapers
old socks
paper clips
paper sacks
paperweight
plastic animals
plastic dolls
puppets
restaurant menus
rubber balls
rubber bands
safety pins
scale
screen
screwdriver
shampoo

shoeboxes
shoehorn
soap
spinners for games
spools
stickers
straight pins
stuffed animals
thermometer
toothpaste
toothpicks
toy telephones
toy trains, cars,
  boats
toy zoo animals
tricycle
tweezers
wagon

Arts and Crafts Supplies
for Making Language Materials

beans
butcher paper
buttons
cardboard
cardboard pizza wheels
clay
construction paper
cotton
crayons
dry macaroni or noodles
felt
felt markers
glue or paste
graph paper
grease pencils
index cards
manila folders
material scraps

paints
paper bags
paper plates
pencils
pipe cleaners
popsicle sticks
rice
ric-rac and braid
rulers
sand
sandpaper
scissors
string
tagboard
tape
tongue depressors
wood scraps
yarn

A Sample List of Reinforcers

Following is a list of reinforcers that can be used in the home or school setting. The reinforcers are in four categories: edible (primary), social, activity, and token. The first three categories are self-explanatory. In the fourth category, token reinforcers, are items that may be used to purchase primary or activity reinforcers.

Edible (Primary) Reinforcers

apple pieces	cookies	orange pieces
bacon bits	crackers	peanut butter
candy	dried fruit	peanuts
carrot sticks	grapes	popcorn
celery	ice cream	potato chips
cereal	juice	raisins
cheese bits	milk	soft drinks
chips	miniature marshmallows	sunflower seeds

Social Reinforcers
Activities

hugging	patting on the head	smiling
nodding approval	shaking hands	tickling
patting on the back	showing thumbs up	winking

Phrases
(alternative ways of saying good)

all right	good choice
best ever	good talking
class, look at (child's name)	good thinking
	great
correct	great piece of work
excellent work	great work
fantastic	I am pleased
fine answer	I like it
give me five	I like that
good answer	I'm proud of you
keep up the good work	that's interesting
marvelous	that's right
nifty	this is your best yet
	very clever
outstanding	wonderful work
perfect	you are doing better
right	you are doing fine
super	you have done well today
terrific	you're improving

Activity Reinforcers
Activities

acting as custodian's helper	helping the librarian
acting as line leader	leading the flag salute
acting as messenger for the principal	listening to records
	looking at a book
acting as messenger for the teacher	operating the movie projector
arranging a party for friends	painting
	playing dot-to-dot games
attending a class party	playing in water or sand
attending athletic events	playing show and tell
being read to	playing with puppets
bowling	raising the flag
coloring	skating
cutting and pasting	spending time in the library
dancing	
distributing and collecting work	taking care of the class pet
getting permission to stay up past bedtime	taking class roll
	taking field trips
having a friend spend the night	tutoring younger children
	using a typewriter
having early recess	using teaching machines
having extra recess	wearing 3-D glasses
having free time	working with a friend
	writing letters
	writing on chalkboard

Materials

balloons	hourglass
beads	makeup kits
blocks	marking pens
clay	model kits
coloring book	movies
comic books	playdough
dolls	puzzles
"dress-up" clothes	soap bubbles
Etch-A-Sketch	tape recorder
games of all types	

Token Reinforcers

"bankbook"	paper slips
behavior charts	plastic or wooden chips
bottle caps	play money
buttons	points
good work slips	poker chips
happy paper faces	punches in cards
letter grades	rubber stamp designs
marbles or pebbles in a	stars
container	stickers
marks on cards	tickets
marks on the blackboard	trading stamps
metal washers	wooden popsicle sticks
money	

Appendix E

An Annotated Bibliography of Parent-Involvement Materials

Following is an annotated bibliography divided into two sections. Section 1 lists and describes materials to aid professionals who work with parents of exceptional children. Section 2 lists and describes materials that can be used by parents themselves.

Section 1 Materials for Professionals

Abidin, R.R. *Parenting skills*. New York: Human Sciences Press, 1976. Guidelines for the professional interested in developing parent training workshops. The book is arranged in modules to facilitate skills in child rearing.

Barsch, R.H. *The parent teacher partnership*. Reston, Va.: Council for Exceptional Children, 1969. A discussion dealing with parents as teachers of their handicapped child. The book stresses the importance of parents and teachers coordinating their efforts in working with the child. An action outline consisting of guidelines for parent training is included.

Bennett, L.M., & Henson, F.O. *Keeping in touch with parents*. Austin, Tex.: Learning Concepts. A multimedia kit that focuses on building skills in communicating with parents, learning how to assist parents in implementing home instructional programs, and techniques to maximize input into the educational process.

Berger, E.H. *Parents as partners in education: The school and home working together*. St. Louis, Mo.: C.V. Mosby, 1981. Suggestions on how to bring parents and schools closer together, based on the author's experience as both parent and educator.

Chinn, P.C.; Winn, J.; & Walters, R.H. *Two-way talking with parents of special children: A process of positive communication*. St. Louis, Mo.: C.V. Mosby, 1978. A book dealing with enhancing communication within the family of an exceptional child. It is also concerned with the communication triad existing between the family, child, and school.

Coletta, A.J. *Working together: A guide to parent involvement*. Atlanta, Ga.: Humanics Limited, 1977. Suggested components and strategies for educators in setting up parent involvement programs. Its guidelines for parent involvement are based on current research in the field.

Cooper, J.O., & Edge, D. *Parenting: Strategies and educational methods*. Columbus, Ohio: Charles E. Merrill, 1978. Eight instructional sessions that give professionals guidelines for training parents in the specifics of behavior change. The book includes 175 problem-solving strategies.

DeFranco, E.B. *Parent education methods and learning activities for pre-school children*. Salt Lake City, Utah: Olympus Publishing, 1975. A structure for teachers to use with parents in home-teaching programs for preschool children. The book provides teachers with numerous activities to suggest to parents in developing their child's language, sensory motor skills, science, and math concepts at home.

Evans, J. *Working with parents of handicapped children*. Reston, Va.: Council for Exceptional Children, 1976. A book designed to help teachers work with parents of young handicapped children. It includes information sources, bibliographies, and forms for parent interviews. It is also available in Spanish.

Kelly, E.J. *Parent-teacher interaction: A special educational perspective*. Seattle, Wash.: Special Child Publications, 1974. A book that looks at parent involvement from the educator's viewpoint. It discusses the advantages and disadvantages of having parents participate in the instructional program.

Kroth, R.L. *Communicating with parents of exceptional children: Improving parent-teacher relationships*. Denver, Colo.: Love Publishing, 1975. A book of specific techniques for teachers and counselors. It tells when to schedule parent conferences and what materials to provide.

Kroth, R.L., & Scholl, G.T. *Getting schools involved with parents*. Reston, Va.: Council for Exceptional Children, 1978. A book that describes exemplary parent involvement programs and tells how to measure the effectiveness of parent programs.

Lillie, D.L., & Trohanis, P.L. (Eds.). *Teaching parents to teach: Education for the handicapped*. New York: Walker Educational Book Corporation, 1976. A book that describes how to plan, organize, and supervise activities that involve parents in early childhood programs for the handicapped. It contains contributions from 18 experienced psychologists and educators.

Losen, S.M., & Diament, B. *Parent conferences in the schools: Procedures for building effective partnerships*. Rockleigh, N.J.: Allyn & Bacon, 1978. A book written by two school psychologists that covers all the steps involved in the parent conference, from the initial contact, to the evaluation and follow-up phases, through the decision-making stage. Special emphasis is given to federal regulations mandating parent involvement in the decision-making process.

McDowell, R.L. *Managing behavior: A parent involvement program*. Roll-
ing Hills Estates, Calif.: B.L. Winch & Associates. A multimedia training program used to train parents in positive behavior management skills.
It includes filmstrips, audio cassettes, and parent log books.

Miehaelis, C.T. *Home and school partnerships in exceptional education*.
Rockville, Md.: Aspen Systems Corporation, 1980. A book that describes how home and school cooperation can enrich the special education
program. The author is both a special educator and the parent of a
handicapped child.

Morrison, G.S. *Parent involvement in the home, school, and community*.
Columbus, Ohio: Charles E. Merrill, 1978. A review of home- and
center-based models for parent involvement, based on a combination of
theory and current practices. The book looks at current trends and issues
in programs that use parents as teachers. It would be useful to the educator
who is seeking a broad view of how to set up a training program that
involves parents in the education of their child.

Pickarts, E., & Fargo, J. *Parent education*. New York: Appleton-Century-
Crofts, 1971. A book for the professional who is seeking guidelines and a
process for developing parent education programs. It deals with the
child's learning process and the role of the parent as a teacher. It examines
several different methods used in parent education and suggests content
for training programs. It compares and contrasts the education of parents
in advantaged circumstances with training programs for parents in low-
income communities.

Ross, A.O. *The exceptional child in the family*. New York: Grune &
Stratton, 1964. A book that offers the professional a view of family
dynamics in response to having an exceptional child in the family. It deals
with parental reactions and attitudes and covers theory and practices for
counseling parents of exceptional children. It specifically deals with the
problems of the child with sensory defects or physical handicaps, the
emotionally disturbed child, the gifted child, and the adopted child.

Simpson, R.L., & Kroth, R.L. *Parent conferences as a teaching strategy*.
Denver, Colo.: Love Publishing Co., 1977. A book whose focus is on the
parent-teacher conference. It contains specific ideas for conducting and
recording the conference.

Stewart, J.C. *Counseling parents of exceptional children*. Columbus, Ohio:
Charles E. Merrill, 1978. A book that combines counseling theory and
practice with an overview of the educational, personal, social, and day-to-
day problems facing parents of handicapped children.

Wagonseller, B.; Burnett, M.; Salzberg, B.; & Bernard, B. *The art of
parenting: A complete training kit*. Champaign, Ill.: Research Press. A
multimedia training program to be used by professionals to train parents in
child-rearing techniques. The five workshop sessions involve the use of
filmstrips, audio cassettes, and workbooks.

Section 2 Materials for Parents
General

Alvord, J. *Home token economy*. Champaign, Ill.: Research Press, 1973.
Guidelines for parents in setting up a token economy system in the home.

Brown, D.L. *Developmental handicaps in babies and young children: A
guide for parents*. Springfield, Ill.: Charles C Thomas, 1972. An explanation of the causes of common handicapping conditions, including
language and speech problems. The book provides parents with a dictionary of terms and suggestions for seeking resources.

Bryant, J.E. *Helping your child speak correctly* (Pamphlet No. 445). New
York: Public Affairs Pamphlets, 1970. A booklet that considers how
parents can help their child who is delayed in developing language or
speech. It deals with causal factors in speech and language problems and
suggests places to seek help when a speech problem is suspected.

Curran, J.S., & Cratty, B.J. *Speech and language problems in children*.
Denver, Colo.: Love Publishing Co., 1978. A nontechnical book written
for the teacher and parent. It contains information and strategies to be used
with four types of speech and language problems: delayed acquisition of
words and sentences, rhythm problems in voice, articulation problems,
and voice disorders.

DeVilliers, P.A., & DeVilliers, J.G. *Early language*. Cambridge, Mass.:
Harvard University Press, 1979. A book that deals with early language
development through a nontechnical approach. It emphasizes how
children begin to develop sounds and words and how they learn grammatical rules to combine words into sentences. It also deals with the child's
experiences and how they affect language learning.

Dreikurs, R., & Grey, L. *Parent's guide to child discipline*. New York:
Hawthorn Books, 1970. A call for a "new tradition" in child rearing.
Special emphasis is placed on parents using logical consequences in
dealing with their children.

The Effective Parent. New York: Parents Magazine Films, 1977. A series of
four sound-and-color filmstrips dealing with the parent as a
teacher—learning in the home, learning through play, and learning away
from home.

Hatten, J.J., & Hatten, P.W. *Natural language*. Tucson, Ariz.: Communication Skill Builders, 1975. A teacher-guided program for parents of
language delayed children. It gives parents suggestions for using natural
and structured activities in three areas of child development: language-re-
lated skills, prelanguage sensory skills, and language skills.

Karnes, M.B. *Creative games for learning: Parent, teacher made games*.
Fifth easy games that parents can make in the home. The games are
intended for children of ages three to eight.

Kirk, S.A.; Karnes, M.B.; & Kirk, W.D. *You and your retarded child*. Palo
Alto, Calif.: Pacific Books, 1968. A book that seeks to answer the
questions of parents of retarded children. It gives suggestions on how
parents can help their children learn to play, become more independent,
learn to talk, gain acceptance, and control their behavior.

Lattman, M., & Seandel, A. *Better speech for your child*. New York:
Wyden Books, 1977. A parent's practical guide to encouraging language
from birth to age five. At each level, characteristics of language growth
and family influences on language are included. Activities for stimulating
language acquisition are included for each developmental stage.

Markel, G., & Greenbaum, J. *Parents are to be seen and heard: Assertive-
ness in educational planning for handicapped children*. San Luis Obispo,
Calif.: Impact Publishers, 1978. Materials designed for parents in work-
book format with over 30 illustrations. The authors contend that assertive
action and knowledge of P.L. 94-142 are required for parents to ensure
that their handicapped children receive an appropriate education.

Molloy, J.S. *Teaching the retarded child to talk*, New York: John Day,
1961. Practical suggestions to help the parents of the young retarded child
who has not yet begun to talk. The book stresses listening skills, combining sounds into words and words into sentences, and using appropriate
social language.

Mopsik, S.I., & Agard, J.A. *An education handbook for parents of handicapped children*. Cambridge, Mass.: Abt Books, 1980. A book that
focuses on the relationship between parents and special educators. It
attempts to answer parents' most frequently asked questions about providing a free and appropriate education for their handicapped children.

Nazzaro, J. *Preparing for the IEP meeting: A workshop for parents*. Reston,
Va.: Council for Exceptional Children, 1979. A mediated training package designed to help prepare parents to be active participants in the IEP
meeting. A 64-page guide, a filmstrip, and reproducible materials are
included.

Patterson, G.R. *Families: Applications of social learning to family life*.
Champaign, Ill.: Research Press, 1975. An approach based on a social

learning theory for dealing with ordinary family interactions. Emphasizing the changeable nature of behavior, it is designed to provide parents with the technical skills for making family life ''work.''

Pushaw, D.R. *Teach your child to talk: A parent guide*. New York: Dantree Press, 1976. Descriptions of normal speech and language development at different age levels and suggested activities to enhance language skills at each developmental level.

Rinn, R.C., & Markle, A. *Positive parenting*. Cambridge, Mass.: Research Media, 1977. An easy-to-read book on parenting. It provides parents with positive techniques for dealing with inappropriate child behavior. It also includes case histories, behavior monitoring systems, and relaxation techniques to combat parental stress.

Rosen, M.; Wesner, C.E.; & Zisfein, L. *Your child can talk, too*. Elwyn, Pa.: Elwyn Educational Materials Center, Elwyn Institute, 1972. A manual to help parents who wish to stimulate the language development of their handicapped child. It gives suggestions for identifying the starting point for home instruction, the importance of keeping a record of the child's progress, and a training procedure for developing receptive and expressive language.

A special need, a special love, children with handicaps: Families who care. New York. Parents' Magazine Films, 1977. A series of four sound-and-color filmstrips for parents of exceptional children. Topics include support from the family, support from educators, support from the helping professions, and support from the community.

Striefel, S. *Managing behavior: Teaching a child to imitate*. Lawrence, Kans.: H & H Enterprises, 1974. A manual for use by parents, teachers, and other professionals. Its purpose is to provide a behavioral procedure for teaching the child how to imitate motor and verbal responses, the skills that are prerequisites to more complex language and social behaviors.

Newsletters and Magazines

Closer Look. Washington, D.C.: Parents' Campaign for Handicapped Children and Youth. A newsletter distributed free upon request by a national information center to the parents of handicapped children. It provides information about educational rights, parent groups and coalitions, and resources in each state.

The Exceptional Parent. Boston, Mass.: A magazine for parents of exceptional children. Its articles deal with physical disabilities, emotional problems, mental retardation, learning disabilities, perceptual disabilities, deafness, blindness, and chronic illness.

The Parent Newsletter. Logan, Utah: Special Education Instructional Materials Center, Utah State University. A monthly newsletter to disseminate helpful information to parents of exceptional children. It is free upon request.

About the Authors

JACK T. COLE, Ph.D., has been an elementary teacher, counselor, school psychologist, and special educator. He is currently an associate professor of special education and the coordinator of the Educational Diagnostician Training Program at New Mexico State University. His main areas of professional interest are the preservice and inservice training of special educators. He has published, taught, consulted, and directed grants in the field of special education. Dr. Cole has been actively involved in regular and special education for over 17 years.

MARTHA L. COLE, M.Ed., is a teacher of children with communication disorders in Las Cruces, New Mexico. She has served as the president of the New Mexico Federation of the Council for Exceptional Children and has been a practitioner in the field of early childhood education and special education for over 17 years. She has served as a clinical/demonstration teacher at the Exceptional Child Center, Utah State University, and has taught university-level courses in the area of special education and early childhood education. She has given numerous presentations and workshops on the language development of language delayed and nonlanguage children.